T0305141

The Challenge of Economic Rebalancing in Europe

The Challenge of Economic Rebalancing in Europe

Perspectives for CESEE Countries

Edited by

Ewald Nowotny

Governor, Oesterreichische Nationalbank, Austria

Doris Ritzberger-Grünwald

Director, Oesterreichische Nationalbank, Austria

Helene Schuberth

Head of Division, Oesterreichische Nationalbank, Austria

PUBLISHED IN ASSOCIATION WITH THE OESTERREICHISCHE NATIONALBANK

Edward Elgar
PUBLISHING

Cheltenham, UK • Northampton, MA, USA

Published by
Edward Elgar Publishing Limited
The Lypiatts
15 Lansdown Road
Cheltenham
Glos GL50 2JA
UK

Edward Elgar Publishing, Inc.
William Pratt House
9 Dewey Court
Northampton
Massachusetts 01060
USA

A catalogue record for this book
is available from the British Library

Library of Congress Control Number: 2015938635

This book is available electronically in the **Elgar**online
Economics subject collection
DOI 10.4337/9781784719807

ISBN 978 1 78471 979 1 (cased)
ISBN 978 1 78471 980 7 (eBook)

Typeset by Servis Filmsetting Ltd, Stockport, Cheshire
Printed and bound in Great Britain by TJ International Ltd, Padstow

Contents

Contributors

Thorsten Beck, Professor of Banking and Finance, Cass Business School, City University London, UK.

Marek Belka, President, Narodowy Bank Polski, Poland.

Sir Suma Chakrabarti, President, European Bank for Reconstruction and Development (EBRD).

Daniel Daianu, Member of the Board, National Bank of Romania, Romania.

J. Bradford DeLong, Professor, University of California, Berkeley, USA.

Nikola Fabris, Vice-Governor, Central Bank of Montenegro, Montenegro.

Martin Gächter, Foreign Research Division, Oesterreichische Nationalbank, Austria.

Martin Geiger, Department of Economics, University of Innsbruck, Austria.

Florentin Glötzl, Department of Socioeconomics, Vienna University of Economics and Business, Austria.

Daniel Gros, Director, Centre for European Policy Studies (CEPS), Brussels, Belgium.

Mario Holzner, Deputy Director, Vienna Institute for International Economic Studies (wiiw), Austria.

Jan in 't Veld, Head of Sector, Model-based Economic Analysis, European Commission.

Richard C. Koo, Chief Economist, Nomura Research Institute, Japan.

Raimondas Kuodis, Deputy Governor, Lietuvos bankas, Lithuania.

Ewald Nowotny, Governor, Oesterreichische Nationalbank, Austria.

Peter Pontuch, Economist, European Commission.

Rafal Raciborski, Economist, European Commission.

Lucrezia Reichlin, Professor, London Business School, UK.

Doris Ritzberger-Grünwald, Director of the Economic Analysis and Research Department, Oesterreichische Nationalbank, Austria.

Helene Schuberth, Head of Division, Oesterreichische Nationalbank, Austria.

Miroslav Singer, Governor, Česká národní banka, Czech Republic.

Lars E.O. Svensson, Professor, Stockholm School of Economics, Sweden.

Till van Treeck, Professor, University of Duisburg-Essen, Germany.

Preface

Six years after the outbreak of the global financial crisis in 2008–2009, debt overhangs and balance sheet repair continue to be important drivers of weak economic growth. Even worse, some countries are still in the middle of a deep recession. Here, self-enforcing negative feedback loops between indebted private sectors, a weak financial sector, and a sovereign under stress constrain aggregate demand and credit supply conditions. When faced with the need to repair balance sheets, economic agents have been placing more attention on reducing debt rather than on increasing consumption or investment. In Europe, balance sheet adjustment seems to be more challenging than in other regions or in previous episodes. Consequently, the rebalancing process is far from complete. While significant progress has been made with the repair of banks' balance sheets, controversial issues such as the difficulty of achieving simultaneous rebalancing across countries and sectors still remain unsolved. In some European countries, simultaneous deleveraging has so far led to negative spillovers, further amplifying the harmful impact of country-specific deleveraging on economic activity.

Against this backdrop, this book examines the multiple challenges and potentially conflicting objectives of sectoral rebalancing in Europe, with a special focus on Central, Eastern and South-Eastern Europe (CESEE).

Part I frames the discussion on rebalancing challenges. Views seem to converge along the following lines. Economies tend to escape the dilemma of either chronic disequilibria or contractive deleveraging by strengthening their industrial base. In order to make rebalancing work all over Europe, they will need to fundamentally improve the macroeconomic environment, presumably by combining supply-side, factor productivity-enhancing measures with policy instruments focusing on the demand side. The remarkable progress of external adjustments observed in countries at the Southern and Eastern European periphery came at the price of high unemployment and a collapse in aggregate demand. The decline in investment was particularly high in those countries. Hence the top priority for Europe, in particular CESEE, is to invigorate innovation, given the exceptionally low levels of public and private spending on research and development, and to reverse the precipitous decline in both public and private investment. In addition, it may be important to address the debt overhang directly, for instance by encouraging financial restructuring of debt of the private sector.

Part II turns the attention to balance sheet recessions, debt overhangs and the associated question of the optimal sequencing of adjustment across institutional sectors. Basically, we can distinguish between 'passive' deleveraging, which is characterized by still positive net credit flows associated with even faster (nominal) growth of gross domestic product, and the much more painful 'active' deleveraging, which is driven by negative net credit flows. Importantly, the cost of private sector deleveraging is apparently considerably higher when it is combined with public sector deleveraging. In almost all European countries, the corporate sector has considerably increased its financial surplus since the outbreak of the global crisis in 2008–2009. The scaling-down of investment went hand in hand with a significant increase of cash holdings among large firms. This indicates that large firms aim at becoming more independent from external funding sources in an environment of high uncertainty.

In a balance sheet recession, despite low interest rates, households are paying down their loans instead of maximizing profits. Following the proponents of a 'balance sheet recession', the government is the only sector still willing to borrow and should therefore step in to increase aggregate demand. However, the Stability and Growth Pact and other restrictive fiscal rules, which have been implemented during the crisis years, are setting narrow limits for government spending. While some of these rules have been too restrictive, hindering growth-enhancing investments, others have been helpful in stabilizing the debt crisis.

Part III deals with an aspect very often overlooked in discussions: the link between macroeconomic imbalances and economic inequality. When comparing the pre-1929 and the pre-2008 decades in the United States, we can observe sharply increasing income and wealth inequality and mounting debt leverage of low- and middle-income households in both episodes. Rising inequality was probably an important driver of debt growth, as top earners save the additional funds while bottom earners borrow to increase consumption. With top earners' rapidly rising income shares, the savings rate in the United States declined and debt increased as low-income households dissaved and borrowed to increase consumption. This resulted in rising current account deficits. The German case is different as it is dominated by small and medium-sized family-owned firms which retained profits within the company instead of distributing bonuses and dividends. Thus the top income shares hardly increased in the boom years, while corporate financial balances increased strongly. Just as in many advanced economies, in some CESEE countries inequalities contributed to credit growth, bubble formation and imbalances, which in turn cemented inequality.

Part IV discusses the future of (central) banking in Europe with a special focus on the interaction between monetary policy and financial stability. It may be argued that in normal times, monetary policy and financial stability should be conducted independently, whereby each policy should be fully informed of, and take into account, the conduct of the other. Cooperation between both types of policy is needed in times of crisis. With the establishment of a Single Resolution Mechanism (SRM) and the Single Supervisory Mechanism (SSM) for banks resident in the euro area and opt-in countries, Europe has made a major step forward.

Finally, Part V looks at the poles between national and global perspectives. This part comprises the views of high representatives of CESEE central banks on their experiences when faced with multiple challenges in the course of the crisis.

As a consequence of the ongoing weak economic performance, the remarkable convergence process of Eastern and Western Europe observed in the two decades prior to the crisis has slowed down, and convergence between the North and the South was reversed. The massive decline in investment further jeopardizes the European convergence process, as the cuts in investment were disproportionately high in the poorer countries. Reversing the decline in investment will be critical to achieving recovery and sustainable growth over the longer term. We hope that this volume will contribute not only to the debate on rebalancing but also provide policy makers with insights helping to improve the chances of prosperous convergence in Europe.

Ewald Nowotny
Doris Ritzberger-Grünwald
Helene Schuberth

PART I

Framing the discussion on rebalancing
challenges

1. European investment to support CESEE and euro area countries

Ewald Nowotny

What do we mean by 'rebalancing', the pivotal term of this book? Obviously, the term signifies a readjustment from a state of imbalance – an economic imbalance in our case. Typically, economists distinguish between external and internal imbalances. By external imbalances, they usually mean disequilibria (mostly deficits) in the current account which, if protracted, might lead to an unsustainable net international investment position. The underlying reason for a current account deficit can differ from case to case: it can be trade-induced via export weaknesses, indicating a lack of competitiveness; it could also reflect strong import demand due to unsustainably high growth. This leads us directly to internal imbalances, such as accumulated private and public debt, asset price bubbles, unemployment or excessive inflation (or deflation). One could also add sectoral or distributional imbalances contributing to uneven growth. Internal and external imbalances are often interlinked, but their interrelation is not always clear-cut.

This chapter is structured as follows: section 1.1 assesses the challenges to the convergence process in Europe revealed by the crisis; section 1.2 elaborates on the investment gap and its solution; section 1.3 takes a historical perspective on rebalancing issues; before the final session summarizes and concludes with a general remark on policy-making.

1.1 HOW TO MAINTAIN MOMENTUM IN THE EU CONVERGENCE?

In 2014 we commemorated three anniversaries, which are crucially linked to the topic of rebalancing: 25 years since the fall of the Berlin Wall, 15 years since the creation of European Economic and Monetary Union (EMU) and 10 years since the – so far – biggest round of European Union (EU) enlargement. This is not only a reason for celebration but also an occasion for honest stock-taking and thoughtful reflection. I think that

3

the developments that followed these events have been broadly successful. For an overwhelming majority of Europeans, the last quarter of a century brought hugely improved living standards and a much higher level of freedom. The Central, Eastern and South-Eastern European (CESEE) region in particular saw a period of accelerated growth rates in the years prior to the global financial crisis. This was a win–win situation not just for the acceding countries but also for the EU in general, and for Austria, with its strong trade and investment links to the CESEE region, in particular. The episode following the introduction of the euro in 1999 and up to the beginning of the financial crisis that started in 2008 was beneficial to the euro area. But those countries which apparently profited the most had to find out that they had built their performance on the untenable foundation of private debt backed by overvalued assets.

The crisis has revealed that the previously remarkable catching-up process is neither automatic nor irreversible (Landesmann, 2013). The new Central European EU member states fared relatively well in terms of trade performance even after the financial crisis. By contrast, a dramatic stop of private financing flows required the economies under stress in the euro area, the Baltics and the Balkans to quickly adjust their external imbalances. Even though they improved their competitiveness, external rebalancing resulted in internal imbalances such as high unemployment and overcapacities, while the development of new export capacities was hampered by financial constraints and weak European and foreign demand. Hence, a lot of the adjustment had to take place via diminished import demand caused by painful cuts in income and employment. Whether this import reduction is sustainable depends on the structural nature of the related economic slump; something we will only know with a sufficient degree of certainty at the beginning of a new cycle.

A very interesting aspect of external imbalances is their relation to the patterns of sectoral specialization in a given economy. The countries featuring the best export performance prior to and after the financial crisis are exactly those that have a large manufacturing sector. The four countries that form the Visegrad Group have been fortunate in terms of foreign direct investment, which enabled their reindustrialization. Via cross-border production networks, these economies are involved in a 'new industrial core' of Europe together with Germany and Austria. Those countries, however, that have not been able to establish sufficient tradeable industries, and have neither abundant natural resources nor tourist attractions, have difficulties in escaping the dilemma of either chronic disequilibria or contractive deleveraging.

1.2 INVESTMENT IS THE KEY

Even worse, investment, which is crucial for future growth, has been cut overproportionally. Six years after the collapse of Lehman Brothers, investment levels in the EU-28 were about 18 per cent below their peak; in some euro area economies under stress, investment was cut by about half. Taking into account some necessary correction of previous overinvestment in the construction sector, a prolonged period of below-trend business investment will certainly weigh on future productivity growth. The investment gap can be partly explained by financial constraints, in particular for small and medium-sized enterprises, start-ups and infrastructure. Another factor is demand uncertainty, triggered by private and public deleveraging – typical for balance sheet recessions.

Having said that, one should not forget that because the level of economic activity differs widely between the euro area average and the CESEE region, the latter has the best long-term growth prospects in Europe, even if convergence will, most likely, proceed more slowly than in the past (with the annual growth differential dropping from up to four to below two percentage points). Thanks to its proximity and its traditional ties to the CESEE region, Austria is in an excellent position to take advantage of this growth process (Oesterreichische Nationalbank, 2014). CESEE's share in Austria's total goods exports rose to roughly 22 per cent (2013), with the euro area countries still accounting for half of all Austrian exports. Conversely, Austrian banks' high international exposure is concentrated with their CESEE subsidiaries despite a slight decline in the respective exposures due to reduced activities in countries such as Hungary and Ukraine. While a tendency toward greater diversity is desirable, banks ought to promote a sustainable growth model in countries with adequate economic and legal conditions, in the spirit of the Vienna Initiative.

How can the hope for convergence be maintained, as enshrined in Article 3 of the Treaty (European Union, 2007), which states that the European Union 'shall promote economic, social and territorial cohesion'? I think that the new European Commission (2014) is setting the right priorities by proposing an investment package combined with regulatory reforms targeted toward fostering smart infrastructure, education, research and energy. This package should not only provide short-term stimulus but also improve the potential for long-term growth in Europe. At the same time, a reform of industrial policy focusing on new companies in the manufacturing sector of vulnerable member states could help create export capacities. At the same time, the process toward a governance structure worth of a 'genuine EMU' as outlined by the Presidents of the European Central Bank, the European Commission, the European

Council and the Eurogroup in 2012 (Van Rompuy, 2012) contributes to confidence-building. While the successful creation of the banking union marked a major step toward completing the architecture of EMU, the other three pillars necessary for this completion – fiscal, economic and political union – are still in the making. To the extent that the new EMU architecture will be able to eliminate economic uncertainty, it may also contribute to economic growth in the euro area and beyond.

1.3   LEARNING FROM HISTORY

Some readers might have noted that an important historic event was missing from the anniversaries I listed above: 2014 also marks the centenary of World War I. This 'great seminal catastrophe' of the twentieth century marked the end of an initial era of globalization and the beginning of a 30- year period of misery and barbarism. Importantly for us, in hindsight, this tragedy was by no means inevitable. Recent work by historians reconfirms the view that European leaders at the time would have had better alternatives, but they made the wrong choices (Clark, 2012; Mombauer, 2013). It took decades to overcome the division of post-war Europe, and in many aspects this process is still under way. The devastation brought about by the wars, however, prompted an unprecedented European peace project: a process of political and economic integration, including monetary integration. The tragic events happening these days just 1500 kilometres east of Vienna should remind us not only of the fact that war destroys lives, but that it also destroys countless opportunities of living in prosperity.

Remembering our past helps us prepare for a better future. In this context, I am glad to advertise the publication of a data volume entitled *South-Eastern European Monetary and Economic Statistics from the Nineteenth Century to World War II* (Bank of Greece et al., 2014). The volume is also available electronically from the Oesterreichische Nationalbank (OeNB) website. It is the result of the work of a joint Data Collection Task Force that comprises the central banks of Albania, Austria, Bulgaria, Greece, Romania, Serbia and Turkey. The book provides the first comprehensive collection of monetary data on South-Eastern Europe for the period between 1830 and 1949. I am grateful to all the contributors and the entire South-Eastern European Monetary History Network (SEEMHN) for their efforts to eliminate the 'white spots' on our map of the region's monetary history and policy. European economic history research had largely neglected South-Eastern Europe, presumably because data were not readily available in the past. Remarkably, what we find today is that the countries covered in this volume already had to deal with problems of imbalances and rebalancing in the period discussed. Thus, the volume allows us to study the particular problems peripheral economies typically face after international crises: credit squeezes, capital flight and fiscal imbalances, all of which lead to strong economic contraction and often collapse.

1.4 CONCLUDING REMARKS

To sum up: internal and external rebalancing has always been a complex challenge. So far, countries at the Southern and Eastern European periphery have made good progress in improving their external competitiveness. Unfortunately, this progress entailed internal disequilibria in terms of high unemployment, contracting demand and sometimes even deflation. Eventually, their rebalancing efforts can only be successful – both externally and internally – if the macroeconomic environment improves all over Europe. Such an improvement, in turn, requires a comprehensive decision-making framework including a set of effective monetary, fiscal and structural policy instruments. Our recent and historical experience suggests that decisions should be taken from a responsible and stability-oriented political perspective; not only for one country alone, but for the whole region concerned.

All too often, we let ourselves be guided by what a famous European leader once has said: 'There is no alternative.' For an economist, there are always alternatives. What we should accept, however, is the trivial truism that any alternative has its costs or risks. There is no free lunch in economics, but we definitely have choices to make. In order to make the right ones, we must learn from each other.

ACKNOWLEDGEMENT

Andreas Breitenfellner, of the Oesterreichische Nationalbank's staff, contributed to this chapter.

REFERENCES

Bank of Greece, Bulgarian National Bank, National Bank of Romania and Oesterreichische Nationalbank (2014), *South-Eastern European Monetary and Economic Statistics from the Nineteenth Century to World War II*, Athens, Sofia, Bucharest, Vienna.

Clark, C. (2012), *The Sleepwalkers. How Europe went to War in 1914*, London: Allen Lane.

European Commission (2014), 'An Investment Plan for Europe, Communication from the Commission', Brussels, 26 November.

European Union (2007), 'Consolidated Version of the Treaty on European Union – Protocols – Declarations Annexed to the Final Act of the Intergovernmental Conference which adopted the Treaty of Lisbon, signed on 13 December 2007', *Official Journal* C 326, 26/10/2012 P. 0001–0390.

Landesmann, M. (2013), 'The New North–South Divide in Europe: Can the European Convergence Model be Resuscitated?', *Vienna Institute Monthly Report*, 2013/1, pp. 3–13.

Mombauer, A. (2013), *The Origins of the First World War: Diplomatic and Military Documents*, Documents in Modern History, annotated edn, Manchester: Manchester University Press.

Oesterreichische Nationalbank (OeNB) (2014), 'Facts on Austria and Its Banks', December, available at http://www.oenb.at/en/Publications/Financial-Market/Facts-on-Austria-and-Its-Banks.html.

Van Rompuy, H. (2012), 'Towards a Genuine Economic and Monetary Union', Report by President of the European Council, Brussels, 26 June.

2. The rebalancing challenge in Europe

J. Bradford DeLong

The purpose of this chapter is – starting from first principles – to provide a large-scale bird's-eye overview of what is to come in this book. Readers will find chapters on monetary policy, balance sheet adjustment and growth, inequality and its role in generating internal macroeconomic imbalances, external macroeconomic rebalancing, and banking sector regulation. They all presuppose that Europe, and within it the regions of Central, Eastern and South-Eastern Europe (CESEE) that we focus on here, have problems that for their solution require more than just higher aggregate demand in the short term. Proper solutions require large-scale sectoral rebalancing. And that sectoral rebalancing needs to be rapid. Why? Because these economies will not grow smoothly without deep structural reforms; these reforms need to be not just at the bottom but at the top, and reforms of institutions, governance structures, and regulatory practices and mandates need to be carried out as well. Note that the need, while urgent in Central Europe, Eastern Europe and South-Eastern Europe, is not necessarily more urgent here than in the other regions of Europe.

So why is the naive Keynesian claim wrong that the only thing that is needed now is higher aggregate demand? And which of the many things that go under the labels of 'rebalancing' and 'structural adjustment' are most needed? And why? If these questions can be answered coherently and convincingly in this chapter, then it will have done its task and provided an appropriate intellectual framework into which the rest of the chapters will fit naturally and form a coherent whole.

To start with, note three dates: 12 September 1683, 18 June 1815 and 19 November 1942. The first date, 12 September 1683, was of course the end of the Turkish imperial project (Hochedlinger, 2002). It was the date of the last truly mass slaughter in Vienna. On that day the defending armies commanded by Ernst Rüdiger von Starhemberg, reinforced by the relieving forces of King John III, Sobieski of Poland, defeated and forced the retreat down the Danube Valley of the armies commanded by Grand Vizier Merzifonlu Kara Mustafa Pasha. That was the last time that this segment, at least, of the Danube Valley saw the chaos, destruction and death of large-scale, long-lasting war. If von Starhemberg and Mustafa Pasha could see South-Eastern Europe now, while they might mourn the loss of power of the dynasties they served, they would both be very pleased at the state of the people who live here; and both be very grateful that the peoples and states are, for the most part, not still locked in what looked then like an eternal region-encompassing destructive war of intolerant, militant faiths.

The second date, 18 June 1815, was of course the end of the French revolutionary-imperial project, with the final defeat at Waterloo in Belgium of the army of the French Emperor Napoleon Bonaparte (Napoleon I) by British, Dutch and German forces under the command of the Irish-born Arthur Wellesley, Duke of Wellington.[1] We all owe a great deal to the implementation and then transmission of the good ideals of the Enlightenment by the French Revolution. We owe less than zero to the habit of deadly ideological purges introduced by the Convention in Paris and in the Vendée. And the practice of introducing and maintaining those ideals by every four years having a French army come through, burning as it went and living off the land, leaving famine in its wake, is something we can live without. If either Metternich or Talleyrand could see right now that we are no longer engaged in the military destruction of the struggle for French dominance over Europe that consumed the sixteenth, seventeenth and eighteenth centuries and that seemed to them to be perpetual, they would be pleased.

And 19 November 1942 was, of course, the end of the Nazi imperial project, with the initial breakthrough of the Soviet Union's Red Army at Stalingrad on the Volga.[2] It was followed by two-and-a-half more years of fire, blood and death, and then a process of reconstruction that hung in the balance in Western Europe for a decade and is still not complete in Eastern Europe. Nevertheless, if those whose job it was to start rebuilding in 1945, the Adenauers and de Gaulles, could see us now, they would be very pleased. Right now the European project is a success. And we could not have said that on 12 September 1683, on 18 June 1815 or on 19 November 1942.

In fact, we can take a much longer perspective in which the post-World War II project of European community, unification and peace has been a success. It was not far from Vienna that the tribes of the Kimbri and the Teutones who had left their previous homes somewhere in or near Jutland crossed the Danube River into Noricum in 113 BC. Was it 111 BC that the Kimbri and the Teutones, having moved down from Jutland to what is now Austria and crossed the Danube, decided they would rather cross the Rhine into the land of feta and olives in the Rhone Valley rather than eat Sauerkraut and sausage – or, back then, probably dried auroch meat – in Noricum, near what is now Salzburg? So they went. And so they looted, burned, ravaged, killed, and ruled until a decade later they were broken at the battles of

Aquae Sextiae and Vercellae by the new-model Roman Republican army commanded by Gaius Marius, seven times consul (Plutarch, n.d.).

Ever since then, by my count, it is every 37 years that a hostile army crosses the Rhine going one way or the other bringing fire and sword. The original Swiss – the Helvetii. Julius Caesar. All of those who claimed to be Julius Caesar's adoptive descendants. The Visigoths heading for Andalusia. Louis XIV commanding his armies to make sure that nothing grew in the Rhinish Palatinate so that his armies attacking Holland had a secure right flank. And, last, the Ludendorff Bridge at Remagen in 1945. Every 37 years, with increasing destructiveness as time passes.

Thirty-seven years after 1945 carries us to 1982. Thirty-seven years after 1982 will carry us to 2019. By 2019 we will have missed two of our appointments with slaughter. Even with Stalin's legacy, the difficulties of post-Cold War transition, everything that has happened in the republics of the Former Yugoslavia, and the current struggle over austerity and adjustment between the northern and southern pieces of the euro zone, things have gone very well indeed recently.

Yet, clearly, most think that we desperately need political union in Europe as insurance to keep the bad old days from 111 BC to 1945 from coming again. We do not want Europe to once again fall victim to the tragedy of great power politics (Mearsheimer, 2014). That means that politicians find some way to union, so that differences are thrashed out in conference rooms in Brussels and Strasbourg rather than in the streets with Molotov cocktails, submachine guns, armed drones, and worse. That is the necessity.

This does not mean that we should minimize Europe's current problems, just note that the problems are not as large as the achievements. The problems facing us are many. A very quick list consists of five. There are two major political problems:

- Incorporating ex-superpowers into the common European home; a problem Europe has faced over and over again since 1600, first with Spain, then with France after 1815, then with Germany after 1870, and now with Great Russia.
- Building institutions for Continental governance in our late-Westphalian nationalist age.

And there are three major economic problems and opportunities:

- Grasping rather than letting drop the enormous fruits of continent-scale economic integration that nearly all studies of economies of scale and economic integration say are there.

- Accelerating the painfully and disappointingly slow convergence of both East and South to North-West European standards. Looking at the Asian Pacific Rim reveals that if we can get the institutions, the trade patterns, and integration more than half-right we can look forward to a regime of convergence in which living standards and productivity levels in a region converge halfway to the standards of that region's core in a generation. We can do it. We have done it elsewhere in the past. We should be doing it now in Central, Eastern and South-Eastern Europe. And, frustratingly, we are not: it is more 'the slow boring of hard boards' than it is 'the 30 glorious years'.
- Successfully resolving and recovering from the shock of 2008 and its aftereffects. This is, mostly, what concerns us today. The other four problems are, mostly, in the background right now.

And the need to do all of this is in a global context that is not terribly supportive. The global context of 2008 is a world that was characterized either by a global savings glut or a global investment shortfall, depending on which blade of the scissors is your favorite to focus on.[3] That imbalance in turn produced what one might call a global overleveraging: the gap between desired global savings at global full employment and planned global investment at global full employment was filled in by credit creation to create funding for long-term investment projects that was not backed by savings commitments to long-run patient capital.[4] One might, alternatively, call it a global shortage of risk tolerance: the gap between desired global savings at global full employment and planned global investment at global full employment was filled in by promising savers that they were not bearing large amounts of systemic business-cycle risk, when in fact they were (Caballero and Farhi, 2013). These are alternative ways of labelling the same underlying economic failure of expectations to be consistent, that focus on somewhat different things: the apocryphal tale of the five wise men and the elephant comes to mind.[5]

We had a world in which there was no global hegemon, in a Keynes–Kindleberger sense, in Washington, willing to take responsibility for managing the level of global aggregate demand, even if the consequences for the domestic United States (US) were potentially unfortunate (Kindleberger, 1973). If in the 1950s and 1960s the US under Bretton Woods had made a durable commitment to serve as the world's importer of last resort, its falling into the same role during what some called Bretton Woods II was contingent and evanescent (Dooley et al., 2009).

Moreover, we had a world in which there was no alternative local continental-scale orchestra conductor focused on balancing effective demand to potential supply over the European continent as a whole.

Instead, there were many countries, some of them very large, most of them focused inward, none of them thinking that responsibility needed to be taken; that, it was thought, was the business of the European Central Bank (ECB), which had the proper monetarist tools to do the job of managing Continent-wide demand. But what if those tools proved insufficient? The ECB did not have the power (Cecchetti and O'Sullivan, 2005), and nobody had the power to do banking regulatory or fiscal policy in Europe on the proper Continent-wide scale.

Plus there was little sense in the years before 2008 of what a North Atlantic-wide Keynes–Kindleberger international economic hegemon would actually do. Such are used to dealing with problems of excessive aggregate demand, de-anchoring inflation expectations, and upward price spirals on the one hand; or with problems of liquidity shortage on the other. But we did not have a liquidity shortage; certainly not after the start of 2009. The monetarist playbook for how the Great Depression ought to have been handled was taken down from the shelf, dusted off and applied. As a result the North Atlantic economy floated on an absolute sea of liquidity from the start of 2009 to the present day: so much has there been a lack of shortage of cash that central bank deposit velocity has fallen to low levels that few observers indeed even a decade ago would ever have thought they might see.

We have, instead, since the middle of 2008 had another kind of deficiency in the macroeconomy: aggregate demand has fallen below potential supply because there has been an excess demand for, and a shortage of, safe assets in the North Atlantic economy. That has been a consequence of an excess of risky assets, of an excess of non-performing loans, of the transformation of assets formerly seen as safe into risky status. These problems are more sophisticated and less tractable to monetary interventions. Open-market operations that simply swap one interest-paying, or potentially interest-paying, government liability with duration for a non-interest-paying government liability with zero duration have next to no effect on the supply and demand for safe assets as a class.[6]

If we view the big shock of 2008 as a collapse, on the demand side, of risk tolerance, and on the supply side as the recognition that very large classes of assets sold as safe were in fact not safe, one driven by events in the United States, then we would think that this collapse is both good and bad. It is good in that savers are no longer easily fooled: people who are in fact bearing systemic business cycle and other forms of risk are now aware that they are doing so, and if full employment is reattained it will not be under the shadow of expectations that are inconsistent and cannot be fulfilled. Creditors will not let debtors borrow until not only their solvency is at risk but the creditors' solvency is at risk as well. It is bad because attaining anything close to full employment in a capitalist market economy requires that savers bear risk. The provision of risk-bearing capacity is an important factor of production that only those who have current wealth (are savers) can provide. And right now they are not doing so on a sufficient scale.

I was told this morning (24 November 2014) that the ten-year Spanish government-bond nominal interest rate is now less than 2 per cent per year. Whatever we think of those who invest in Spanish government bonds, 2 per cent per year nominal for ten years in euros does seem a little low, given the existence of a great deal of value in the world today in the form of potentially storable commodities, and given the existence of political uncertainties – 'black swans' – over the next decade that are not things we can today quantify or even imagine. Compare a sub −1 per cent per year German ten-year nominal bond rate to the 6 per cent per year real earnings yield on a diversified portfolio of equities of European non-financial operating companies. With a 2 per cent per year inflation target, $6 + 2 - 1 = 7$. 7 per cent/year is a huge premium return to get on equity investments in a diversified portfolio of corporations rather than government bonds subject to inflation risk; especially when one reflects that this is not a duration risk, for dividends plus stock buybacks today make up a very healthy cash payout, and the covariance of interest rates and corporate profits further reduces the effective duration of equities (DeLong and Magin, 2008).

That suggests that the collapse of risk tolerance has gone much too far. Right now we are in a world in which savers do not view the risks and opportunities of the world with clear eyes, but rather with eyes that perceive through a distorted negative bubble. Financial markets thus seem to be failing on a very large scale to successfully mobilize the risk tolerance of economies. This is doubly unfortunate. To undertake new enterprise or to invest to produce economic growth requires that someone peer through the veil of time and ignorance. That means that somebody must provide the risk-bearing capacity, must be willing to bear the losses if something goes wrong.

Back in 2008, I gave many speeches about how we were experiencing a shock that boosted demand for safe liquid savings vehicles, and that this shock was going to trigger a sharp downturn in the North Atlantic economies. But, the consensus of economists thought and said that the downturn would be short. At first, the consensus of economists concluded it was going to just be a liquidity squeeze; and we knew how to deal with liquidity squeezes by using open-market operations to boost the money supply. Then it became clear that it was more than a liquidity squeeze. Yet even though it was not a liquidity crisis – even though taking down, dusting off, and applying the monetarist depression-fighting playbook would not be sufficient (Friedman and Schwartz, 1963) – the examples of the Great Depression and of Japan since 1990 would provide a guide for what not to do. So, the majority of economists believed – and so I said publicly at the time – that the North Atlantic would quickly resolve insolvent institutions and write down unpayable debts. The recession would be sharp. But recovery would be rapid. And afterwards the global economy would have been reknit into much the same pattern it was in before 2008. This was wrong.

We have not reknit the global economy into the same pattern. We have not restored the long-run growth path that the North Atlantic was on before 2007. After a liquidity squeeze is brought to an end, asset prices return to normal, the sea becomes calm again and, broadly, patterns of the societal division of labour that were profitable before the squeeze are profitable again. Hence all that needs to be done to reattain full employment is to reknit the same division of labour. Not true this time.

This time, there has been no recovery of risk tolerance; whether because of incomplete deleveraging, or the inability to reattain levels of risk tolerance that turned out *ex post* to be absurd but that nevertheless those engaged in enterprise required and expected, or for other reasons. Since there has been no recovery of risk tolerance, the previous division of labour across Europe cannot be profitably and sustainably reknit. There must be structural adjustment before anything like full employment can be reattained (Groshen and Potter, 2003). Now nobody thinks that there ought to be a full recovery of risk tolerance to its levels in the days when a simple demonstration involving mark-to-model finance would convince a rating agency that a security deserved AAA, with which it could then be marketed at a spread of less than 25 basis points over the debt of creditworthy sovereigns like Germany.

The pre-2008 European convergence equilibrium employed peripheral labour in Eastern, South-Eastern and Southern Europe in extremely risky long-duration enterprises: bets on the value of long-lived construction, bets that governments would resolve unresolvable public finance problems and bets that human capital would emerge to make profitable enterprises that would use new infrastructure. All of these bets seemed reasonable because risk tolerance was high. And perhaps most of them were reasonable, in the context of permanently high risk tolerance. Hence the strong demand pushed relative real wages in peripheral Europe high, relative to the regions' relative productivity at producing tradable goods (Gourinchas, 2002).

All this came to an end in 2008. Now, in order to properly rebalance – even though rebalancing has been ongoing for six years – peripheral workers in Europe must either boost their productivity in making tradable goods or find something 'safe' to do, must find something that does not require the mobilization of any substantial amount of European core risk tolerance in order to make the financing work, or must accept large real wages declines. These are the options. If it were not for the existence of the euro zone, all or nearly all peripheral European economies would choose the third: real wage reduction via depreciation of the currency. But for many that is not an option, or not a good option, or not seen right now as the best of the bad options. Peripheral depreciation for countries not in the euro zone, and peripheral internal deflation for countries that are, may in the end be the road chosen, in spite of all the economic pain and chaos it is generating now and will generate in the future. Euro-core inflation – 'structural adjustment' in the northern core rather than in the periphery – is another possibility.

Real structural reforms that 'successfully' and substantially boost productivity in making tradable goods would be an option, if that unicorn could be found. The problem is that structural reform too often stands as a placeholder for all good things that would increase an economy's productivity. The danger is when commitments to structural reform are not accompanied by any political economy strategy to successfully disrupt the current stakeholders blocking reforms in order to confiscate their current rents.

Attempting to restore financial-market risk tolerance – but, we hope, not to 'go–go' levels – is another possible strategy. A 7 per cent per year gap between the returns to properly diversified real European equity baskets and the returns to lending money to the German government could be greatly lessened without, in my judgement, running any risk of a new round of bubble finance. The governments' powers to tax could mobilize the risk-bearing capacity of Europeans Continent-wide; but if taxpayers are bearing the risk they deserve the returns of enterprise as well, and history has not been kind to those who think that governments' interventions in industry can take the form of a very large and high-return investment portfolio. Better, probably, for governments to boost the supply of safe assets via deferring the taxation to ultimately amortize expenditures they ought to be undertaking anyway, than to involve governments on a larger scale as venture capitalists and industrial financiers.

This would be the case even were there not the additional problem that the risk-bearing capacity of taxpayers is mostly in the core of Europe, while the need for additional demand right now is mostly on the periphery. In the United States economic flows between states are not tracked, as Europe tracks flows between nations. The US does not assign its national debt to individual states. It does not have to worry about this. In the United States back in 1991–1992 after the collapse of the Savings and Loan bubble, the

United States central government transferred to Texas a sum equal to 25 per cent of a year's Texas gross domestic product (GDP) – an amazing no-strings bailout – without there being any complaint or worry about fiscal transfers or about encouraging a feckless culture of moral hazard in 'rattlesnake country'. Part of it was that Americans did not notice. Part of it was that the senior senator from Texas was in the key position of being Chair of the Senate Finance Committee. Europe cannot do the equivalent or anything close, without political upset.

Or else? If structural reform and demand management are not both successfully performed, the alternative for Europe is then a long and uneven depression. Such might produce political pressures to set European economic integration into reverse. That, however, is a low-probability scenario. The higher-probability scenario in the event of the failure of structural reform and demand management is for the European Union and the euro to be held together, year after year, by just enough fiscal transfers and debt relief from the core to keep the grinding pain of deflation in the euro periphery from becoming so great as to trigger reversal. This would, in the end, be a much more expensive strategy for the core's taxpayers than one of biting the bullet and immediate resolution and debt write-down.

What can be said about the roads toward structural adjustment, toward an economic configuration that could sustain Continent-wide full employment without relying on unreasonable expectations of risk and return? For some countries, exchange rate policy is possible. Exchange rate policy is very effective medicine. It is a very good way of improving competitiveness and sharing social burdens. The problem is that it is so only as long as inflation expectations are anchored in domestic nominal terms. When they are not – especially when inflation expectations become anchored to inflation in import prices – relying on exchange rate depreciation is worse than useless. It is a medicine that is effective until resistance develops, and the fear is that alongside resistance there will also develop addiction to this mechanism. Hence it should be resorted to gingerly, lest overuse lead to high inflation and to even more intractable structural problems. Nevertheless, if the largest global financial shock in a century is not a time to resort to it for those countries that can, when would the proper time to resort to it be? But how can we know whether tolerance has developed? To that question there is no good answer.

Within the euro zone, internal devaluation is not a possibility. External devaluation – chiefly vis-à-vis the dollar, hoping that the United States will once again be willing to take on the role of importer of last resort – is a possibility. However, it does not resolve Europe's internal structural problems. What it does do is make life very pleasant for the export powerhouse that is Germany. And while life is pleasant for Germany, perhaps its politicians can be induced to make concessions and provide funding and take policy steps that do resolve Europe's internal structural problems.

There is the possibility of replacing the missing private risk tolerance for large-scale loan guarantees, asset purchases, or public spending to create demand for products that enterprises in peripheral regions can produce. That requires that European politicians know and understand and be willing to use the debt capacity of Europe's core for the benefit of primarily the periphery, but also the euro zone as a whole. There is structural reform, and the knotty question of whether structural reform is harder when unemployment is high or when it is low. Those in Frankfurt and Berlin are sure that structural reform can be accomplished only when unemployment is high and politicians feel a sense of crisis in their bones. Those in Washington are sure that structural reform can be accomplished only when unemployment is low and politicians can assemble fleshpots of resources to be distributed to assemble majority political coalitions. We economists avoid taking a stand on this issue by saying that we are, after all, just economists. It is, however, important to note that the fact that at most one of these can be true does not mean that at least one of these is true.

And, as noted above, inflation in the European core and deflation in the European periphery round out the list. We have not had much of the first. We have had a lot of the second. A 2 per cent per year inflation rate for the euro zone as a whole, with a 0 per cent per year inflation rate in the euro zone's poorer half, means 4 per cent per year inflation in the euro zone's richer half. It is difficult to see how much that is good could come out of a monetary target that turns into a mandate that inflation in the European core must always be less than 2 per cent per year. Whether all who staff the ECB fully understand this, is not clear.

But among all these possibilities, why choose? These all seem to be not substitutes, but complements. Yet the political economy of today in Europe seems curious: these are all, overwhelmingly, posed as either–or substitutes, as mutually exclusive alternatives. And observers hear the same thing in the United States. Yet this is difficult to understand. I, at least, have always thought that the best and obvious strategy is to attempt them all; and to be willing to, pragmatically, reverse course on those that appear to turn out to have implementation costs greater than their potential benefits.

As of now, those who favour a broad-front approach have been waiting for five years for advocates of narrow single-measure solutions to convincingly outline why the broad-front approach, that would appear obvious and best to the naive, is not in fact the obvious and best one. And yet we are all still waiting.

NOTES

1. Roberts (2014): the best recent (although definitely excusing Napoleon) biography of the Emperor, and of the French Revolution through his eyes.
2. Glantz (2009): the best English-language study of the turning point of World War II.
3. Bernanke (2005): truly a path-breaking speech and argument by the former Federal Reserve Chair.
4. Gorton (2010): still the best study of the origins of our current economic crisis.
5. Wolf (2014): the best work on the structural changes that created the vulnerabilities necessary for a small financial-market trigger to cause a worldwide depression of this magnitude.
6. Koo (2011): Richard Koo is the economist who has, in the general view, succeeded in providing the most comprehensive systemic view of the balance sheet view of the downturn.

REFERENCES

Bernanke, B. (2005), 'The Global Savings Glut', available at http://www.federal-reserve.gov/boarddocs/speeches/2005/200503102/.

Caballero, R. and E. Farhi (2013), 'A Model of the Safe Asset Mechanism (SAM): Safety Traps and Economic Policy', NBER Working Paper No. 18737, available at http://www.nber.org/papers/w18737.

Cecchetti, S. and R. O'Sullivan (2005), 'The European Central Bank and the Federal Reserve', *Oxford Review of Economic Policy*, 19(1), available at http://people.brandeis.edu/~cecchett/Jpdf/J32.pdf.

DeLong, J.B. and K. Magin (2008), 'The US Equity Return Premium: Past, Present, and Future', *Journal of Economic Perspectives*, available at http://delong.typepad.com/sdj/2007/04/the_us_equity_r.html.

Dooley, M.P., D. Folkerts-Landau and P.M. Garber (2009), 'Bretton Woods II Still Defines the International Monetary System', NBER Working Paper No. 14731, available at http://www.nber.org/papers/w14731.

Friedman, M. and A. Jacobson Schwartz (1963), *A Monetary History of the United States, 1867–1960*, Princeton, NJ: Princeton University Press.

Glantz, D. (2009), *Armageddon in Stalingrad: September–November 1942*, Lawrence, KS: University Press of Kansas.

Gorton, G. (2010), *Slapped by the Invisible Hand: The Panic of 2007*, New York: Oxford University Press.

Gourinchas, P. (2002), 'Discussion of Olivier Blanchard and Francesco Giavazzi, "Current Account Deficits in the Euro Area: The End of the Feldstein-Horioka Puzzle?"', Brookings Papers on Economic Activity 2002:2, available at http://www.brookings.edu/~/media/Projects/BPEA/Fall%202002/2002b_bpea_blanchard.PDF.

Groshen, E. and S. Potter (2003), 'Has Structural Change Contributed to a Jobless Recovery?' *Current Issues in Economics and Finance*, 9(8), available at http://www.newyorkfed.org/research/current_issues/ci9-8/ci9-8.html.

Hochedlinger, M. (2002), *Austria's Wars of Emergence, 1683–1797*, New York: Routledge.

Kindleberger, C. (1973), *The World in Depression*, Berkeley, CA: University of California Press.

Koo, Richard (2011), 'The World in Balance Sheet Recession: Causes, Cure, and Politics', Tokyo: Nomura Research Institute, available at http://www.paecon.net/PAEReview/issue58/Koo58.pdf.

Mearsheimer, J. (2014), *The Tragedy of Great Power Politics*, New York: W.W. Norton.

Plutarch (n.d.), *Lives of the Noble Greeks and Romans*, available at http://www.gutenberg.org/files/14114/14114-h/14114-h.htm.

Roberts, A. (2014), *Napoleon: A Life*, New York: Viking Penguin.

Wolf, M. (2014), *The Shifts and the Shocks: What We've Learned – and Have Still to Learn – from the Financial Crisis*, New York: Penguin.

3. Mid-term growth perspectives for CESEE

Marek Belka

The objective of this chapter is to discuss medium-run growth perspectives in Central, Eastern and South-Eastern European (CESEE) countries, as assessed in November 2014. The discussion will focus on Poland but many of the insights I would like to offer have a much broader scope of applicability.

3.1 REAL CONVERGENCE PROCESSES IN CESEE ECONOMIES

As a convenient starting point, let me observe that since these countries' political and economic transition in the early 1990s, the region has been a huge beneficiary of real convergence processes. Real gross domestic product (GDP) per capita in Poland at purchasing power parity (PPP)[1] more than doubled between 1995 and 2012 (102 per cent increase) while the respective increase in the European Union (EU)-15 was just 22 per cent. This translates into a large part of the development gap which has been covered in this period: while in 1995, Poland's GDP per capita stood at about 36.1 per cent of EU-15 average, it reached 59.7 per cent in 2012. It is natural to attribute this outstanding performance primarily to real convergence, because at the same time we observed a significant build-up of capital stocks across the region, driven to a large extent by foreign investments. Unlike other continents, Europe has not observed the so-called 'Lucas paradox': capital has indeed been systematically flowing from richer to poorer countries. This has been exemplified by substantial inflows of foreign direct investment (FDI) to countries such as Poland, including greenfield investments, as well as – after Poland joined the EU in May 2004 – substantial amounts of resources from EU structural funds which have helped to co-finance important investments in infrastructure, private enterprise and human capital. It is clear that real convergence processes have been a powerful driver of regional growth over the last decades.

However, as we well know from economic theory, real convergence cannot last forever and the closer Poland gets to its wealthier neighbours in terms of real GDP, the smaller its impact is. The need to seek alternative sources of growth for the future will therefore continue to be more and more pressing.

3.2   IMPROVEMENTS IN THE QUALITY OF FACTOR INPUTS

Let us then look at the alternatives. Taking the macroeconomic production function perspective, there are two alternatives to physical capital accumulation, the main force behind real convergence. First, real convergence processes can also be supported by the improvements in quality of capital and labour inputs. Second, increases in total factor productivity (TFP) can offer growth perspectives which are not constrained by the limits of real convergence. The latter category, related to the technology used for production, the economy's innovativeness and firms' willingness to adopt new ideas, as well as to the evolving sectoral structure of the economy, will be discussed further below. Let me now proceed to the composition of capital and labour.

It is often acknowledged that the quality of physical capital inherited by post-communist economies from their previous regime is generally dubious. However, as shown in a study conducted recently at Narodowy Bank Polski (NBP) (Gradzewicz et al., 2014), only about 3 per cent of the observed GDP increase in Poland between 1996 and 2013 can be attributed to the improvement in the composition of the capital stock, mainly due to an increase in the share of machinery, equipment and intangible fixed assets in the entire capital stock, at the cost of non-residential buildings and structures. Moreover, this effect had already essentially disappeared back in 2001 and it is unlikely that it will speed up convergence process in the future. In contrast, physical capital accumulation as such has contributed as much as 42 per cent of total GDP growth.

Remaining with physical capital, let me also note that – outside of the simplifying logic of growth accounting – its accumulation does not always translate into increased capabilities to generate value added in the economy. The recent world economic crisis has uncovered the fact that some European countries, notably the Mediterranean members of the euro zone, have fallen victim to exuberant growth, with their overinvestment in transport infrastructure, residential and non-residential buildings, and so on. While this generally has not been the case in the CESEE region so far, one has to remain careful to avoid such pitfalls in the future, and to monitor the ways in which capital gains are allocated and consumed. As an aside, let me also observe that during the recent crisis, the exchange rate regime seems to have played an important role, insofar as the 'floaters' had a visibly better record than 'fixers' in curtailing the boom–bust cycle and avoiding exuberant growth before the outbreak of the crisis. Still, EU cohesion policy aside, it is internal rather than external sources of financing which should be counted upon in the coming years.

The accumulation of human capital, augmenting labour – the second input in the production process – is a much more powerful driver of economic growth over the medium run. The aforementioned NBP study by Gradzewicz et al. (2014) has estimated that improvements in the composition of labour are responsible for about 21 per cent of total GDP growth in Poland. These effects accrue, in turn, mostly to the huge increases in educational attainment of Poles over the recent decades. Unlike capital composition, labour composition effects have been strengthening real convergence processes in Poland throughout the period 1996–2013 and are expected to be active in the future as well. Their future importance is constrained, however, by decreasing returns to human capital accumulation and the already very high share of the population with a university degree. Moreover, worrying demographic trends and projections across CESEE economies imply that while some potential can still be tapped by increasing the labour force participation rate (particularly among women and individuals above 55 years of age), these gains will soon be outweighed by the declining working-age population as the societies continue to age. Viewed in this light, it is particularly problematic for CESEE economies given that, after EU accession, we have observed a substantial wave of emigration which was led primarily by relatively young and well-educated individuals, leading to the so called 'brain-drain' effect.

Summing up: the prospects for future growth stemming from traditional sources related to factor accumulation are rather gloomy, both for Poland and for many other CESEE countries. The only exceptions are improvements in human capital, but these gains cannot last forever.

3.3   STRUCTURAL CHANGE

Turning to the question of other available sources of medium-run growth in CESEE countries, let me begin by observing that the aggregate productivity of an economy can be driven by change in its sectoral structure. This can indeed be a powerful source of income disparities across the globe: as shown repeatedly in the literature, cross-country differences in aggregate labour productivity tend to be much larger than differences observed within the manufacturing sector. What drives these gaps are differences within the agricultural and (to a lesser extent) services sector, and their respective shares in total employment.

The political and economic transition of the 1990s unleashed market forces which have led to a partial withdrawal from communist-era emphasis on industry, and heavy industry in particular, and a rapid build-up of service activities. At the same time, increased market opportunities have attracted workers to leave unproductive agriculture in favour of either of the other two large sectors. In Poland, the share of agricultural workers plummeted from 26.1 per cent in 1995 to 12.6 per cent in 2012, while the employment share in services increased from 27.4 per cent to 37.1 per cent. The shares of the respective sectors in value-added creation were much more stable because agricultural productivity remained very low and labour productivity growth was – just like virtually everywhere else in the world – strongest in manufacturing, due to ongoing technological progress, which Poland largely absorbs from abroad.

To assess the potential of this reallocation to affect growth perspectives over the medium run, it is useful to compare the trends in labour productivity and TFP within manufacturing and services. As shown in a recent publication by the NBP staff (Growiec et al., 2014), despite the dynamic growth in industrial labour productivity in Poland, its level remained below that of services throughout the entire period 1995–2012. It follows that labour reallocation towards services was contributing to overall productivity growth during these years. However, extrapolating the observed trends forward creates the expectation that these levels are about to converge very soon, indicating that this 'bonus' growth effect of sectoral shifts will no longer help the Polish economy. Additionally, cross-country evidence indicates that the (somewhat unexpected) result that labour productivity is higher in services than in manufacturing in Poland is not repeated for other countries. In advanced economies such as, for example, Germany, the United Kingdom and the United States, manufacturing has been relatively more productive[2] throughout; in other countries of the region (Czech Republic, Slovakia, Hungary), this has been the case since about 2005. This suggests that productivity growth in the future will be lower due to the ongoing sectoral shifts. A similar argument has been recently put forward by Young (2014): as the demand for many services is income-elastic and price-inelastic, services account for a rising percentage of GDP over time, in line with economic growth. And since services are more sluggish in productivity growth, and are being weighted more heavily in output, we can expect economy-wide productivity rates to decline.

We may also think of the consequences of the structural change for the cyclical volatility of sectoral employment and value added. In line with economic intuition, it is found that business cycles in the services sector are of a substantially smaller magnitude and frequency. It therefore seems fair to conclude with the expectation that in the future, the ongoing process of labour reallocation from manufacturing and towards services in CESEE countries will provide a systematic drag on average economic growth rates, while simultaneously reducing the volatility of growth and employment over the business cycle.

At this point I would like to mention another structural issue, potentially important from the perspective of future productivity growth, namely the energy sector. Poland is very homogenous in this respect so far: about 90 per cent of energy is generated from domestically available coal and lignite. Poland is now to make crucial decisions on its investment strategy that will shape its future energy mix. I see many advantages of maintaining the status quo in this area, energy security being one. But on the other hand, a significant diversification of energy sources, as well as finding a smart way to attract the new technologies needed to develop gas processing facilities, facilities based on renewable sources (mainly solar and wind), or even nuclear energy, could lead to positive productivity spillovers and increased innovation in the economy. By saying 'a smart way', I mean importing the technologies needed to develop local industries supplying equipment, parts and components to the renewable energy sector, and not just importing the final product. The car industry in Poland, which nowadays consists of not only car assembly factories, but also a huge net of local suppliers of parts, can be used as a good example in this respect.

3.4 INNOVATION AND TECHNOLOGY ADOPTION

Having discussed technology and innovation, let me now turn to the impact of innovation and TFP growth within sectors, on medium-term growth perspectives in CESEE. Here, I would like to emphasize that it is not enough to be more innovative: one ought to successfully reap the economic benefits of these innovations as well. As the road from research and development (R&D) expenditures to measurable increases in aggregate TFP can be long and rugged, it is important to carefully discuss all the essential milestones.

The starting point has to be R&D expenditures. Indeed, one of the obvious reasons for the arguably small impact of domestic innovation on economic growth observed so far, is the relatively small and inefficiently addressed R&D outlays. It must be noted that significant progress has been recently attained in this respect in Poland. The share of GDP spent on R&D increased to 0.90 per cent in 2012, advancing the country from the very bottom of the EU list, and now it only has ninth-lowest R&D share in the EU. Despite the dynamic upward trend, the level of R&D expenditures in Poland still falls short of the EU-wide average of 2.07 per cent, as well as the Lisbon objective of 3 per cent of GDP. Similarly, substantial progress has also been obtained with respect to cooperation between the universities and the private sector. In 2012, about 37 per cent of R&D expenditures in Poland came from the business enterprise sector, a major increase from 30 per cent in 2011. Yet again, given that the EU average stands at about 63 per cent, Poland still has a long way to go. And it is important to reach a better structure of R&D funding, because – although basic research is necessary and will always be funded mostly by state funds – privately funded R&D has the advantage over publicly funded R&D that it is more likely to find immediate commercial applications, and thus directly increase the country's TFP. Another challenge for the region is to improve the allocative efficiency of R&D funds by attributing a larger fraction to grants, financed on a competitive basis, and to begin exploiting agglomeration externalities in R&D.

One could argue that R&D may sometimes become a wasteful expenditure in a converging economy, lagging behind the world technology frontier. Why innovate, while research is inherently risky, research effort cannot be directly monitored by authorities, and there is still a substantial pool of untapped technological potential abroad? Well, there are at least two replies to this criticism. First, technologies which are being constantly introduced elsewhere do not diffuse instantaneously and are often protected by costly patents. This implies a barrier to the follower (adopter) economy, precluding its full convergence in terms of GDP per capita, and instead leading it to what is sometimes referred to as the 'middle income trap', a parallel but permanently lower growth path. Second, economic literature (most notably, Griffith et al., 2004) suggests that for technological follower countries such as Poland, an important role can be played by domestic R&D (the so-called 'second face of R&D') which is aimed at facilitating technology adoption. Specifically, there is a documented impact of domestic R&D on productivity growth across Polish manufacturing industries (Kolasa, 2008). It has been shown that local firms in Poland benefit from foreign presence in the same industry and in downstream industries. The absorptive capacity of domestic firms is highly relevant to the size of spillovers: vertical spillovers are larger for R&D-intensive firms, while firms investing in other (external) types of intangibles benefit more from horizontal spillovers.

I now turn to the question of how the R&D outcomes could be effectively commercialized. My view on this issue is that the regulatory framework in Poland is a mixture of unnecessary bureaucratic barriers which may discourage new entrepreneurial action in risky sectors, and on the other hand, substantial, probably excessive generosity which can, in the negative scenario, lead to indolence on the side of established manufacturing and service companies. The former condition of the economic environment of the business enterprise sector, especially with regard to legal and tax regulations, is captured by Poland's position in the World Bank's 'Doing Business' classification. In its release for 2015, after a favourable change in methodology, Poland ranks 32 out of 189 countries, and 14 out of the 28 EU members. According to the World Bank, Poland's institutions are found to be particularly harmful to business in the categories 'Getting electricity', 'Starting a business', 'Paying taxes' and 'Dealing with construction permits'. Hence, the ability of the Polish economy to exploit innovative ideas can be seriously hindered when innovators find it difficult to establish start-up companies and plants. By the same token, risky entrepreneurial actions are also discouraged by the complicated, time- and effort-consuming bankruptcy laws.

On the other hand, owners of Polish companies enjoy low tax rates and low labour costs. The flat corporate income tax rate of 19 per cent is notably lower than the EU average of 22.8 per cent, itself biased downwards by the newer EU countries (for example, 10 per cent in Bulgaria, 15 per cent in Lithuania and Latvia). The capital share of GDP at factor prices, corrected for mixed income of the self-employed, increased from about 30 per cent in 1995 to 40 per cent in 2013. Furthermore, despite substantial increases in educational attainment, wage cost growth has been moderate throughout the period, keeping unit labour costs in check and maintaining the country's cost competitiveness. This, coupled with the geographic proximity of the big, open, integrated EU market, and a flexible labour market with a large percentage of temporary employment contracts, creates very favourable business conditions for established enterprises even without adopting new technologies. Hence, one could speculate, in line with the Schumpeterian 'creative destruction' theory, that making money more difficult to earn could potentially speed up technology adoption in countries like Poland. While the net growth effects of such policy changes are unclear, it must also be remembered that even without taking any policy measures, cost competitiveness as a source of dynamic growth will likely dry up soon. Once labour costs become too large to guarantee profitability when just doing 'business as usual', firms will be forced either to make risky decisions regarding their technological profile, or to shut down. Appropriate policy measures and technological developments can help to increase TFP and labour productivity so that more firms can 'jump ahead' before this dilemma really kicks in.

3.5   THE POSITION OF CESEE COUNTRIES IN THE GLOBAL VALUE CHAIN

Another economic issue which translates into the level of country-wide TFP, and – temporarily – to its growth dynamics, is the country's position in the global value chain. It is generally argued that value-added creation is typically concentrated in more downstream economies, that is, in economies that are closer to the final good or service. As a consequence, if real convergence, structural change or technology adoption could cause an economy to move down along the global value chain, this can also bring about measurable increases in TFP over the medium run.

During the period of economic transition, manufacturing in most of the newer EU countries has experienced faster productivity growth than the services sector, despite the relatively low level of R&D expenditures. One of the important factors driving productivity and output growth was the ongoing internationalization of the manufacturing sector: opening up to exports, intermediate goods imports and the inflow of foreign capital (Bijsterbosch and Kolasa, 2010). There is also evidence that in Poland there have been sizeable productivity spillovers from foreign firms to domestic firms. Recent meta-analyses show that this phenomenon was present in the 25 years of transition in many CESEE countries, but was weakening over time (Hanoušek et al., 2011). In Poland the spillovers were mostly vertical: where foreign firms operating in a given sector induce productivity growth in their domestic counterparts. However, significant backward spillovers have been found as well, with foreign buyers of intermediate goods making their upstream domestic manufacturing firms more productive (Hagemejer and Kolasa, 2011).

The above findings are in line with the theoretical literature that claims that internationalized firms are more productive than their counterparts without links to foreign markets. Therefore the process of opening up of CESEE economies was closely associated with continuous productivity growth. Yet this process has also overlapped with the global process of increasing fragmentation of manufacturing. Fragmentation manifests itself in the overall increase in the length of the production chain: an increase in the number of stages required to manufacture a product. The position of a producer in the production chain determines the ability to reap the benefits of the participation in the process. The so-called 'smile-curve' suggests that the largest gains come from the very first stage of product design (R&D) and the very last (marketing) (Veugelers, 2013). The manufacturing process is related to a relatively low share of overall value added. However, manufacturing value added goes up with the decreasing distance from final demand.

Where are the newer EU member states in the global value chain? They started up relatively far from final demand, exporting mainly natural resources and products of a relatively small degree of processing. Over time, imports of intermediate goods contributed to an increasing portion in the production costs and these economies have gradually moved towards the global final demand in relative terms. The ongoing relocation of manufacturing production to the newer EU members has led to convergence in the overall distance of the final demand of the newer EU members relative to the EU-15 in the period of 1995 to 2011. As far as manufacturing exports are concerned, the position of newer EU members is not different from that of the EU-15 (Hagemejer and Ghodsi, 2014). Moreover, exports of newer EU members are visibly more downstream than imports, also suggesting the relative movement towards final demand.

The devil is, however, in the detail: the share of the manufacturing sector is much higher in the newer EU members than in the EU-15 and therefore the overall economy distance from the final demand is much larger in the former. Moreover, the four important manufacturing sectors of the region are transport equipment, machinery, electrical and optical equipment, but also basic and fabricated metals. In motor vehicles and machinery, sectors that expanded the most in transition, the goods supplied by CESEE are far from final demand. Organisation for Economic Co-operation and Development (OECD, 2013) studies show that in Poland the domestic share of value added in both sectors is very low and most of the value added is captured elsewhere in the production chain. Newer EU members are as downstream as the EU-15 in optical and electrical equipment, but here the level of domestic value added in exports is also low.

It may also be argued that the productivity gains due to internationalization have already materialized to a large extent, as global value chains were established across Europe, through the reallocation of resources. Most importantly, Germany is an important centre of European economic activity in the global value chain. Therefore the growth prospects of a large part of the global value chain depend on the developments in the German economy. German-centred global value chains specialize in medium-technology intensive goods unlike those of the United States or Japan. To what extent participation in Germany-centred global value chains will involve ongoing innovation and productivity growth is yet to be seen. Finally, let me also note that despite the above caveat, the distance from the final demand should clearly attract more attention in the discussion on the desired model of CESEE exports. The optimal placement within the global value-added chain, which brings largest gains in terms of innovation and productivity as well as the largest share of domestic value added, should be an important element of an effective growth-promoting policy.

3.6   CONCLUSION

To wrap up, let me reiterate that a point has now been reached after which medium-term growth perspectives for countries in the CESEE region will no longer be shaped only by the classical forces of real convergence. The remarkable past achievements in this respect have caused this source of development to gradually dry up. The only way to ensure rapid growth in GDP per capita in the future is to encourage ongoing increases in total factor productivity. This calls for a well-crafted policy related to the issues of R&D, technology adoption, and these countries' positions in the global value chain.

NOTES

1. OECD data, GDP per capita in constant prices of 2005, corrected for purchasing power parity (PPP).
2. The exceptions are France and Italy where the levels of labour productivity have been similar in both sectors since 2000.

REFERENCES

Bijsterbosch, M. and M. Kolasa (2010), 'FDI and Productivity Convergence in Central and Eastern Europe: An Industry-level Investigation', *Review of World Economics* (Weltwirtschaftliches Archiv), 145(4), 689–712.
Gradzewicz, M., J. Growiec, M. Kolasa, Ł. Postek and P. Strzelecki (2014), 'Poland's Exceptional Performance During the World Economic Crisis: New Growth Accounting Evidence', NBP Working Paper No. 186.
Griffith, R., S. Redding and J. Van Reenen (2004), 'Mapping the Two Faces of R&D: Productivity Growth in a Panel of OECD Industries', *Review of Economics and Statistics*, 86(4), 883–95.
Growiec, J., M. Gradzewicz, J. Hagemejer, Z. Jankiewicz, P. Popowski, K. Puchalska, P. Strzelecki and J. Tyrowicz (2014), 'Rola usług rynkowych w procesach rozwojowych gospodarki Polski' (The Role of Market Services in Development Processes of the Polish Economy), Materiały i Studia NBP nr 308.
Hagemejer, J. and M.M. Ghodsi (2014), 'Up or Down the Value Chain? The Comparative Analysis of the GVC Position of the Economies of the New EU Member States', mimeo, University of Warsaw.
Hagemejer, J. and M. Kolasa (2011), 'Internationalisation and Economic Performance of Enterprises: Evidence from Polish Firm-level Data', *World Economy*, 34(1), 74–100.
Hanoušek, J., E. Kočenda and M. Maurel (2011), 'Direct and Indirect Effects of FDI in Emerging European Markets: A Survey and Meta-Analysis', *Economic Systems*, 35(3), 301–22.

Kolasa, M. (2008), 'Productivity, Innovation and Convergence in Poland', *Economics of Transition*, 16(3), 467–501.
OECD (2013), 'Global Value Chains: Poland', available at http://www.oecd.org/sti/ind/GVCs – POLAND.pdf.
Veugelers, R. (ed.) (2013), 'Manufacturing Europe's Future', Brussels: Bruegel Blueprint Series, No. 21.
Young, A. (2014), 'Structural Transformation, the Mismeasurement of Productivity Growth, and the Cost Disease of Services', *American Economic Review*, 104(11), 3635–67.

4.   Rebalancing the CESEE economies: a crucial agenda for future years
Sir Suma Chakrabarti

Against the backdrop of conditions in 2014, 'rebalancing' is a topic that some might think of as backward looking. After all, rebalancing the economies of Central, Eastern and South-Eastern Europe (CESEE) has been under way for some time. Indeed, the rapid withdrawal of international liquidity from the markets of countries in which the EBRD is active, and the sharp spike in risk premia in the immediate aftermath of the 2009 crisis in essence forced the EBRD to address a number of vulnerabilities.

National banking systems have adopted much more balanced funding: less foreign and more local sources of funding. As foreign wholesale and parent bank funding was rapidly withdrawn, banks began to compete more for domestic deposits. The loan-to-deposit ratio has come down significantly as a result. More recently, we have seen good success in opening domestic bond markets to bank refinancing, for instance in Romania, and a number of countries have pressed forward with developing a framework for securitised transactions. The European Bank for Reconstruction and Development (EBRD), since 2010, has strongly supported the development of local currency and capital markets through its dedicated initiative.

But well-structured and managed use of foreign capital should not be abandoned. We should not throw the baby out with the bath water, as they say in Britain. Central and Eastern Europe needs to continue its convergence and grow considerably faster than advanced Europe. Capital inflows should accordingly flow from advanced to emerging Europe. It has been, and will remain, a good business overall, both for advanced country investors and the recipient countries.

Some rebalancing is occurring in the ownership structure of banks too, including with regard to foreign and domestic ownership. As long as it is taking place on the basis of market principles – some banks withdraw from non-core markets and budding domestic investors take their place – then this can be a healthy and welcome development. However, the EBRD does not believe in 'targets' for national ownership in any sector. One of

Europe's main achievements has been its single market, and it needs to be maintained and protected.

We have seen some success in fiscal consolidation that has, at the same time, helped create fiscal space in some countries. The EBRD's research has shown that quite a few countries in the region have fiscal space in terms of debt sustainability as well as absorptive capacity. The latest World Economic Outlook (WEO) at the time of writing, published in October 2014, has demonstrated that, if well designed and executed, infrastructure projects actually can be self-financing (International Monetary Fund, 2014). We at the EBRD are supporting clients and countries in the region to help prepare and select high-quality investment, which is a key precondition of growth-enhancing high impact infrastructural projects. We of course support and catalyse infrastructure investment with projects.

Finally, we have recently seen domestic consumption becoming a more meaningful driver of demand. Improving labour market dynamics in Central Europe, and some revival in consumer credit, have underpinned household spending. Given the renewed concerns over the euro zone this rebalancing comes not before time.

So, while we have gone through the recovery of the immediate post-crisis phase, this book addresses a crucial agenda for future years. As the euro area continues to go through simultaneous public and private sector deleveraging, growth prospects in the European Union (EU) remain modest. Within emerging Europe, policy space for crisis management policy is heavily circumscribed, and as regards the financial sector it is thoroughly exhausted. A sustainable growth model is needed that is rooted in domestic productivity growth.

It is worth recalling that we have seen a significant divergence in growth paths in emerging Europe. Most notably this is evident in Poland, where the economy expanded by 20 per cent from 2010 to 2014, while the euro zone still remains more than 2 per cent below the pre-crisis peak. The growth picture in the Western Balkans remains very disappointing, and Croatia and Serbia remain in recession.

Since overcoming the immediate challenges of the post-crisis period we have seen a slowdown in structural reforms, as was demonstrated in the EBRD's 'Transition Report 2013: Stuck in Transition?' (EBRD, 2013). In fact, in an attempt to boost growth some countries have regressed in what we previously thought of as key goals in economic transition, and we have seen a series of reform reversals. For growth and convergence, it is indispensable that structural reforms are revitalised in the transition region.

But let me point out four challenges that are shared by most of the EBRD countries of operations. First is the post-crisis overhang of non-performing loans. As in many other emerging markets that have experienced an abrupt stop to a credit boom and contraction in domestic activity we have seen a sharp rise in the level of non-performing loans. The earliest and sharpest rise came in the Baltic countries. It is instructive that active bank restructuring and reforms in the legal context for insolvency laws brought about an equally rapid decline. Proactive provisioning policies by the National Bank of Romania have recently activated the non-performing loan sales market there. And, sure enough, we saw reductions in non-performing loans in the second half of 2014. By contrast, economies in South-Eastern Europe – whether in the EU or not – have seen a steady rise in loan delinquency. Non-performing loan ratios above 20 per cent now impair the very functioning of the banking system, undermining investment and growth across the economy.

Along with other international institutions the EBRD has supported its countries of operation in trying to understand the necessary regulatory and tax reforms, and we have long called for action by the public sector and the banking community alike. I am therefore very pleased that the resolution of non-performing loans has become a renewed priority under the Vienna Initiative; at this point focusing on implementation and action plans in affected countries. In addition to the strong engagement by a number of bank groups, holders of bad assets, we are helping to introduce outside investors to the region who could assist in the needed restructuring effort.

A second and related challenge lies in addressing corporate debt distress. In many countries the flip-side of banks' non-performing loans problem is excessive leverage in the corporate sector. All too often enterprises took on credit from a large and unwieldy group of creditor banks. Empirical studies leave little doubt that debt distress translates into a weaker record on investment, productivity growth and employment. The EBRD countries of operations are no exception.

What is needed is a legal environment that encourages financial restructuring, on the back of which investment and operational performance will recover. In many cases that will require new equity investors to contribute risk capital and fresh strategies. We at the EBRD have been engaged in a number of such restructuring cases – typically a complex and extensive process. Slovenia is a good example. But increasingly we seek to bring specialist investors to the region who can handle such processes on a more efficient scale, freeing up banks' capacity to again focus on fresh lending. We welcome in this regard the initiative by Austrian parent bank groups to adopt harmonized principles to corporate restructuring.

A third challenge is presented by the precipitous decline in investment, both public and private. Europe's rate of capital formation is still more than 15 per cent below the pre-crisis peak. Years of underinvestment – in some sectors a shrinkage of the value of real capital – will translate into weaker trend growth, compounding the investment malaise. As I mentioned above, infrastructure investment would likely have a particularly potent link to trend growth, and concerns over short-term debt dynamics should be assessed in the light of such growth effects.

Some of our countries have recognized this weakness and, despite stretched public finances, have designed innovative investment schemes that seek to attract commercial funding into priority sectors. The new EU Commission has proposed a €300 billion scheme with similar ambition (European Commission, 2014). The EU structural and cohesion funds remain the principal source for a range of investments, and the EU Commission encourages member states to blend public with private investment sources. We at the EBRD have for 23 years endeavoured to harness capital markets for a range of public and private investment priorities. We can attest to the benefits that private capital can bring to the crucial process of project selection and structuring.

Finally, a fourth challenge lies in invigorating innovation. To date much of the growth in our countries has been based on factor accumulation and the redeployment of factors of production away from unproductive sectors. These relatively easier gains will soon be exhausted; in particular as foreign direct investment inflows will likely remain scarce, and the challenges of an ageing and shrinking workforce are increasingly setting in.

But plenty of gains remain where enterprises raise efficiency and productivity. Lifting the exceptionally low levels of public and private spending on research and development is one aspect of this agenda. Yet much promise also lies in encouraging firms to adopt technologies of products that already exist in other markets or structuring management processes more efficiently. The EBRD's 'Transition Report 2014' provides great detail on this issue.

Twenty-five years of economic transition comprised a deep early recession, then a rapid convergence, and in 2009 a crisis that exposed the risk from overly rapid financial expansion and excessive dependence on foreign funding. Going forward, growth will need to be more balanced. The EBRD countries of operations will seek balance between different sectors of the real economy, between domestic and external demand, and between different forms of funding. Crucially, the search for a new growth model is advancing. But one thing remains clear: we all need to support reforms that will underpin the return to the path of economic convergence.

REFERENCES

European Bank for Reconstruction and Development (EBRD) (2013), 'Transition Report 2013: Stuck in Transition?', available at http://tr.ebrd.com/tr13/images/downloads/357_TR2013.pdf.

European Bank for Reconstruction and Development (EBRD) (2014), 'Transition Report 2014: Innovation in Transition', available at http://www.ebrd.com/news/publications/transition-report/transition-report-2014.html.

European Commission (2014), 'An Investment Plan for Europe', available at http://ec.europa.eu/priorities/jobs-growth-investment/plan/docs/an-investment-plan-for-europe_com_2014_903_en.pdf.

International Monetary Fund (2014), 'World Economic Outlook. Legacies, Clouds, Uncertainties', World Economic and Financial Surveys, available at http://www.imf.org/external/pubs/ft/weo/2014/02/pdf/text.pdf.

PART II

Balance sheet adjustments and economic
growth

5. Fighting balance sheet recessions: a Japanese lesson for the euro zone

Richard C. Koo

After the years of economic stagnation since 2008 and an alarming fall in inflation rates, some European policy-makers are beginning to pay attention to Japan's experience of a 'lost decade'. This is in sharp contrast to the Obama administration in the United States (US), which recognized within the first two years of the global financial crisis that the US was suffering from the same kind of balance sheet recession that had plagued Japan and managed to steer clear of its dangers by fully utilizing lessons learned from Japan. This chapter argues that once the European predicament is understood to be a case of balance sheet recession, it will become clear that the crisis can be resolved with two modifications to the structure of the euro without resorting to an injection of German taxpayer money or additional monetary easing by the European Central Bank (ECB), including quantitative easing.

5.1 JAPANESE AND US EXPERIENCES WITH BALANCE SHEET RECESSIONS

A balance sheet recession happens when a debt-financed asset price bubble bursts and leaves the private sector with a large debt overhang. In order to climb out of its negative equity hole, the private sector shifts priority from maximizing profit to minimizing debt. Although that is the right thing to do for individual households and firms, a huge fallacy of composition problem is created when a substantial portion of the private sector moves to minimize debt at the same time. This is because if one group is saving money or paying down debt, another group must borrow and spend money to keep the national economy going.

In a normal economy, this function of matching savers and borrowers is performed by the financial sector, with interest rates moving higher or lower depending on whether there are too many or too few borrowers. But when the private sector as a whole is minimizing debt to repair damaged

39

balance sheets, there will not be enough borrowers even at zero interest rates. Nor will there be many lenders if the financial institutions themselves are facing balance sheet problems. That means the savings that find no borrowers even at zero interest rates (unborrowed savings) will be bottled up in financial institutions and leak out of the economy's income stream. If this leakage or deflationary gap is left unattended, the economy will continue shrinking by the amount of the leakage each year until the private sector finally becomes too poor to save. That outcome is typically called a depression. This deleveraging process was what caused the US to lose 46 per cent of its gross national product (GNP) in just four years following the New York stock market crash in October 1929.

When the private sector as a whole is deleveraging or saving, the money multiplier also turns negative at the margin, which means the money supply cannot grow no matter how much base money the central bank injects into the banking system. During the four years of the Great Depression mentioned above, the US lost over 30 per cent of its money supply largely for this reason.[1]

Japan avoided that outcome after its bubble burst in 1990 and kept its gross domestic product (GDP) and money supply above bubble peak levels for the next 24 years because the government elected to borrow and spend the unborrowed savings of the private sector. As a result, the Japanese unemployment rate never climbed above 5.5 per cent, averaging just 4.0 per cent during the same period. This is no mean achievement in view of the fact that commercial real estate prices fell 87 per cent nationwide and the private sector has been deleveraging to the tune of 8 per cent of GDP per year on average for the last 15 years. Although two big mistakes were made in the form of premature attempts at fiscal consolidation in 1997 and 2001 – both of which not only delayed the recovery but actually increased the deficit – the Japanese private sector successfully completed its balance sheet repairs by 2005.

The post-2008 US policy-makers who understood Japan's lessons on balance sheet recessions were determined to avoid the mistakes of 1997 and 2001 and issued a strong warning against premature fiscal consolidation by using the expression 'fiscal cliff'. The US economy was indeed in a precarious state when they started using the term, with the private sector saving nearly 10 per cent of GDP in spite of zero interest rates (although that number was subsequently revised downwards). US policy-makers understood that in the absence of private sector borrowers, both GDP and the effectiveness of monetary policy depend on the last borrower standing, that is, the government. If the government opts to borrow and spend the unborrowed savings of the private sector, not only is the leakage from the economy's income stream eliminated, but the money multiplier remains positive, which prevents the money supply from shrinking. Although the US came very close to falling off the fiscal cliff on a number of occasions – including the government shutdown, the sequester and the debt ceiling disputes – it ultimately managed to steer clear of this outcome. That is the main reason why it is doing better than its European counterparts today.

5.2 MISTAKING BALANCE SHEET PROBLEMS FOR STRUCTURAL PROBLEMS

European leaders, on the other hand, did not realize that they are facing an unusual disease called a balance sheet recession, which was never taught at universities and which strikes only in the aftermath of a nationwide asset price bubble. With no leaders issuing warnings about a fiscal cliff, even though governments have been the only borrowers across the euro zone since 2008, euro zone countries in balance sheet recessions have fallen off the fiscal cliff one after another, with devastating human consequences.

European leaders also repeated the Japanese error of mistaking balance sheet problems for structural problems not once but twice, and it was these two mistakes that led to the current economic crisis. The first was made by Chancellor Gerhard Schroeder when the German economy was suffering from a severe balance sheet recession triggered by the bursting of the dotcom bubble in 2000. The Neuer Markt, Germany's equivalent of the Nasdaq, rose tenfold during the bubble years only to lose 97 per cent of its value afterwards (Figure 5.1).

This crash devastated the balance sheets of both households and businesses in Germany, forcing them to dramatically increase savings thereafter. German flow-of-funds data (Figure 5.2) show that prior to the dotcom bubble the German household sector was a net saver (financial surplus) while the German corporate sector was a net borrower (financial deficit). After 2000, however, both sectors increased savings sharply, and by 2004 the two sectors combined were saving as much as 8 per cent of GDP in spite of interest rates that were at a post-war low of 2 per cent. The massive shift in household behaviour is illustrated in Figure 5.3, which shows that while households were saving money before 2000, they were also borrowing money to buy houses and so on. After 2000, however, they stopped borrowing altogether in spite of such low interest rates, reflecting an aversion to debt that continues to this day.

The fact that the private sector as a whole was a net saver means that the money multiplier for the German private sector was negative at the margin. This explains why the German economy failed to respond to ECB monetary accommodation from 2001 to 2005. The slow growth in the

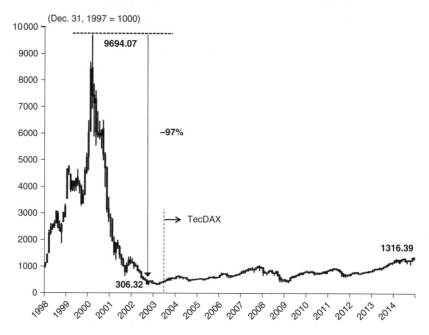

Note: The TecDAX tracks the 30 largest technology companies listed in the prime standard segment of Deutsche Börse.

Source: Bloomberg, as of Dec. 17, 2014

Figure 5.1   Collapse of the Neuer Markt in 2001 pushed the German economy into balance sheet recession

German money supply translated to slow growth in German wages and prices.

The German recession was also exacerbated by the fact that the Maastricht Treaty prohibited member governments from running budget deficits in excess of 3 per cent of GDP, even though the German private sector was saving as much as 8 per cent of GDP. Although the actual deficit was frequently greater than 3 per cent because of a weakening economy, Treaty constraints kept the German government from using fiscal stimulus proactively to fight the recession.

The economy's inability to respond to monetary easing led many to label Germany the 'sick man of Europe' and prompted its policy-makers to assume that the economy was shackled by structural problems. This is exactly the same mistake that the Hashimoto (1996–1998) and Koizumi (2001–2006) administrations made in Japan when they pushed

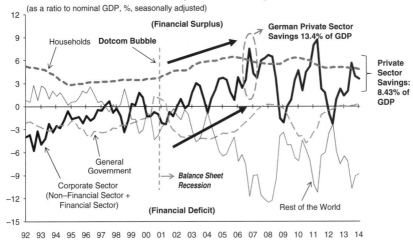

Financial Surplus or Deficit by Sector
(as a ratio to nominal GDP, %, seasonally adjusted)

Notes: The assumption of Treuhand agency's debt by the Redemption Fund for Inherited Liabilities in 1995 is adjusted. All entries are four-quarter moving averages. For the latest figures, four-quarter averages ending in 2014 Q1 are used.

Source: Nomura Research Institute, based on the data from Bundesbank and Eurostat

Figure 5.2   *The German private sector refused to borrow after the dotcom bubble*

for structural reforms that included fiscal consolidation. In both cases the Japanese economy weakened further and the fiscal deficit actually grew because of the stuttering economy (Figure 5.4).

When the Hashimoto government implemented six major structural reforms – including fiscal consolidation – in 1997 under strong pressure from the International Monetary Fund (IMF) and the Organisation for Economic Co-operation and Development (OECD), the economy collapsed and the deficit actually widened by 72 per cent, underscoring the fact that these international organizations had no understanding of balance sheet recessions back then. Another attempt by Prime Minister Koizumi in 2001 to substitute structural reforms for fiscal stimulus also ended in tears, with deficits increasing in spite of fiscal consolidation efforts. It took Japan ten years to bring its deficit back down to pre-1997 levels. These failed attempts demonstrated that structural reforms are no substitute for the fiscal stimulus needed during this type of recession.

Of course structural reforms have their own merits, some of which are substantial and long-lasting. But when an economy that was responding

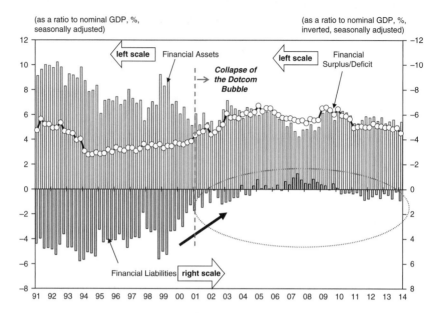

Note: Seasonal adjustments by Nomura Research Institute. Latest figures are for 2014 Q1.

Sources: Nomura Research Institute, based on flow of funds data from Bundesbank and Eurostat

Figure 5.3   German households stopped borrowing altogether after the dotcom bubble

well to ordinary macro policies suddenly stops responding, the cause of this shift cannot be blamed on structural problems that have existed for years, if not decades, before the shift. Moreover, all economies that experienced this shift did so after an asset bubble burst, which suggests that balance sheet problems and not structural problems are the cause.

Fortunately for the Germans, the peripheral countries of the euro zone were not caught up in the dotcom bubble, and the balance sheets of their private sectors were clean. When the ECB took interest rates down to what was then a post-war low of 2 per cent to save the German economy, the peripheral nations responded in textbook fashion by borrowing money to invest in real estate, fuelling huge housing bubbles (Figure 5.5). Figures 5.6 and 5.7 show flow-of-funds data for the Spanish and Irish household sectors, respectively. Traditionally conservative households in both countries were unable to resist the lure of 2 per cent interest rates, a level not seen in generations, and plunged headfirst into real estate. This is in sharp

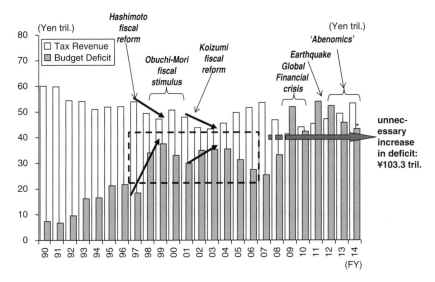

Notes: Latest figures(*) are estimated by MOF. From FY2011, figures include reconstruction taxes and bonds.

Source: Ministry of Finance, Japan

Figure 5.4   *Japan's fall from the fiscal cliff in 1997 and 2001 weakened the economy, reduced tax revenues and increased the deficit*

contrast to Germany, where house prices declined 10 per cent from 1995 to 2005 as households refused to borrow money after the dotcom bubble burst.

The strong demand for funds in peripheral countries meant that their money multipliers were strongly positive, and their money supplies grew rapidly. German banks, facing a severe shortage of borrowers at home, also lent eagerly to these countries. With money supply growing rapidly, peripheral countries' wages and prices also increased rapidly. Figure 5.8 illustrates money supply growth in Germany and the euro zone (excluding Germany). Rebased to 100 at 2000, Germany's money supply grew only to 156 by mid-2008, while the money supply in the rest of euro zone increased to 217, opening up a huge competitiveness gap between the two. That allowed the Germans to export their way out of their balance sheet recession, since German wages had become increasingly competitive vis-à-vis the rest of the euro zone.

Figure 5.9 illustrates the composition of German trade surpluses. It shows that Germany was able to surpass Japan and China to record the

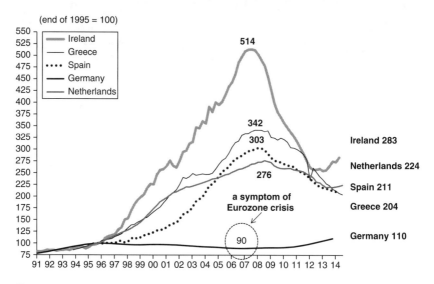

Notes:
1. Ireland's figures before 2005 are existing house prices only.
2. Greece's figures are flats' prices in Athens and Thessaloniki.

Sources: Nomura Research Institute, calculated from Bank for International Settlements data.

Figure 5.5   Europe (excluding Germany) also experienced housing bubbles

world's largest trade surplus by exporting to its euro zone neighbours, where wage and price increases outstripped those of Germany. In other words, the fact that Germany was in a balance sheet recession while other economies were not is crucial to understanding why the euro zone competitiveness gap grew to such an extent.

5.3   STRUCTURAL REFORM IS RESPONSIBLE FOR ONLY HALF OF THE COMPETITIVENESS GAP

The three lines at the bottom of Figure 5.8 are an attempt to compare the competitiveness gap created by Germany's balance sheet recession with the gap due to Chancellor Schroeder's painful structural reforms. First, in the euro zone (excluding Germany) M3, the broad measure of money supply expanded by 117 per cent between the collapse of the dotcom bubble in 2000 and Lehman's bankruptcy in 2008 Q3. That growth led to

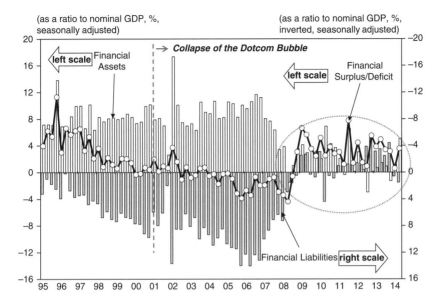

Notes: Seasonal adjustments by Nomura Research Institute. Latest figures are for 2014 Q2.

Sources: Nomura Research Institute, based on flow of funds data from Banco de España and National Statistics Institute, Spain

Figure 5.6   *Spanish households increased borrowings after the dotcom bubble but are now deleveraging*

corresponding increases in wages and prices. But in Germany, where the collapse of the dotcom bubble prompted the private sector to focus collectively on minimizing debt, the money supply grew only 56 per cent over the same period. That served to depress price and wage inflation relative to the rest of Europe.

As the third line from the top in Figure 5.8 shows, unit labour costs in the rest of the euro zone rose from 100 (rebased) in 2000 to 129.9 in 2008 Q3, for an increase of 29.9 per cent. In Germany, shown by the bottom line in Figure 5.8, they edged up to 100.6, for an increase of just 0.6 per cent. If we assume that German workers were no more competitive than their counterparts in the rest of the euro zone in 2000, the implication is that by 2008 Q3 workers in the rest of the euro zone had grown 29.3 percentage points more expensive relative to their German counterparts.

The next question is how much of this 29.3 percentage point gap was attributable to the microeconomic factor of Germany's painful structural

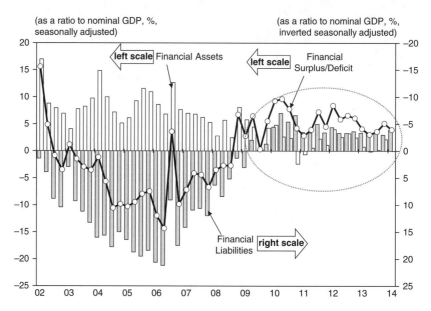

Notes: Seasonal adjustments by Nomura Research Institute. Latest figures are for 2014 Q1.

Sources: Nomura Research Institute, based on flow of funds data from Central Bank of Ireland and Central Statistics Office, Ireland

Figure 5.7   Irish households increased borrowings after the dotcom bubble but are now deleveraging

reforms and how much was due to the macroeconomic factor of the nation's balance sheet recession. The following calculations suggest a roughly equal split between the two factors.

The money supply in the euro zone (excluding Germany) grew 117.0 per cent during this period, while unit labour costs rose 29.9 per cent. The regression results shown at the bottom of Figure 5.8 indicate that each percentage point increase in the money supply lifted unit labour costs by 0.318 per cent. This means if money supply growth in the euro zone (excluding Germany) had been the same as in Germany, unit labour costs in the rest of the euro zone would have risen by 15.2 per cent, not 29.9 per cent. In other words, money supply growth was responsible for 14.7 percentage points (29.9 per cent – 15.2 per cent), or 50.2 per cent, of the 29.3 percentage point gap in unit labor costs.

Meanwhile, unit labour costs in Germany rose only 0.6 per cent during this period, which means that 14.6 percentage points (15.2 per cent – 0.6

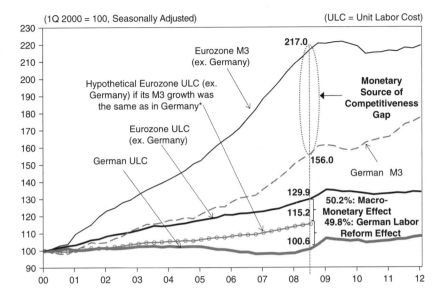

Note: *Parameters obtained from the regression result on Eurozone ULC (ex. Germany) on Eurozone M3 (ex. Germany), log(Eurozone ULC (ex. Germany)) = 3.155506 + log(Eurozone M3 (ex. Germany)) × 0.318227, applied to German M3 data indexed to 1Q 2000 = 100.

Sources: Nomura Research Institute, based on ECB, Eurostat and Deutsche Bundesbank data

Figure 5.8   The German–euro zone (excluding Germany) competitiveness gap has macro (50.2%) and micro (49.8%) factors

per cent) of the 15.2 per cent estimated growth in unit labour costs cannot be explained by money supply growth and is attributable instead to Germany's structural reforms. These 14.6 percentage points represent 49.8 per cent of the total 29.3 percentage point gap.

Although this simplified calculation has a number of shortcomings, it provides a starting point for measuring the impact of structural reforms vis-à-vis the impact of Germany's balance sheet recession. It suggests that while the microeconomic factor of German structural reforms was certainly important, those reforms explain less than half (49.8 per cent) of the overall gap in competitiveness. The remaining 50.2 per cent is attributable to the fact that Germany was in a balance sheet recession while the rest of the euro zone was enjoying brisk economic performance and money supply growth.

Ultimately the ECB lowered rates out of concern for Germany, but the

Source: Deutsche Bundesbank

*Figure 5.9   Germany recovered from the post-dotcom balance sheet
recession by exporting to other euro zone countries*

German economy did not respond because it was in a balance sheet recession. Instead, the low interest rates fuelled housing bubbles in countries on the European periphery, causing both GDP and the money supply in these nations to surge, along with prices and wages. Germany finally succeeded in pulling itself out of its balance sheet recession by massively increasing exports to these countries.

5.4   PRIVATE SECTOR SAVINGS HAVE SURPASSED FISCAL DEFICITS SINCE 2008

The bursting of the housing bubble in 2008 pushed peripheral countries into serious balance sheet recessions as can be seen from a complete disappearance of borrowings in Figure 5.6 and 5.7 in spite of near-zero interest rates. But German politicians and others who had never understood this type of recession began demanding that peripheral countries also cut their deficits and implement structural reforms, thus repeating the mistake they themselves made eight years earlier. This second mistake plunged the euro zone into an unprecedented economic crisis, because this time there were no businesses or households willing to borrow and spend the unborrowed savings generated elsewhere in the euro zone.

When Germany was the only country in the euro zone suffering from a balance sheet recession, it could count on the private sectors of other euro zone economies to borrow and spend its unborrowed savings. Indeed, German banks lent enthusiastically to those countries to make up for a severe shortage of borrowers at home. But at the time of this writing in early 2015 there is not a single country in the euro zone where the private sector is a net borrower, and that includes Germany. In other words, the entire euro zone is now characterized by both a deflationary gap and a negative money multiplier. That explains why all the monetary easing measures implemented by the ECB have failed to produce the expected results.

Within the euro zone, only Greece is running a fiscal deficit that is larger than its net private savings. In all other countries, the private sector is saving far more than the government is borrowing, as shown in Figure 5.10, which combines into one line all private sector entries from each country's flow-of-funds data; that is, the household, corporate and financial sectors. It shows that the private sectors of all these countries were major net borrowers during the bubble era but turned into huge net savers after the bubble burst. The fact that they are saving or deleveraging despite zero interest rates indicates that these countries are all in serious balance sheet recessions.

Unfortunately, most policy-makers in Europe remain unaware that private sector savings are in excess of government deficits. In fact, most have never seen the savings data shown in Figure 5.10. Instead, they are obsessed with the fact that their deficits exceed the 3 per cent (of GDP) limit imposed by the Maastricht Treaty. But whether a deficit is too large or too small for an economy should be judged in the context of private sector savings. If savings exceed the deficit, even at zero interest rates, then the deficit is too small to stabilize the economy even if it is larger than the 3 per cent limit imposed by the Treaty.

5.5 THE MAASTRICHT TREATY IS DEFECTIVE AND SHOULD BE REVISED IMMEDIATELY

The above disregard for the size of private sector savings leads one to the first of the two structural flaws specific to the euro zone: namely, that the Maastricht Treaty is a defective agreement that makes no provisions for balance sheet recessions. In particular, the Treaty says nothing about how to counter a deflationary spiral brought about by a private sector that is saving far more than 3 per cent of GDP at zero interest rates. The Treaty

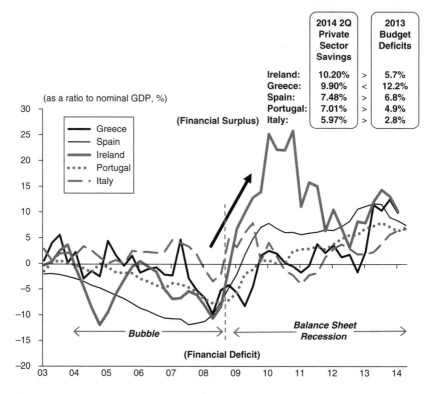

Notes:
1. Private sector = Household Sector + Non-Financial Corporate Sector + Financial Sector
2. All entries are four-quarter moving averages. For the latest figures, four-quarter averages ending in 2014 2Q (only Ireland and Greece, 2014 1Q) are used. Budget deficits in Euro area in 2013 are from Oct. 21, 2014 release by Eurostat.

Sources: Bank of Greece, Banco de España, National Statistics Institute, Spain, The Central Bank of Ireland, Central Statistics Office Ireland, Banco de Portugal, Banca d'Italia and Italian National Institute of Statistics

Figure 5.10   Europe in balance sheet recession: private sector savings exceed fiscal deficits in the euro zone

never envisioned a situation in which the private sector would behave in such a manner, because economics textbooks say that the private sector should be borrowing at such low rates. But the private sectors of all Western countries (except Australia and Canada) and Japan are currently increasing savings despite zero interest rates.

Spain's private sector (households + non-financial corporations +

financial institutions) was saving 7.5 per cent of GDP in 2014 even with zero interest rates, but under the Maastricht Treaty the government can borrow and spend only 3 per cent of GDP. The remaining 4.5 per cent becomes a deflationary gap that causes the Spanish economy to contract. The Treaty makes no mention of what to do in a situation where the private sector is saving more than 3 per cent of GDP in spite of zero interest rates. That is perhaps to be expected, as the concept of balance sheet recessions was unknown outside Japan when the details of the Treaty were being worked out in the 1990s. If policy-makers had been aware of this risk and had incorporated it in the Treaty, the response of the ECB and the German government to the collapse of the dotcom bubble would have been very different indeed.

If the Treaty had requested – if not required – countries in balance sheet recessions to respond with sufficient fiscal stimulus to prevent distortions in the ECB's monetary policy or other euro zone economies, Germany would not have had to rely as much on exports after the dotcom bubble, and the ECB would not have had to lower interest rates as far as it did to rescue Germany, creating housing bubbles in Spain and Ireland in the process. And if German banks had been able to invest in their own government's bonds, far less money would have flowed into Spanish assets and US subprime securities. In that sense, the euro crisis was caused in part by policy distortions brought about by the fact that the Maastricht Treaty makes no allowances for balance sheet recessions. This is something that needs to be rectified as soon as possible.

Countries that are recognized by a panel of experts as being in a balance sheet recession (that is, the private sector saving more than 3 per cent of GDP at near-zero interest rates) should not only be freed from the 3 per cent deficit constraint but should also be encouraged – if not required – to administer adequate fiscal stimulus so that their economic weakness does not cause problems for the ECB or the rest of the euro zone. Only then will the Treaty be suitable for both balance sheet recessions and ordinary economic conditions.

A 3 per cent cap on fiscal deficits makes a certain amount of sense in an ordinary (non-balance sheet recession) world. But it is completely counterproductive during a balance sheet recession, when government borrowing and spending becomes the only policy tool available to arrest the economy's deflationary spiral.

With major political parties in the euro zone unable or unwilling to consider modifying the Treaty, increasingly impoverished and desperate voters are flocking to 'populist' eurosceptic parties that are at least willing to think outside the box of this defective arrangement. If the present trend is not corrected, not only the institution of the euro but also Europe's democratic structures themselves may come under threat as the economic crisis continues.

I have been warning about this defect in the Treaty ever since my first English book, *Balance Sheet Recession* (John Wiley, 2003), where I argued that 'of the three regions – Japan, the US and Europe – Europe is by far the most vulnerable when it comes to balance sheet recession because of the restrictions placed on it by the Maastricht Treaty' (p. 234). I also warned in my second English book, *The Holy Grail of Macroeconomics* (John Wiley, 2008), that 'forcing an inappropriate policy on a nation already suffering from a debilitating recession can actually put its democratic structures at risk by aggravating the downturn . . . the euro zone needs a treaty that is designed to cope with both ordinary and balance sheet recessions' (p. 250). Unfortunately my warnings went unheeded, and my worst fears are in the process of being realized in some of these countries.

5.6   WHY THE POLARIZATION OF EURO ZONE GOVERNMENT BOND YIELDS?

There is one more euro zone-specific problem that stands in the way of countries suffering from balance sheet recessions. Whereas government bond yields in the United States, the United Kingdom (UK), the Nordic countries and Japan, all of which are experiencing balance sheet recessions, dropped to historical lows to provide fiscal spaces for the governments, government bond yields surged in the periphery countries, which are also in balance sheet recessions (Figure 5.11). This bifurcation of yields reflects the second structural flaw specific to the euro zone.

During a balance sheet recession which occurs when the private sector moves collectively to pay down debt or increase savings, the financial institutions responsible for investing those private savings have only a limited range of investment options. Because the private sector as a whole is striving to minimize debt, fund managers cannot, in aggregate, lend to their own private sectors. Of course they have the option of buying domestic equities or foreign securities, but investors such as pension funds and life insurers are subject to regulations that prevent them from taking on excessive principal or currency risk.

These large institutional investors therefore tend to buy fixed-income assets that are denominated in the local currency and offer safety of principal. The only asset satisfying those conditions in a balance sheet recession is domestic government bonds. Institutional investors therefore head en masse to their own government bond market, pushing yields down to levels unthinkable under normal economic conditions. The steep drop in

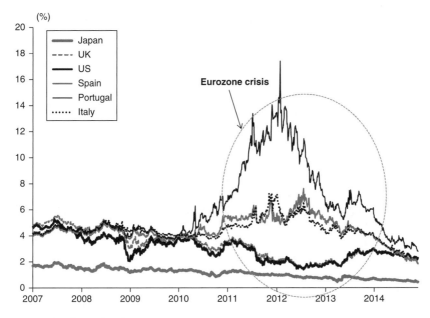

Note: As of Dec. 3, 2014.

Source: Bloomberg

Figure 5.11   Peripheral bond yields jumped on destabilizing capital flows

yields provides support for fiscal stimulus and thereby serves as an important self-corrective mechanism during a balance sheet recession. This
mechanism was first observed in Japan 20 years ago, and it has since been
witnessed in the UK, the United States and Sweden.

5.7   THE EURO ZONE ALLOWS INVESTORS TO BUY SAFER GOVERNMENT BONDS WITH NO CURRENCY RISK

This self-corrective mechanism failed to operate in many parts of the euro
zone because institutional investors concerned about the size of their own
governments' fiscal deficits can buy bonds issued by other, less fiscally
challenged euro zone governments without taking on any currency risk.
This is because all government bonds in the euro zone are denominated in
the same currency, giving investors 18 markets to choose from.

Today Spanish pension funds and life insurers who have qualms about Spanish government debt can just as easily buy bonds issued by the German or Finnish governments. Spain's large surplus of private savings will then flow to Germany, causing Spanish government bond yields to rise. When that happens, the government tends to panic because higher yields indicate that the market is shunning its bonds and that the country has no 'fiscal space'. Even worse, it may be forced to undertake deficit reduction efforts, the single worst thing a government can do during a balance sheet recession. Conditions then deteriorate further in what becomes a vicious cycle.

In November 2011, I had the opportunity to lead a seminar of large institutional investors in Madrid, and when I asked how many had moved funds out of Spain and into Germany, they all raised their hands. Their purchases contributed to a €426 billion increase in foreign holdings of German government bonds from 2008 to 2012.[2] Countries such as Spain, Ireland and Portugal that were in balance sheet recessions watched as their rapidly growing private savings – the cause of those recessions – fled to Germany's government bond market, driving yields on their own debt higher and making it impossible for them to administer the necessary fiscal stimulus. In other words, the self-corrective mechanism for balance sheet recessions does not function in the euro zone.

There would be no reason for the broader euro zone economy to contract if the German and Dutch governments elected to borrow and spend the private savings of countries like Spain and Ireland. Such actions would also provide an indirect boost to the economies experiencing an outflow of savings. However, the Maastricht Treaty's 3 per cent deficit rule has kept Germany and the Netherlands focused on fiscal consolidation. As a result, the unborrowed savings of peripheral countries became the unborrowed savings of the broader euro zone. The fact that the self-corrective mechanism no longer functions is a critical structural flaw in the euro zone that should be addressed as soon as possible.

Euro zone fund flows were moving in the opposite direction prior to the global financial crisis. As noted above, the collapse of the dotcom bubble in 2000 plunged Germany into a severe balance sheet recession, forcing local banks and other financial institutions confronting a shortage of domestic borrowers to seek the higher-yielding debt of Southern European nations. The resulting fund outflows from Germany fuelled housing bubbles in these countries.

The problem with such shifts is that they are highly destabilizing and tend to amplify swings in the real economy. Funds flow into countries that are experiencing bubbles and are in no need of further liquidity, pouring more fuel on the asset fire, while governments facing balance sheet recessions must stand by and watch as the funds they desperately need flow elsewhere, making it impossible for them to administer the necessary fiscal stimulus and accelerating the vicious cycle.

5.8 THE MEANING OF 'FISCAL SPACE' DIFFERS INSIDE AND OUTSIDE THE EURO ZONE

From around 2012 more people – including some among the euro zone authorities – have come to understand that fiscal stimulus is essential during a balance sheet recession. Yet many of them continue to believe that fiscal stimulus is an option only for countries with 'fiscal space', while the rest must undertake deficit reduction efforts. However, most are unaware that this term has a very different meaning depending on whether the country is inside or outside the euro zone.

By definition, an economy in balance sheet recession has in its financial system enough unborrowed private savings to fund the fiscal stimulus needed to close the deflationary gap. The existence of unborrowed savings, after all, is the cause of the recession. Many fund managers charged with investing those funds have no choice but to buy bonds issued by the government, which is the sole remaining borrower during a balance sheet recession, and that will provide the needed fiscal space for the government to implement fiscal stimulus. Hence the balance sheet recessions in the US, the UK and Japan have led to a sharp drop in government bond yields, providing these countries with all the fiscal space they need.

In the euro zone, however, countries that would have more than adequate fiscal space if they did not belong to the euro zone find the unborrowed savings of their private sectors fleeing for the government bond markets of other euro zone members. Consequently, their fiscal space disappears. Spain's private sector, for instance, is currently saving at the annual rate of 7.5 per cent of GDP, an amount more than sufficient to finance the Spanish government's fiscal deficit, which amounted to 6.8 per cent of GDP in 2013. If Spain were not a euro zone member, it would have ample fiscal space and its government bond yields would have fallen sharply long ago. The same is true for Ireland and Portugal. And there would have been no fiscal crisis to begin with if government bond yields in these countries had come down in line with yields in the US, the UK and Sweden. The euro crisis, after all, was sparked by surging government bond yields in the periphery.

The reality, however, is that a substantial portion of both the Spanish savings and the foreign savings that entered Spain during the bubble years fled for the perceived safety of foreign shores. The resulting surge in bond yields and the lack of fiscal space has forced governments to undertake deficit reduction efforts, plunging these economies into a deflationary spiral.

5.9 DIFFERENT RISK WEIGHTS SHOULD BE APPLIED TO DOMESTIC AND FOREIGN GOVERNMENT DEBT

To counter this capital flight problem, a different set of risk weights should be introduced for the domestic and foreign government bonds held by euro zone financial institutions and institutional investors. Specifically, the risk weight for holding domestic government bonds should be kept at or close to the current figure of zero, while risk weights for holding other government bonds should be raised significantly.

The concept of risk weights has been widely adopted by financial regulators around the world since the BIS capital rules for banks were introduced in the 1990s. Risk weights are based on the view that financial institutions should have to set aside more capital against riskier loans or investments. The original purpose of this rule was to prevent institutions from taking on excessive risk, but the goal of the present proposal is to see that euro zone investors in government bonds face conditions as similar as possible to those confronting investors in countries outside the euro zone such as Japan, the US and the UK.

The justification for assigning a lower risk weight to domestic government bonds is that domestic investors have the best understanding of local economic conditions and the local bond market.

Investors in Japan, the US and the UK are able to buy financial instruments from all over the world, but a substantial portion of their funds ends up in domestic government bonds because of regulations limiting the amount of principal and currency risk they can assume. This ring-fencing of the domestic government bond market by foreign exchange risk has produced a sharp decline in government bond yields during the balance sheet recession, thereby providing these governments with the fiscal space they need. If similar conditions could be created in the euro zone, member countries would also enjoy enhanced fiscal space and see the self-corrective mechanism restored.

The proposed risk weights would also have a minimal impact on the improvements in private sector productivity and efficiency brought about by the single currency because they apply only to the holdings of domestic versus foreign government bonds. Spanish fund managers are still free to buy German equities, and German fund managers are still free to buy Spanish corporate bonds.

The assignment of different risk weights to domestic and foreign government bonds would also work only for banks and institutional investors that are under the supervision of the monetary authorities. But if these investors began buying more domestic government bonds, yields would fall accordingly, creating the fiscal space these countries need.

5.10 THERE IS NO REASON FOR THE ECB TO IMPLEMENT QUANTITATIVE EASING

This would also mean that there is no reason for the ECB to pursue quantitative easing (QE). Expectations of QE grew because so many euro zone countries are seen as having no fiscal space, therefore necessitating additional monetary stimulus. But balance sheet recession is fundamentally caused by a lack of borrowers; adding the central bank to the list of lenders does not solve anything. More importantly, private sector savings actually exceed budget deficits in all of these countries except Greece. If the adoption of different risk weights prompted sufficient domestic savings to flow to their government bonds, yields would come down, assuring governments the fiscal space they need.

If the introduction of different risk weights were accompanied by changes to the Maastricht Treaty that allowed countries in balance sheet recessions to implement the necessary fiscal stimulus, these countries would begin to recover, since their greatest problem – the shortage of borrowers – would disappear.

It is true that QE has been credited with the recovery of the US and UK economies as well as the renewed strength of the Japanese economy under Abenomics. But a careful observation suggests that QE has not been as effective as it is often portrayed to be. Figure 5.12 shows the amount of base money injected by the central banks of the US, UK and Japan after 2008. Central banks have indeed increased the monetary base, from 100 at the time of the Lehman failure to 452 in the US, 474 in the UK and 304 in Japan. But for this base money to enter the real economy, the financial institutions receiving the liquidity must lend it to borrowers in the real economy; they cannot simply give the money away.

The bottom three lines in Figure 5.12 show credit to the private sector, that is, how much money was actually lent to the private sector. It shows that in the US and Japan, credit to the private sector grew only 7 and 8 per cent, respectively, during this six-year period, which is next to nothing. Credit growth in the UK was a negative 15 per cent. These numbers suggest that most liquidity supplied by the central banks was unable to enter the real economy due to a lack of borrowers. That explains why inflation rates have

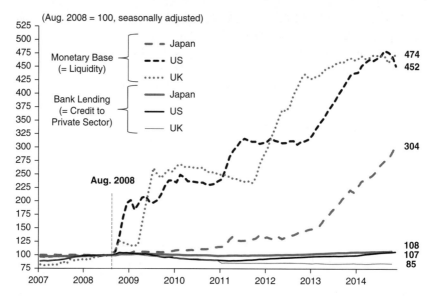

Notes:
1. US monetary base and UK's reserve balances data are seasonally unadjusted.
2. UK's bank lending data exclude intermediate financial institutions.

Source: Nomura Research Institute, based on FRB, Bank of England and Bank of Japan data.

Figure 5.12   Drastic liquidity injections resulted in minimal increases in credit

been so low in all of these countries in spite of massive quantitative easing: the money simply was not reaching the real economy.

Increasing lenders via QE when the problem is a lack of borrowers also creates massive problems later when the borrowers return and QE has to be unwound. Although the huge problems associated with the unwinding of QE are beyond the scope of this chapter, a more detailed discussion of this challenge is found in Chapter 2 of my *The Escape from Balance Sheet Recessions and the QE Trap* (John Wiley, 2014).

5.11   GERMANY BENEFITED MOST FROM THE EURO

Had Germany not been part of the euro zone, the ECB would not have lowered rates as far as it did after the dotcom bubble, and there would have been no reason for the housing bubbles in the periphery nations to expand to the extent they did. In that case, the only way Germany could have addressed its balance sheet recession – at a time when the economy was not responding to monetary policy – is by devaluing the Deutschmark, which was anathema to the Bundesbank, or by administering a massive dose of fiscal stimulus by running a large budget deficit, as Japan did in the past and the United States is doing today.

In that sense, Germany benefited more than any country from the euro. The only reason that its fiscal deficits did not widen substantially after the dotcom bubble collapsed was that the ECB, in order to rescue Germany, created housing bubbles in other euro zone countries that had sidestepped the dotcom bubble. After the housing bubbles burst in the periphery nations that had provided such an economic fillip to Germany, their economies weakened and attention suddenly focused on their lack of competitiveness. But people should question whether Germany is in a position to criticize these nations. After all, it was only because the ECB lowered short-term interest rates to 2 per cent in an attempt to rescue Germany that these countries experienced asset price bubbles, rapid money supply growth and reduced competitiveness vis-à-vis Germany, and ultimately fell into balance sheet recessions. It was not peripheral countries' policy choices that led to this outcome.

If Germany had addressed its balance sheet recession with fiscal stimulus, there would have been no need for the ECB to ease monetary policy to the extent it did, and the competitive gap between Germany and the periphery nations would never have grown as large as it did. This lack of synchronicity among euro zone economies will persist as long as some countries in the zone are suffering from balance sheet recessions while others are not. Countries in balance sheet recessions must therefore be urged to administer fiscal stimulus so that the ECB need not engage in excessive monetary accommodation, fomenting bubbles elsewhere in the euro zone. This lack of synchronicity also means that fiscal union is no solution to the problem either, because different parts of the euro zone would need different fiscal policies.

5.12 THE EURO CAN BE SAVED WITH TWO REPAIRS

The euro represents one of humanity's greatest achievements. The structures underpinning it were erected over decades by a large group of capable individuals who took into account a multitude of possibilities. It was because of their ceaseless efforts that the actual transition to the euro went so smoothly.

But just as the launch of a new aircraft inevitably reveals a variety of problems, the introduction of the euro brought to light two flaws. The first was that the Maastricht Treaty had made no allowance for balance sheet recessions, and the second was the extremely procyclical and destabilizing capital flows brought about by having a plurality of government bond markets within the same currency zone. The lack of understanding of these two problems among both the authorities and market participants increased the severity of the euro crisis. However, the euro would function beautifully as a unified currency – and would have a long future ahead of it – if only these two defects were remedied.

Encouraging – if not requiring – countries certified as being in balance sheet recessions to administer fiscal stimulus is essential to saving both those economies and the broader euro zone. That will require changes to the Maastricht Treaty, but it will also prevent distortions in monetary policy by freeing the ECB from having to take on an excessively broad role in rescuing balance sheet recession countries, a role it is ill-equipped to perform.

The relatively minor regulatory change of attaching different risk weights to holdings of domestic versus foreign government bonds would go a long way towards reducing procyclical and destabilizing capital flows among government bond markets. And if it succeeds in preserving the tremendous achievement that is the euro, it will have been a very small price to pay.

Countries such as Germany are worried that their costs will increase if the periphery nations fail to undertake deficit reduction efforts, but those fears are based on ignorance and misunderstandings. All of these countries – with the exception of Greece – have massive pools of unborrowed private sector savings that are sufficient to finance their fiscal deficits as long as those savings can be channelled to their own government bond markets. If that can be achieved with differentiated risk weights, governments facing balance sheet recessions will be able to implement necessary fiscal stimulus without costing German taxpayers anything.

Achieving the consensus needed for these changes will probably take time, because today's policy-makers never learned about balance sheet recessions in their studies at university. But the efforts required will have been more than worth it if these two simple modifications can put the finishing touches on the grand project of the euro.

NOTES

1. A more detailed treatment of this phenomenon can be found in Chapter 3 of my book, *The Holy Grail of Macroeconomics: Lessons from Japan's Great Recession* (John Wiley, 2008).
2. This figure, calculated as the difference between the outstanding foreign holdings of German government bonds from 2008 to 2012, is from Deutsche Bundesbank Balance of Payment Statistics, International Investment positions, September 2014.

6. Post-crisis recovery in slow-motion mode: the role of the non-financial corporate sector

**Martin Gächter, Martin Geiger,
Florentin Glötzl and Helene Schuberth**

The aftermath of the global financial crisis that started in 2008 is characterized by a very sluggish economic recovery, particularly due to the weakness of corporate investment. Against this backdrop, we examine the role of private sector balance sheet repair – particularly in the non-financial corporate sector – as a drag on investment. Sectoral deleveraging needs may seriously impair investment expenditures, and thus might have long-term effects on potential growth rates. In 2013, the average level of real gross fixed investment in the European Union (EU) and the euro area was still 17 per cent and 18 per cent, respectively, below the peak reached in 2008 (European Commission, 2014). The decline in investment has been particularly large in stressed economies of the euro area, where investment has fallen by up to more than 50 per cent, while the fall has been less severe in Central, Eastern and South-Eastern Europe (CESEE).

A consensus view seems to be emerging that this extraordinary decrease in investment activity is caused by the combined effect of credit constraints and demand-driven factors, and that the associated negative feedback loops push some of the countries into a balance sheet recession. In this context, demand-driven factors, such as the balance sheet position of firms (and households) per se may exercise an impact on investment decisions, irrespective of the existence of credit constraints. When the bubble bursts, asset prices collapse, but liabilities denominated in nominal terms remain, forcing households and the corporate sector to increase savings or to pay down debt despite low or zero interest rates, resulting in a massive drop in investment activity.

In this chapter, we highlight a number of stylized facts associated with the rebalancing challenge in Europe. For this purpose, we exploit both aggregated macro data as well as firm-level data.[1] We trace debt developments from different angles to investigate whether we can identify deleveraging efforts and whether these efforts materialize in a reduction of sectoral debt levels. Subsequently, we depict the development of the gap between saving and investment, linking the findings to future growth perspectives and the European catching-up process. As suggested by Bakker and Zeng (2013), national economic environments as well as the need to adjust balance sheets are extremely heterogeneous among European economies. While we are able to identify deleveraging efforts in almost all countries, these efforts do not systematically cause the ratios of debt to gross domestic product (GDP) to go down, primarily due to low growth and deflationary pressures in a number of countries. Against the backdrop of prevailing rebalancing needs, deleveraging efforts are therefore likely to continue to drag on the recovery, as well as on the catching-up process. The main conclusions we draw from our analysis can be summarized as follows:

- Across Europe, a number of countries suffer from a massive drop in private sector demand. Even the non-financial corporate sector, which is typically a net borrower, has become a net lender in many countries.
- Rebalancing mostly comes at cost of investment activities, which has resulted in a dramatic reduction of aggregate investment across Europe.
- External rebalancing within Europe, as exemplified by a considerable improvement of current account balances of pre-crisis deficit countries, is mainly driven by a decline in investment rather than an increase in national saving.
- Determinants of both corporate investment and corporate saving (that is, the propensity to hold cash) have strongly changed in the course of the crisis. In the post-crisis regime, firms rely more heavily on internal financing and exhibit a higher propensity to save cash out of cash flow.
- Besides its implications for the weak recovery, the investment decline also jeopardizes the convergence process among European economies.

6.1 PRE-CRISIS COUNTRY CHARACTERISTICS AND POST-CRISIS BALANCE SHEET ADJUSTMENT

Empirical research suggests that accelerated financial sector growth is often followed by financial contractions (Jordà et al., 2011; Aizenman et al., 2013). For the global financial crisis starting in 2008, we find the same pattern in our sample of European economies. The more countries increased their total debt levels, the lower their GDP growth during the crisis period, and the stronger the increase of unemployment during the crisis.

From a historical perspective, the increase in private debt during boom periods tends to be reversed during the following recession (see Tang and Upper, 2010). Looking at sectoral developments in Figure 6.1, we see that in most of the European economies, the private sectors (defined as corporations plus households) have indeed shown deleveraging tendencies in recent years, as indicated by considerably increased net lending/ net borrowing (NLNB) balances. The NLNB balance essentially reflects the balance between saving and investment by institutional sector.[2] Thus, a negative NLNB balance should be reflected either in increasing (gross) debt levels (that is, if the financing gap is funded externally) or decreasing (financial) assets in the same sector. It is important to note that our data do not allow us to study *ex ante* saving decisions as they always measure *ex post* outcomes. If a sector shows some deleveraging efforts (or, alternatively, if one sector is forced to reduce its debts), this should materialize in positive NLNB balances or at least in an increasing trend. The private sectors in more or less all countries (except for Luxembourg, Belgium and Austria) have considerably increased their NLNB[3] as a reaction to the global crisis, with Bulgaria (27 percentage points), Slovenia (23), Greece (23), Cyprus (22), Estonia (21) and Spain (20) showing the strongest increase in NLNB balances. In other words, within six years some of the countries lost a considerable share of private sector demand. Those adjustments appear even more distinct when considering the slow recovery path in the euro area, where many of the economies mentioned above have not achieved their pre-crisis peaks in terms of GDP at the time of writing in early 2015. Deleveraging efforts were particularly strong in the corporate sector,[4] although households also increased their NLNB balances in most countries. The public sector, on the contrary, was leveraging up in almost all countries, although governments were not able to fully compensate for the massive private sectors' drop in aggregate demand. Figure 6.1 also shows, however, that NLNB balances of private sectors remained more or less unchanged in some large countries (including Germany, France and the United Kingdom), highlighting the considerable heterogeneity of the impact of the crisis across Europe.

Figure 6.2 shows the development of NLNB balances and corresponding debt ratios as a percentage of GDP for various sectors in the euro area (households, government, non-financial corporations, financial corporations and the rest of the world). In the run-up to the crisis, the euro area's total debt-to-GDP ratio was rising significantly. Surprisingly, even after

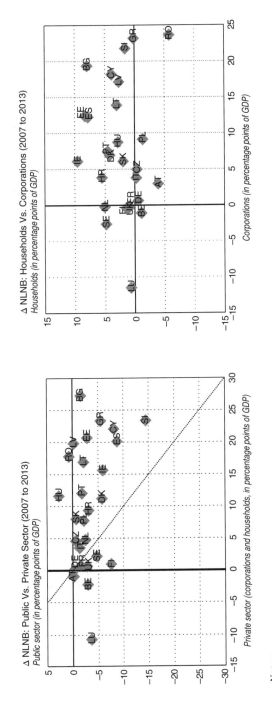

△ NLNB: Households Vs. Corporations (2007 to 2013)
Households (in percentage points of GDP)

Corporations (in percentage points of GDP)

△ NLNB: Public Vs. Private Sector (2007 to 2013)
Public sector (in percentage points of GDP)

Private sector (corporations and households, in percentage points of GDP)

Notes:
NLNB = net lending/net borrowing, AMECO = Annual macro-economic database of the European Commission, GDP = gross domestic product.
AT = Austria, BE = Belgium, BG = Bulgaria, CY = Cyprus, CZ = Czech Republic, DE = Germany, DK = Denmark, EE = Estonia,
ES = Spain, FI = Finland, FR = France, GR = Greece, HR = Croatia, HU = Hungary, IE = Ireland, IT = Italy, LT = Lithuania, LU =
Luxembourg, LV = Latvia, NL = Netherlands, PL = Poland, PT = Portugal, RO = Romania, SE = Sweden, SI = Slovenia, SK = Slovakia, UK
= United Kingdom.

Source: European Commission, AMECO.

Figure 6.1   Net lending/net borrowing (NLNB) balances by sector

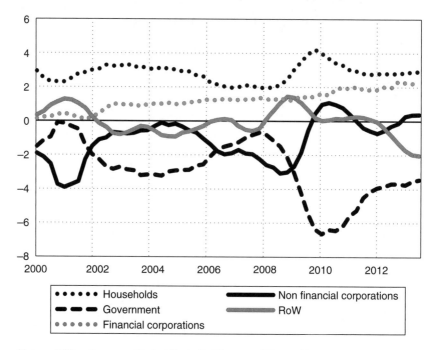

Note: ECB = European Central Bank, RoW = rest of the world.

Source: *ECB-Euro Area Accounts.*

Figure 6.2   Euro area: net lending/net borrowing (% of GDP)

2008, debt-to-GDP ratios continued to increase in most European countries. The sectoral NLNB balances, however, reveal significant adjustments
in saving and investment behaviours of households and non-financial
corporations. Until 2010, the latter exhibited persistently negative NLNB
balances (that is, an excess of investment over saving), but since then the
non-financial corporate sector has shifted to positive values. This quite
significant adjustment in the euro area was associated with a sharp decline
in the (total) investment ratio from 22.0 per cent of GDP in 2008 (Q2) to
18.1 per cent in 2013 (Q2). More than half of this decline was due to lower
investment of the non-financial corporate sector.

The household sector, on the other hand, exhibited positive NLNB balances prior to the crisis, although surpluses decreased in the boom phase
before 2008. The reaction to the crisis was rather similar to that of the
corporate sector, as households increased their NLNB balance between
2008 and 2010, but then started to decrease their NLNB again. The public

sector exhibited negative NLNB balances, reflecting budget deficits that increased sharply in 2008. But in 2010, the public sector started to consolidate and to increase its NLNB balance. While the NLNB balance of the private sector has remained in positive territory in recent years, the adjustment in public sector NLNB to less borrowing (lower public deficits) was associated with a decrease in the balance to the rest of the world, that is, an increase in the euro area current account surplus. Interestingly, despite the deleveraging efforts of the private sector as well as the public sector, total debt ratios across sectors still increased considerably (from 280 per cent to 326 per cent of GDP) during the first five years after the crisis (ending in Q2 2013).

In a next step, we further investigate why widespread increases of NLNB in private sectors did not lead to a systematic reduction in gross debt ratios. For that purpose, we decompose the change of sectoral debt ratios (in per cent of GDP) into contributions from the numerator (that is, transactions and other changes) and the denominator (that is, contributions from real GDP growth and inflation), respectively (for a similar approach, see Cuerpo et al., 2013). Increasing values of the denominator (real GDP growth and inflation) reduce the real debt burden. On the contrary, an increase of the numerator consisting of actual transactions (that is, credit flows) and other changes (such as write-downs, write-offs as well as revaluation and reclassification effects) raise the real burden of debt.[5] These contributions as well as the corresponding debt ratios in the non-financial corporate sector in the euro area are shown in Figure 6.3. While actual transactions have decreased substantially in the course of the crisis, GDP growth and inflation have decreased considerably throughout the euro area, thereby contributing to rising debt-to-GDP ratios in a number of European economies. Overall, despite visible deleveraging efforts across Europe, debt-to-GDP ratios have remained high or have even increased further across Europe.

An analysis of debt ratio changes on the country level[6] reveals quite heterogenous patterns across countries. While inflation rates helped to dampen debt-to-GDP ratios in most countries (particularly in Germany and the United Kingdom, but also in France, Sweden, Italy and Poland, among others), such a relieving effect was not present in Spain and in other peripheral countries, such as Greece and Ireland, where (partly) negative inflation rates and low or negative GDP growth increased the real debt burden.[7]

Although public sectors reacted to the crisis with increasing deficits, those stimulation policies were not able to increase aggregate demand sufficiently in many countries, leading to unfavourable debt dynamics both for the private sector and the public sector. In other words, subdued

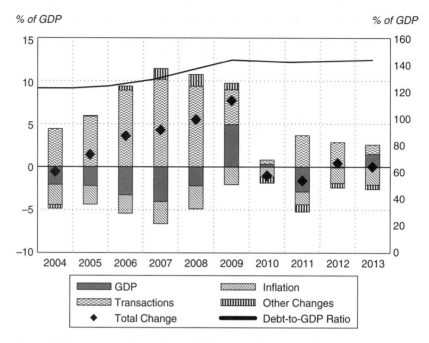

Note: ECB = European Central Bank, GDP = gross domestic product.

Source: ECB-Euro Area Accounts, own calculations.

Figure 6.3   Euro area: change in debt ratio of non-financial corporations

output growth associated with low (or even negative) inflation rates have significantly undermined deleveraging efforts in stressed economies, particularly in the private sector. In many countries of the euro area, but also in the CESEE region, current deleveraging efforts are therefore not associated with a reduction in debt ratios. This conundrum is reminiscent of the Keynesian 'paradox of thrift', namely that the attempt of businesses and households to save more actually leads to lower total savings due to lower consumption, investment and aggregate demand.

6.2   AGGREGATE INVESTMENT AND REBALANCING IN EUROPE

The increase of sectoral debt ratios during the pre-crisis boom was accompanied by a strong rise of capital inflows, cross-border credit and external imbalances, particularly in peripheral economies of the euro area. Massive capital inflows, not least from core countries of the euro area, led to significant reductions of interest rates. Consequently, debt ratios in the corporate sector and also in the household sector (particularly in countries which suffered from a housing boom) increased markedly. While the current account of the euro area as a whole was more or less balanced in the years prior to the crisis, imbalances within the euro area increased strongly. Increasing current account balances of surplus countries masked increasing negative current account balances in deficit countries, also reflecting the surplus in the financial account due to massive capital inflows. Starting in 2009, however, deficit countries reduced their current account deficits continuously, and by 2013 more or less all pre-crisis deficit countries exhibited (almost) even or positive external balances. This rebalancing process was however not accompanied by decreasing current account balances in surplus countries, and thus resulted in a pronounced increase of the current account balance of the euro area as a whole. In most of the peripheral countries, rebalancing was mainly driven by low import demand rather than rising exports. Furthermore, the improvement of the euro area current account balance was associated with significant changes in sectoral saving and investment rates across countries, which will be analysed in depth below.

When recalling some basics of macroeconomics, the current account balance can basically be defined in three different ways. First, a current account surplus is defined as a positive balance of exports minus imports (under consideration of factor income and current transfers), which is probably the most common definition. Secondly, it can be seen as a financial account deficit, that is, the current account surplus is mirrored by capital outflows of the same amount. Finally, a current account surplus can also be interpreted as an excess of saving over investment across sectors within the corresponding country. The three mentioned perspectives on the current account are identities: that is, they must hold empirically by definition, whereas a causal effect in one direction cannot be identified.

The upper panel in Figure 6.4 shows the ratio of (overall) saving and fixed investment relative to GDP, as well as the current account balance in per cent of GDP for the euro area. The middle and the bottom chart show decompositions of gross fixed capital formation (investment) and saving by institutional sector in the euro area. The current account balances of the euro area fluctuated around zero between 2008 and 2012. Between 2008 and 2010, as a reaction to the crisis, both saving and investment ratios decreased considerably by about 4 percentage points of GDP. Since then, overall saving rates recovered marginally, while investment has decreased even further since 2012. Thus, from this perspective, the current account

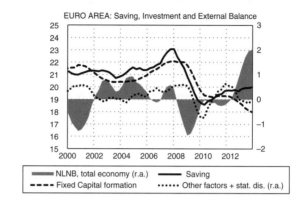

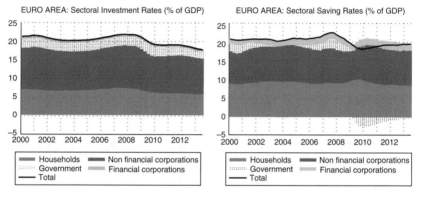

Notes:
NLNB = net lending/net borrowing, ECB = European Central Bank, GDP = gross
domestic product.
r.a. = right axis.
stat. dis. = statistical discrepancy.

Source: ECB-Euro Area Accounts

Figure 6.4   Euro area: saving, investment and external balance

surplus of the euro area does not result from higher saving, but rather from
lower investment.

Figure 6.5 shows the corresponding results for individual countries
by decomposing the total change in net lending/net borrowing (total
economy)[8] between 2007 and 2013 in contributions from saving, investment and other factors. From such a simple decomposition, some interesting patterns become visible. First, since 2007, investment ratios have
been decreasing in all economies (as shown by positive contributions to

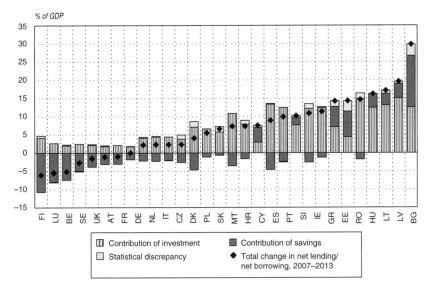

Notes: AT = Austria, BE = Belgium, BG = Bulgaria, CY = Cyprus, CZ = Czech Republic, DE = Germany, DK = Denmark, EE = Estonia, ES = Spain, FI = Finland, FR = France, GR = Greece, HR = Croatia, HU = Hungary, IE = Ireland, IT = Italy, LT = Lithuania, LU = Luxembourg, LV = Latvia, MT = Malta, NL = Netherlands, PL = Poland, PT = Portugal, RO = Romania, SE = Sweden, SI = Slovenia, SK = Slovakia, UK = United Kingdom.

Source: *European Commission-AMECO.*

Figure 6.5 *External rebalancing: change in net lending/net borrowing (total economy), 2007–2014*

the total change in NLNB), although the magnitude of the decline differs strongly across countries. Second, external rebalancing developments in countries which exhibited significantly negative current account balances prior to the crisis were consistently associated with a strong decrease in investment rather than an increase in saving rates (with the exception of Bulgaria, Hungary and Romania, where increased savings also contributed significantly to the ongoing rebalancing). In fact, overall saving rates have even decreased in most stressed economies (Cyprus, Spain, Greece), and thus, external rebalancing is driven by a stronger decrease of investment as compared to saving. Third, in countries affected by strong declines in house prices, such as Spain and the United Kingdom, households (and also businesses in the case of Spain) reacted with a strong increase in saving rates, as their net worth plummeted. The decline of household investment in those countries is likely to be part of a necessary rebalancing in the housing market. At the same time, however, investment ratios of the corporate sector also fell, particularly in Spain. Interestingly, despite increased private savings, the overall saving rate decreased in both countries due to strong measures by the government to cushion the recession.

6.3   DETERMINANTS OF CORPORATE SAVING AND INVESTMENT IN POST-CRISIS EUROPE

To investigate the channels through which the crisis has affected investment, we subsequently examine the determinants of firms' investment and saving decisions before and after the crisis at the micro level. We are specifically interested in whether the drop in investment is only due to lower demand, or whether firms have also adjusted their investment decisions because of changes in their financing patterns. Thereby, we aim at examining the role of balance sheet adjustment for the observed investment decline.

Following Fazzari et al. (1988), the intuition of our approach is that in a benign economic environment, and given that a firm exhibits a healthy balance sheet, the firm should be able to perfectly substitute between external and internal financial funds, as suggested by the famous Modigliani–Miller (1958) theorem. If this is not the case, we assume that the firm faces (or anticipates) some kind of financial friction. In such a situation, the firm's opportunity cost of internal funds (that is, retained earnings or net operating profits) can be substantially lower than the cost of external finance. If this is the case, investment spending will depend not only on the availability of positive net present value projects, but also on the availability of internal funds. Thus, Fazzari et al. (1988) propose to examine the cash flow sensitivity of investment, as financially constrained firms should exhibit a positive link between cash flow and investment. The magnitude of this external finance premium varies by type of firm, depending on the degree of asymmetric information and other capital market imperfections.

Almeida et al. (2004) study the role of financial constraints in the corporate sector from a different, but closely related angle. As firms anticipating financing constraints should rely on cash holdings to finance future investment, financial constraints should be positively associated with the propensity to save cash out of cash flow, which is referred to as the 'cash flow sensitivity of cash'. Firms which are unconstrained, on the other hand, should not exhibit any systematic relationship between (operating) cash flow and cash holdings.

To examine corporate investment decisions and liquidity preferences, we exploit a newly developed unique database – the European Records of IFRS Consolidated Accounts (ERICA) – covering the time period 2005–2012. The data cover stock market listed firms in eight euro area economies.[9] Due to the composition of participating countries, it is reasonable to regard our data as a representative sample of large (listed) European companies. Interestingly, it is often argued that external financing constraints are mostly an issue among small and medium-sized enterprises (SMEs). With our data, however, we are able to examine firm behaviour and financing constraints for large (stock market listed) firms in the euro area. Furthermore, the geographical focus on the euro area enables us to draw direct policy conclusions for current economic policy in Europe, while most other studies are based on data within individual countries, most often for the United States.

To examine the effect of the crisis on corporate saving and investment decisions, we estimate two regression equations with investment and cash holdings as dependent variables. The investment equation reads:

$$\mathrm{Inv}_{i,t} = \alpha + \beta \mathrm{Inv}_{i,t-1} + \gamma OCF_{i,t} + Z'_{i,t}\delta + \lambda_t + v_{i,t},$$

where i, t denotes the individual firm and time (years), respectively. Investment (Inv) is measured as investing cash flow relative to total assets. The same applies to operating cash flow (OCF), which is also taken as a ratio to total assets. $Z'_{i,t}$ is the itth observation on a number of control variables and $v_{i,t}$ is an error term. Furthermore, we include time dummies λ_t in all our specifications to control for time fixed effects. The cash equation reads:

$$Cash_{i,t} = \alpha + \beta \mathrm{Inv}_{i,t-1} + \gamma OCF_{i,t} + Z'_{i,t}\delta + \lambda_t + v_{i,t},$$

where $Cash_{i,t}$ are cash holdings relative to total assets. Both equations are estimated in a dynamic panel framework using the feasible system generalized method of moments (GMM) estimator proposed by Blundell and Bond (1998).

A number of different specifications and robustness checks of the two regression models are discussed in Gächter et al. (2014). In the following analysis, for the sake of brevity, we only present the main conclusions which we draw from our analysis. The γ-coefficients for the main variables of interest attained from our preferred specifications are shown in Table 6.1.

The impact of operating cash flow on investment – that is, the cash flow sensitivity of investment – is not significantly different from zero prior to the crisis, while becoming significantly positive in the course of the crisis.

Table 6.1   Specifications and robustness checks

γ-coefficients	Pre-crisis estimates (2005–2008)	Post-crisis estimates (2009–2012)
Investment equation	0.117 (0.191)	0.133 (0.000)
Cash equation	0.179 (0.010)	0.299 (0.000)

Notes:
p-values are shown in parenthesis.
Control variables included in the investment model: lagged investment, firm size, lagged sales, employment, lagged cash holdings.
Control variables included in the cash holdings model: lagged cash holdings, firm size, investment, lagged leverage.

This pattern suggests that in the post-crisis period firms increasingly rely on internal sources of financing for capital expenditures. Possible reasons for this changing pattern are either effects related to the financial accelerator – that is, that access to external finance is limited even for large firms (see Bernanke et al., 1996, Vermeulen, 2002) – or alternatively, firms rely more heavily on internal sources to become increasingly independent from external sources of funding (that is, a demand-driven precautionary saving motive), which is also likely to be associated with an additional build-up of cash holdings.

Our findings regarding the cash flow sensitivity of cash complements our conclusion from the investment equation in an instructive way. We do not distinguish between financially constrained and financially unconstrained firms as it has been done in earlier papers (e.g. Almeida et al., 2004). Hence, it is interesting that operating cash flow exerts a significantly positive impact on cash holdings in our estimation for pre- as well as post-crisis periods. While this result is remarkable, we would be cautious to interpret it as evidence for existing financial constraints even prior to the crisis due to the well-known issue of controlling for investment opportunities; that is, operating cash flows might contain some information on investment opportunities, and firms might build up some cash for this purpose.[10] Even more remarkable, however, is the pronounced increase of the coefficient for the cash flow variable from the pre- to the post-crisis period.

Hence, from a firm-level perspective, we find rather unambiguous evidence that since the onset of the crisis firms rely more heavily on internal funds and therefore constrain investment activities while increasing their cash holdings. This marked increase in cash preference for large stock market listed firms in the euro area after the crisis can be ascribed to either increased economic uncertainty and/or (anticipated) external financing constraints.

6.4   INVESTMENT AND THE CATCHING-UP PROCESS

The dramatic drop in investment across Europe may also imply a structural break in the European convergence process. Recent studies point to a marked slowdown of income convergence across the European Union since the global financial crisis (see, e.g., Gächter et al., 2013). While the growth differential between the euro area and the EU countries in Central, Eastern and South-Eastern Europe (CESEE) amounted to 3–4 percentage points prior to 2008, it decreased considerably in the aftermath of the crisis. Although this large pre-crisis growth differential was partly cyclical, empirical evidence suggests that the differential in potential growth rates is likely to have decreased as well (Gächter et al., 2013).

In this context, recent developments indicate that the slowdown of the European catching-up process might indeed be structural, both for new EU members (in CESEE) and for peripheral euro area members. Figure 6.6 shows the relationship between the share of gross fixed capital formation in a country's GDP (excluding the construction sector, to control for pre-crisis housing booms) and the corresponding GDP per capita (in purchasing power standards, PPS). While there was a strong negative link between the two variables before the crisis – that is, 'poorer' countries exhibited a higher share of (productive) investment – this relationship essentially broke down after the crisis. Thus, besides the fact that the investment share has decreased in virtually all economies, it is also alarming that countries with lower GDP per capita (and typically lower capital stocks) do not invest overproportionally any more. Lower investment rates, however, are likely to imply decreased potential output growth in the future, and thus a significant slowdown in income convergence across Europe. While the decrease in economic activity in countries with stronger credit and housing booms, as suggested by, for example, Claessens et al. (2009), is not really surprising, the broken link between investment ratios and GDP per capita should be a cause for great concern for policy-makers.

6.5   CONCLUSION

Despite marked differences across European economies, net lending/net borrowing patterns show considerable similarities in deleveraging efforts,

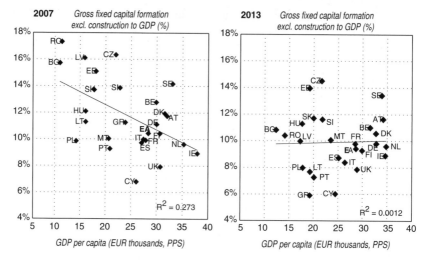

Notes:
GDP = gross domestic product, EUR = euro, PPS = purchasing power standards,
R² = coefficient of determination.
AMECO = annual macroeconomic database (of the European Commission),
AT = Austria, BE = Belgium, BG = Bulgaria, CY = Cyprus, CZ = Czech Republic,
DE = Germany, DK = Denmark, EA = euro area, ES = Spain,
FI = Finland, FR = France, GR = Greece, HR = Croatia, HU = Hungary, IE = Ireland,
IT = Italy, LT = Lithuania, LU = Luxembourg, LV = Latvia, MT = Malta,
NL = Netherlands, PL = Poland, PT = Portugal, RO = Romania, SE = Sweden,
SI = Slovenia, SK = Slovakia, UK = United Kingdom.

Source: European Commission-AMECO, own calculations.

*Figure 6.6   GDP per capita and gross fixed capital formation excluding
construction*

particularly in corporate and household sectors. Interestingly, the decline
in credit transactions so far has not led to a significant reduction of sectoral debt-to-GDP ratios in many countries, because subdued output growth
and low or even negative inflation rates have undermined the deleveraging
process and contributed to an increase of real debt burdens in a number of
European economies. Furthermore, this effect could even be reinforced in
the medium term, as most of the ongoing rebalancing – in terms of both
debt levels as well as current account deficits – is based on a strong decline
in investment (both in the private sector as well as the public sector) rather
than an increase in saving, which might lead to considerably lower potential growth rates in the future.

From an economic policy perspective, our findings raise questions about the optimal speed of fiscal consolidation after a financial crisis. In the course of the sovereign debt crisis, the view has emerged that the European approach to solving the crisis, including austerity packages and measures to sharply decrease external imbalances, might have been suboptimal, and that stressed economies need more time to ensure an orderly adjustment, as simultaneous deleveraging across sectors and trading partners might be associated with high costs in terms of real GDP and deflation developments. Blanchard and Leigh (2013) argue that in an environment where monetary policy is stuck at the zero lower bound, credit constraints exist in the financial sector and the economy is facing a negative output gap, fiscal multipliers are likely to be larger than in 'normal' times in the future. Together with the dangers of low growth and pronounced hysteresis effects, these arguments would plead for back-loaded fiscal consolidation. Severe debt overhang and the risk of multiple equilibria, on the contrary, would rather speak for front-loaded consolidation. Thus, when bank deleveraging is ongoing and credit demand by the private sector is low, public debt consolidation should be gradual and conditioned on the strength of private demand.

Clearly, the reasonableness of fiscal consolidation also depends on the nature of consolidation measures. In particular, growth-enhancing public investment should not be cut in a situation when private investment is already at subdued levels, as long-run growth prospects could be severely impaired in an environment of declining capital stocks. Moreover, the commonly praised strong rebalancing of current account deficits in recent years is viewed in a different light when it is decomposed in developments of domestic saving and investment. That is, rebalancing is mainly based on a strong decline of investment expenditures, which in turn is likely to hamper future growth prospects.

ACKNOWLEDGEMENTS

An adapted version of this chapter with a slightly different focus has been published in: *Focus on European Economic Integration*, Q1/2015, OeNB, 8–23. We are grateful for very helpful comments from our colleagues Peter Backé and Julia Wörz.

NOTES

1. A detailed description of the dataset is available in Gächter et al. (2014, 2015).
2. NLNB is derived by comparing gross capital formation plus the net acquisition of non-produced, non-financial assets with gross saving plus net capital transfers. If saving plus net capital transfers received exceeds non-financial investment, a sector has a surplus of

funds and becomes a net lender to other sectors and/or the rest of the world (https://www.ecb.europa.eu/stats/pdf/eaa/Background_note.pdf, p. 3).

3. An increase of the NLNB balance indicates an increase of saving (that is, of the difference between disposable income and consumption expenditures) and/or a decrease of investment by institutional sector. Please note that in the context of NLNB, an increase of the balance can indicate either a change in saving or investment behaviour, or both.
4. In the European Commission's annual macroeconomic (AMECO) database, the corporate sector entails both non-financial and financial corporations.
5. Note that – by construction – this simple method of decomposition yields a small and positive difference between the sum of contributions and the absolute change in the debt level, which is negligible in magnitude for our calculations. This difference is assigned to other changes.
6. Individual country results and other sectors are not shown for the sake of brevity. The respective figures are available upon request.
7. On the other hand, lower inflation rates are desirable to regain trade competitiveness in international markets, as nominal depreciations are not possible within a currency union. It is obvious, however, that such a (necessary) adjustment in prices and wages is more difficult in a low-inflation environment, which is currently the case in Europe.
8. The net lending /net borrowing (NLNB) balance of the total economy corresponds to the current account balance plus net capital transactions with the rest of the world. As the latter factor is typically small, NLNB (total economy) is roughly equal to the current account balance.
9. The database comprises of data from Austria (AT), Belgium (BE), France (FR), Germany (DE), Greece (GR), Italy (IT), Portugal (PT) and Spain (ES).
10. In well-functioning financial markets, however, even in a setting where firms expect favourable investment opportunities, a build-up of cash holdings would not be necessary, as firms should be able to obtain funding from financial markets (that is, from banks or directly from capital markets). Our results indicate that at least some firms had already chosen to hoard cash prior to the crisis, when financial constraints were probably less pronounced.

REFERENCES

Aizenman, J., B. Pinto and V. Sushko (2013), 'Financial sector ups and downs and the real sector in the open economy: up by the stairs, down by the parachute', *Emerging Markets Review* 16(0), 1–30.
Almeida, H., M. Campello and M.S. Weisbach (2004), 'The cash flow sensitivity of cash', *Journal of Finance* 59(4), 1777–804.
Bakker, B.B. and L. Zeng (2013), 'Dismal employment growth in EU countries: the role of corporate balance sheet repair and dual labor markets', IMF Working Paper No. 13/179, International Monetary Fund.
Bernanke, B., M. Gertler and S. Gilchrist (1996), 'The financial accelerator and the flight to quality', *Review of Economics and Statistics* 78(1), 1–15.
Blanchard, O. and D. Leigh (2013), 'Fiscal consolidation: at what speed?', 11 December, available at http://www.voxeu.org/article/fiscal-consolidation-what-speed.
Blundell, R. and S. Bond (1998), 'Initial conditions and moment restrictions in dynamic panel data models', *Journal of Econometrics* 87(1), 115–43.
Claessens, S., M.A. Kose and M.E. Terrones (2009), 'What happens during recessions, crunches and busts?', *Economic Policy* 24 (60), pp. 653–700.

Cuerpo Caballero, C., I. Drumond and P. Pontuch (2013), 'Assessing the private sector deleveraging dynamics', *Quarterly Report on the Euro Area*, Vol. 12, Brussels: European Commission, pp. 26–32.

European Commission (2014), 'Annual Macroeconomic Database (AMECO)', available at http://ec.europa.eu/economy_finance/ameco/user/serie/SelectSerie. cfm.

Fazzari, S.M., R.G. Hubbard and B.C. Petersen (1988), 'Financing constraints and corporate investment', *Brookings Papers on Economic Activity* 19(1), 141–206.

Gächter, M., M. Geiger, F. Glötzl and H. Schuberth (2015), 'Post-crisis recovery in slow-motion mode: the great rebalancing challenge in Europe', *Focus on European Economic Integration*, Q1/15, 8–23.

Gächter, M., M. Geiger and H. Schuberth (2014), 'Liquidity preferences and corporate investment: new evidence from the euro area', mimeo.

Gächter, M., A. Riedl and D. Ritzberger-Grünwald (2013), 'Business cycle convergence or decoupling? Economic adjustment in CESEE during the crisis', in E. Nowotny, P. Mooslechner and D. Ritzberger-Grünwald (eds), *Achieving Balanced Growth in the CESEE Countries*, Cheltenham, UK and Northampton, MA, USA: Edward Elgar Publishing, pp. 47–70.

Jordà, O., M. Schularick and A.M. Taylor (2011), 'Financial crises, credit booms, and external imbalances: 140 years of lessons', *IMF Economic Review* 59(2), 340–78.

Modigliani, F. and M.H. Miller (1958), 'The cost of capital, corporation finance and the theory of investment', *American Economic Review* 48(3), 261–97.

Tang, G. and C. Upper (2010), 'Debt reduction after crises', *BIS Quarterly Review* (Sept.), 25–38.

Vermeulen, P. (2002), 'Business fixed investment: evidence of a financial accelerator in Europe', *Oxford Bulletin of Economics and Statistics* 64(3), 217–35.

7. Private and public sector deleveraging in the EU[1]

Jan in 't Veld, Peter Pontuch and Rafal Raciborski

The recovery from the worst financial and economic crisis in a generation has been much slower than usual after recessions in the euro area and the European Union (EU). Potential output growth has been on a declining trend for decades, due to a slowdown in total factor productivity (TFP) growth and population ageing, but this trend has worsened further after the crisis. The credit boom in the early 2000s brought a misallocation of investment and resources, which now poses a weight on the recovery. There is also the risk of 'hysteresis' effects, as long spells of unemployment can induce a loss in human capital endowments, leading to longer-lasting exclusion from the labour market. Historical evidence indicates that financial crises are associated with deep recessions, abnormally weak recoveries, and prolonged, even permanent, reductions in the level of output (Reinhart and Rogoff, 2009). Parallels are drawn with the lost decade that Japan faced after the bursting of its bubble in the 1990s (Koo, 2011). In contrast to 'normal' business cycle recessions, balance sheet recessions are deeper and more prolonged. They follow when debt-financed bubbles burst and asset prices collapse, while liabilities remain. In order to repair balance sheets, households and firms are forced to increase savings and/or pay down debt. This deleveraging process causes demand to decline and forms a significant and persistent drag on growth.

In this chapter we describe debt developments and deleveraging in EU member states. We then use the Commission's (global macroeconomic) QUEST model to illustrate the main channels through which private sector deleveraging affects the economy. The sovereign debt crisis has also put pressure on governments to reduce public debt, and simultaneous public sector deleveraging reinforces the private sector deleveraging needs and increases the costs to the economy. While deleveraging pressures are most severe in countries that experienced strong debt-fuelled booms, Central and Eastern European countries are not immune to it, and also suffer from

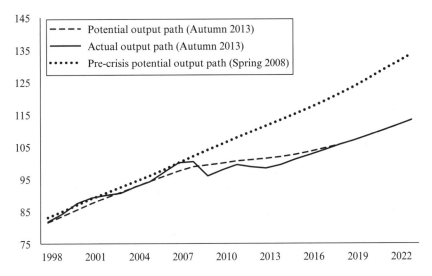

Source: European Commission (2013).

Figure 7.1 Euro area: various potential and actual output paths

cross-border spillovers that can be significant. The effects of deleveraging on gross domestic product (GDP) and demand are sizeable and long-lasting (see Figure 7.1). Although some deleveraging has already taken place, further deleveraging is likely to continue to hold back the pace of recovery. In the final section we discuss what policy options can facilitate the deleveraging process and boost growth.

7.1 DEBT DEVELOPMENTS AND DELEVERAGING IN PRIVATE AND PUBLIC SECTORS IN THE EU MEMBER STATES

The deleveraging process in the non-financial private sector is under way, as household and corporate debt-to-GDP ratios have peaked and started declining in a large majority of EU member states. Nevertheless, if one takes 2008 as a reference year, a reduction of private indebtedness can only be seen in a dozen EU countries and, more importantly, the extent of the adjustment is only a fraction of the pre-crisis increase in most cases (see Figure 7.2). Germany stands out as the only EU country that deleveraged throughout the 2000s and has continued to do so recently.

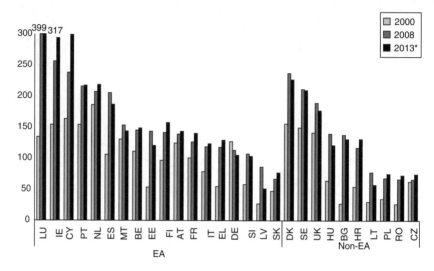

Notes:
Household and corporate sector indebtedness, consolidated at the sector level.
AT = Austria, BE = Belgium, BG = Bulgaria, CY = Cyprus, CZ = Czech Republic,
DE = Germany, DK = Denmark, EE = Estonia, EL = Greece, ES = Spain, FI = Finland,
FR = France, HR = Croatia, HU = Hungary, IT = Italy, LU = Luxembourg,
LT = Lithuania, LV = Latvia, MT = Malta, NL = Netherlands, PT = Portugal,
RO = Romania, SI = Slovenia, SE = Sweden, SK = Slovakia, UK = United Kingdom.
Initial observation: 2001 for SI, HR and IE, 2004 for MT, 2006 for LU. 2013* estimated
from 2013Q4 data, except for CY, BG, RO, LU, HR, where the 2012 figure is presented.

Source: Eurostat, own calculations.

Figure 7.2   Private non-financial sector indebtedness, % of GDP

The comparison against the 2008 levels conceals recent deleveraging
activity, as household and corporate indebtedness in most countries
peaked later than 2008. As can be seen from Figure 7.3, notable corporate debt reductions relative to their peaks have, for example, occurred
in Latvia, Sweden, Denmark, Lithuania and Spain. Firms' indebtedness
in Ireland continued to increase through 2012, then reversed sharply in
2013. As regards households, significant household deleveraging has been
observed in some countries, including Ireland, the Baltic states and the
United Kingdom.

It is useful to study the drivers of ongoing deleveraging in order to
identify different deleveraging modes and to be able to assess their
likely effects on economic activity. Indeed, the reduction of a sector's
debt-to-GDP ratio can be driven to a different extent by the numerator

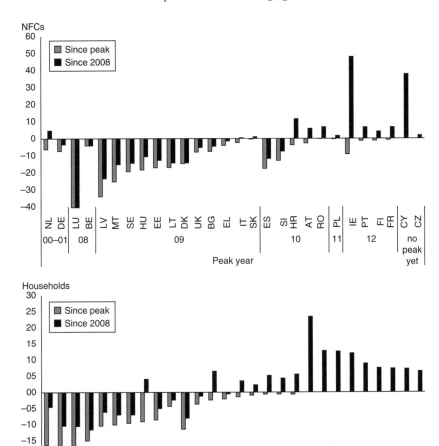

Notes:
Figures are consolidated at the sector level. Debt includes loans and securities other than
shares, excluding financial derivatives.
e = estimated. For country codes, see Figure 7.2.
The initial observation is 2001 for SI, HR and IE, 2004 for MT, 2006 for LU. The 2013e
observation is estimated from 2013Q4 data, except for CY, BG, RO, LU, HR where the 2012
figure is presented.

Source: Eurostat, own calculations.

*Figure 7.3   Change in private indebtedness as of 2013 since 2008 and since
peak, % of GDP*

(active repayment of debts or default) or by the denominator (real GDP growth or inflation).

An 'active deleveraging' mode is one mostly driven by negative net credit flows (the result of credit supply and/or credit demand pressures), which is likely to lead to a nominal contraction of balance sheets. Active deleveraging may face headwinds from the effects of falling or stagnating economic activity, or very low inflation, on nominal GDP (because of the denominator effect). A 'passive deleveraging' mode is one where the debt-to-GDP ratio is gradually reduced while net credit flows remain moderately positive. The nominal debt stock increases at a rate lower than nominal GDP growth, leading to a fall in the indebtedness ratio. An 'unsuccessful deleveraging' mode is one where the debt-to-GDP ratio stagnates, or even increases, despite significant negative net credit flows. In that case the contraction of aggregate demand, in part induced by private deleveraging especially if occurring together with fiscal consolidation or another factor affecting aggregate demand, has deflationary effects on GDP.

Negative credit flows have so far been the main driver of the cumulative reduction in debt-to-GDP ratios, leading to knock-on effects on economic activity and asset markets (see Figure 7.4 illustrating the case with household indebtedness). The active deleveraging effort has faced headwinds from low nominal GDP growth in countries such as Ireland, Estonia, and Spain (bottom left corner of the graph). Greece is the only EU country where negative credit flows have not succeeded in reducing total private debt/GDP, owing to a sharp contraction in nominal GDP (top left corner). Examples of passive deleveraging (through moderate positive net credit flows at a rate below the nominal GDP growth) in the recent past include, among others, the UK and Austria.

A range of potential remaining deleveraging needs is presented in European Commission (2014), where the estimates are based on two methods. The first method defines a sustainable level of indebtedness by estimating debt that is consistent with households' and firms' assets, corrected for valuation effects (see Cuerpo et al., 2015). The second method is based on the typical extent of deleveraging in past episodes, and is a function of the preceding debt increase. This preliminary analysis suggests total private sector deleveraging needs of 30 per cent of GDP or more in Greece, Cyprus, Spain, Ireland, Portugal, Bulgaria and Sweden. Needs between 20 per cent and 30 per cent of GDP are identified in Croatia, Denmark, the Netherlands and the UK. Estonia, Italy, Hungary and Slovenia could face needs of 10 per cent to 20 per cent of GDP. Deleveraging needs in other countries are considered more moderate. These deleveraging needs do not necessarily imply that the same deleveraging patterns can be expected going

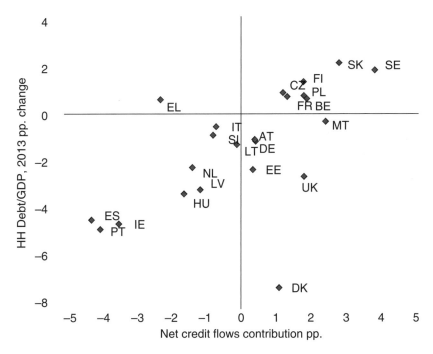

Notes: For country codes, see Figure 7.2

Source: Eurostat, own calculations.

Figure 7.4 Active versus passive deleveraging: household debt, 2013

forward, in terms of the degree of active versus passive deleveraging, of the horizon of adjustment, and of the likelihood of over- or undershooting.

Simultaneously, the public sector has also seen a sharp increase in indebtedness, which has given rise to concerns of debt sustainability in some countries and led to the introduction of consolidation measures. Figure 7.5 shows the increase in gross debt-to-GDP ratios in EU member states. While the changes between 2000 and 2008 were relatively small, and debt-to-GDP ratios actually fell in many countries, after the financial crisis there has been a sharp increase in government debt. Highly indebted periphery countries have been forced into taking wide-ranging austerity measures, when sovereign risk premia increased and some faced losing access to financial markets. However, debt ratios continued to increase, reaching more than 170 per cent of GDP in Greece in 2014, and levels above 100 per cent in Italy, Portugal, Cyprus, Ireland and Belgium. The

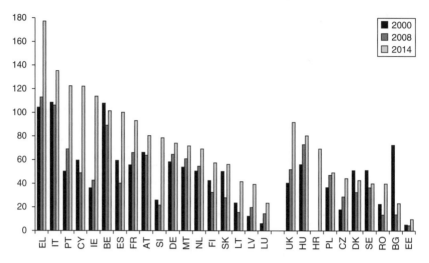

Notes: For country codes, see Figure 7.2

Source: AMECO database (European Commission).

Figure 7.5   General government consolidated gross debt, % of GDP

need to bring sovereign debt back to a sustainable path means that further public sector deleveraging is likely to accompany private sector deleveraging in the coming years.

7.2   DELEVERAGING CHANNELS

As the ongoing deleveraging process is likely to last for many years it is important to understand the impact of deleveraging and underlying balance sheet adjustment on the dynamics of the main macroeconomic aggregates. The scenarios shown in this section, based on a structural macroeconomic model, assess the effects of private sector deleveraging on the real economy. We also look at the channels when private and public sectors are deleveraging simultaneously and consider the cross-border spillovers.

7.2.1   Private Sector Deleveraging

The first scenarios are based on a three-region version of the European Commission's QUEST model. QUEST is an open economy new-Keynesian dynamic stochastic general equilibrium (DSGE) model, incorporating various real, nominal as well as financial frictions.[2] These model-based scenarios of deleveraging illustrate the main economic channels, through which deleveraging impacts the economy. The model variant used here includes heterogeneous agents and distinguishes between borrowers and lenders. Borrowers are credit-constrained and indebted against the value of their collateral, in the form of the housing stock, up to an exogenously given loan-to-value (LTV) ratio (Kiyotaki and Moore, 1997; Iacoviello, 2005). Exogenous shocks to the LTV ratio, as well as (exogenous or endogenous) fluctuations in the value of their wealth (housing stock) describe the deleveraging process for households in these model scenarios. In the model this affects consumption and then also investment, employment and output. The three-region version used here consists of a medium-sized euro area economy, calibrated on Spain, characterized by a relatively large initial household debt-to-GDP ratio, the rest of the euro area and the rest of the world, thus allowing the study of spillovers effects between regions.

In the baseline scenario (see Figure 7.6), a drop in credit availability captured by a negative LTV ratio shock and by a fall in house prices are calibrated so that the household-to-GDP ratio is reduced by about 20 percentage points after ten years and house prices fall by around 15 per cent, in line with the deleveraging needs identified for Spain in Cuerpo et al. (2015).

The simulation results displayed in Figure 7.6 show that a combined reduction in access to credit (LTV ratio shock) and drop in house prices (housing risk premium shock) lead to a relatively speedy deleveraging process: after six years, the household debt-to-GDP ratio falls by about

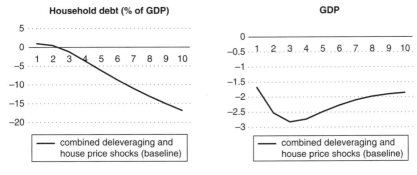

Source: Cuerpo et al. (2015).

Figure 7.6 Deleveraging scenario

nine percentage points. The speed of deleveraging is roughly in line with empirical studies mentioned in Cuerpo et al. (2015). This speedy and sizeable household debt reduction leads to a marked contraction in output. GDP falls by a maximum of around 3 per cent with the trough reached after three years. Output starts climbing back after this period towards its initial level, but at a slow pace.

There are different channels via which deleveraging affects output. First, falling household demand leads to a significant contraction in housing investment and consumption, which has a direct negative effect on output. Second, there is an additional effect due to the so-called debt–deflation spiral: falling prices slow down the speed of deleveraging in terms of the real debt, which forces households to deleverage more aggressively. In consequence, households have to shed relatively more nominal debt, which pushes prices further down. The deleveraging shock leads also to lower investment in capital as the real interest rate rises: without an independent monetary policy the nominal interest rate does not fall sufficiently to offset the decrease in prices. These mechanisms lead to a fall in output that is both relatively more prolonged and stronger than in 'normal' recessions.

7.2.2   Public Deleveraging, 2011–2013

The process of private sector deleveraging coincided with public deleveraging. The impact of this has further intensified the economic costs. Fiscal multipliers are larger at the current juncture than in normal times, due to stronger financial constraint and interest rates being constrained by the zero lower bound.[3] The economic effects of fiscal consolidations depend on the specific measures. Short-term multipliers are typically found to be larger for expenditure shocks (government consumption and investment) than for tax and transfers shocks. Output effects are also significantly larger as consolidations occurred simultaneously, which led to significant spillovers across the euro area.

The analysis shown by in 't Veld (2013) illustrates this for the consolidations in the euro area over the period 2011–2013, as presented in Table 7.1. The version of the model used here includes seven countries separately (Germany, France, Italy, Spain, Ireland, Portugal and Greece) and the rest of the euro area as an aggregate block. All simulations assume that measures were proportionally distributed over expenditure and revenue components, and are based on the assumption that monetary policy was not able to react but interest rates were constrained by the zero lower bound. The dashed lines in Figure 7.7 show the simulated GDP effects of the consolidations if each country was acting alone; the bold lines show the effects of all countries acting together. The latter capture the negative impact of each

Table 7.1   Changes in primary structural balance general government (% of potential GDP)

	Consolidation effort			Cumulative		
	2011	*2012*	*2013**	*2011*	*2012*	*2013**
Germany	*1.42*	*1.16*	*0.03*	1.42	2.58	2.61
France	*1.37*	*1.02*	*1.30*	1.37	2.38	3.68
Italy	*0.47*	*2.75*	*0.73*	0.47	3.22	3.95
Spain	*0.68*	*2.32*	*1.45*	0.68	3.00	4.45
Ireland	*1.63*	*0.64*	*1.77*	1.63	2.27	4.04
Portugal	*3.50*	*2.72*	*0.51*	3.50	6.22	6.73
Greece	*4.82*	*2.24*	*1.85*	4.82	7.06	8.91
Rest of EA	*0.46*	*0.62*	*0.46*	0.46	1.08	1.54

Source: AMECO database (European Commission).

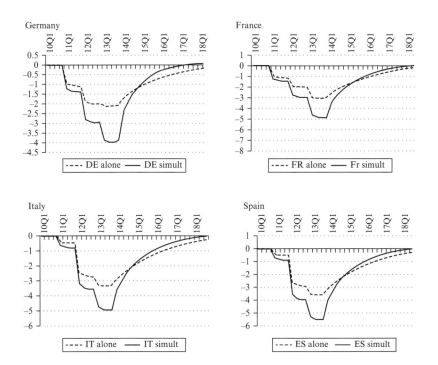

Source: In 't Veld (2013).

Figure 7.7   Spillovers, simultaneous consolidations (GDP, %), 2011–2013

country's own measures as well as the negative spillover effects of other countries' consolidation measures. The differences capture the size of spillovers. The maximum drop in GDP is larger when countries undertake a simultaneous consolidation than when each member state acts alone (by between 1.6 and 2.6 per cent). Public sector deleveraging in the countries shown is estimated to have lowered GDP by between 4 and 5.5 per cent over these three years. In the first years, all domestic demand components are negatively affected by the measures, with sharp declines in consumption and investment. The benefits from an improvement in competitiveness boosting domestic exports are also partly lost due to other countries implementing the same measures. A recovery starts taking place after three years, when no further consolidation measures are assumed to be introduced and positive confidence effects linked to expectations of lower debt and lower future taxes bring about a gradual recovery and ultimately higher output.[4]

7.2.3   Simultaneous Private and Public Sector Deleveraging

Public sector deleveraging also has an impact on the process of private sector deleveraging. While the simulations in the above section considered public sector deleveraging in isolation, in the following we consider the same private sector deleveraging scenario as in Figure 7.6 (bold lines in Figure 7.8), but with a hypothetical simultaneous public sector deleveraging scenario aiming at a permanent improvement of the budget balance by 2 per cent of GDP *ex ante*. Here too the fiscal measures are equally distributed over the revenue and expenditure side.

Public sector deleveraging in a period of private sector deleveraging is found to be challenging (Figure 7.8, dashed line): public sector deleveraging aggravates the fall in GDP and all domestic demand components, when compared to the baseline scenario. There is now an additional direct effect: falling public demand leads to a larger fall in GDP. However, since private deleveraging deteriorates the government's budget balance by itself, the government needs to undertake substantial and credibly permanent restrictive fiscal policy measures to achieve a reduction in the public debt-to-GDP ratio over the medium term, implying additional second-round effects. Moreover, increased taxes and lower demand for labour result in weakened demand and costlier supply, hence further amplifying the negative GDP effect of deleveraging. Finally, as in the case of the debt–deflation spiral, real public debt is also affected by emerging deflation: falling prices increase the level of real debt which further increases the debt-to-GDP ratio.[5]

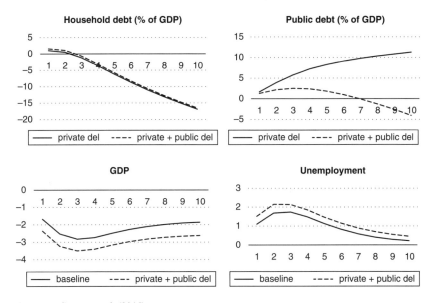

Source: Cuerpo et al. (2015).

*Figure 7.8   Private sector deleveraging scenario with simultaneous public
           sector deleveraging*

7.3   CROSS-COUNTRY SPILLOVERS

Demand shocks can have significant cross-country spillovers, as was
shown above. Table 7.2a reports the spillover effects from consolidations, measured as the ratio between the foreign GDP effect over the
GDP effect in the shock-originating country. The larger and the more
open the shock-originating country is, the larger the spillovers to other
member states. The ratio is largest for shocks originating in Germany
(20–25 per cent) and smallest for those originating in Portugal, Ireland
and Greece. Table 7.2b shows the GDP effects of private sector deleveraging shocks in the euro area periphery onto Germany, Poland and the
Czech Republic. Even for the latter two, the spillovers can be as large as
10–20 per cent.

   How does simultaneous deleveraging affect the deleveraging process?
The following scenario assesses the impact of deleveraging in one currency
union member state (Spain) when deleveraging is simultaneously occurring
in the rest of that currency union. Deleveraging in the rest of the currency
union is captured by the same type of shocks described above and it is

Table 7.2a   GDP spillover ratios for fiscal consolidations

	DE	REA	FR	IT	ES	IE	PT	EL
Germany	1.00	0.19	0.18	0.17	0.09	0.01	0.01	0.02
Rest of EA	0.25	1.00	0.17	0.16	0.09	0.02	0.01	0.02
France	0.22	0.17	1.00	0.16	0.10	0.01	0.01	0.02
Italy	0.21	0.16	0.16	1.00	0.09	0.01	0.01	0.02
Spain	0.22	0.16	0.18	0.16	1.00	0.01	0.02	0.02
Ireland	0.25	0.23	0.20	0.18	0.11	1.00	0.02	0.02
Portugal	0.23	0.17	0.18	0.17	0.18	0.01	1.00	0.02
Greece	0.23	0.17	0.18	0.18	0.10	0.01	0.01	1.00

Note: GDP spillovers by originating country, by column. The spillover ratio is defined as the ratio of foreign GDP over GDP in the shock-originating country, after three years, for balanced composition multi-year consolidations measures.

Source: In 't Veld (2013).

Table 7.2b   GDP spillovers household deleveraging shock in euro area periphery

	Periphery	Germany	Poland	Czech rep.
GDP	1	0.3	0.1	0.2

Source: European Commission simulations.

assumed in the simulations that the size of deleveraging in the rest of the currency union is one-third of that in the member state considered (Spain). The currency union central bank is supposed to be restricted by the zero lower bound (ZLB) in the first three years.

Simultaneous deleveraging in various euro area countries is found to amplify the negative impact of deleveraging when compared to the baseline scenario (Figure 7.9, dashed line). The deleveraging in the rest of the currency union has a negative impact on the country considered because of the falling external demand from abroad. However, the size of the spillover crucially depends on the absence of monetary easing during the first three years of the simulation (recall that in this scenario the monetary union as a whole is assumed to operate on the zero lower bound during this period). Given that the deleveraging is now assumed to take place in all member states of the monetary union, allowing the central bank to operate freely would lead to substantial easing of the monetary

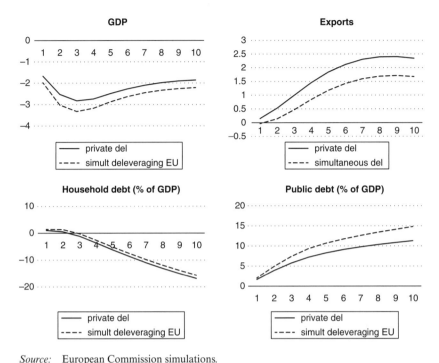

Source: European Commission simulations.

Figure 7.9 *Private sector deleveraging scenario with simultaneous deleveraging in EU*

conditions. This effect would to a large extent cushion the negative impact of deleveraging on the monetary union and hence neutralize negative spillovers.[6]

7.4 POLICY ACTIONS AND CONCLUDING REMARKS

Deleveraging needs in many EU countries are shown to remain significant. The fact that further deleveraging can be expected both in the private sector and in the public sector, and simultaneously in many EU countries together, suggests that this is likely to remain a persistent drag on growth. What policy actions could help to alleviate the economic costs of deleveraging?

It is important to open discussion on a broad range of policy initiatives

and assess their cost–benefit balance. One of the policy priorities should be
to foster the recognition of actual losses by creditors through write-offs of
bad debts. This would have to be accompanied by a simultaneous strengthening of banks' capital positions, in order to prevent a further contraction
in credit flows to other parts of the economy. To complement this process,
insolvency frameworks in many countries should be improved and made
fully accessible to both insolvent firms and households at affordable cost
and in reasonable time. For households in particular, the relief provided
following insolvency or foreclosure should be a key feature in the current
debate.

Going beyond the recognition of bad debts, creditors and debtors could
be encouraged to adopt a forward-looking attitude and resort to preventive debt restructuring measures before actual insolvency occurs. Policy
could also improve incentives for creditors to voluntarily reduce outstanding balances to close-to-insolvent debtors, debt-to-equity swaps, and debt
rescheduling (depending on the economic situation of debtors).

Going forward, it is important to guarantee that once financing conditions normalize, the adjustment process of private sector indebtedness
does not get reverted, leading to a new build-up of an imbalance. The
right financial supervision tools must be in place to guarantee that the
new lending supports the rebalancing process, possibly in tandem with
tax reforms (such as amending favourable fiscal treatment on debt-related
instruments). The reinforcement of micro- and macroprudential supervision are of utmost importance in this context, with additional emphasis on
the supervision of cross-border banking and coordination in macroprudential measures, especially at the euro area level.

Concerning macro policies, what is needed is a combination of structural, fiscal and monetary policies in an integrated growth-friendly way.
The fact that monetary policy is constrained by the zero lower bound
aggravates the impact of deleveraging shocks as highlighted in the simulations shown in this chapter, Although interest rates are at the zero lower
bound, this does not mean that monetary policy is powerless. Monetary
policy can alleviate the costs of the deleveraging process thorugh unconventional measures, expanding the central bank's balance sheet and channelling liquidity to the real economy. Fiscal policy can also support growth.
Although public sector deleveragng needs remain a pressng issue, further
consolidations should be designed in a growth friendly way. Countries
with fiscal space should use this to boost public infrastructure investment.
Figure 7.10 shows the GDP effects of a temporary two year increase in government investment in core euro area countries (Germany and rest of the
euro area, REA) of 1 per cent of GDP. The impact multiplier in Germany
and the rest of the core euro area block is not particularly large (between

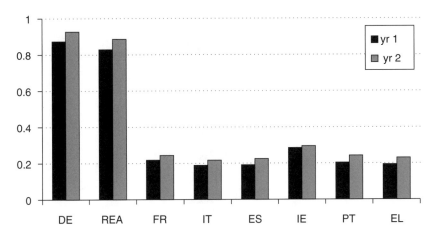

Notes:
First- and second-year GDP (percentage difference from baseline) and current account (percentage of GDP) for temporary increase in public investment of 1 per cent of GDP in Germany and rest of the core euro area.
DE = Germany, REA = rest of the euro area, FR = France, IT = Italy, ES = Spain, IE = Ireland, PT = Portugal, EL = Greece.

Source: In 't Veld (2013).

Figure 7.10   GDP effects of fiscal stimulus in Germany and the rest of the euro area

0.8 and 1) due to the relatively high degree of openness of these countries. But the GDP effect is persistent even after the stimulus is discontinued, as productivity is higher. Import leakage leads to relatively high spillovers to other euro area countries, boosting GDP by between 0.2 and 0.3 per cent, with the smallest increase occurring in Italy and Greece and the largest in Ireland. This shows how a fiscal stimulus in those countries that have the fiscal space can raise potential growth there and also support growth in other countries through positive spillovers.[7]

Finally, structural reforms can alleviate the negative impact of deleveraging (Figure 7.11). Varga and in 't Veld (2014) show the potential growth effects if countries close half the gaps in different structural indicators vis-à-vis best performers. Closing only half the observed gaps should be a realistic and not unattainable goal. It can boost GDP by up to 8 per cent after ten years for the countries most lagging behind. While the short-run impact of structural reforms can be deflationary and hence contractionary in the first year, this effect is only short-lasting. As shown in Vogel (2014), in a larger macroeconomic model like QUEST, the contractionary

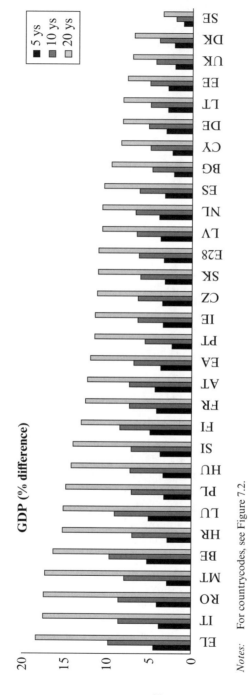

Notes: For countrycodes, see Figure 7.2.

Source: Varga and in 't Veld (2014).

Figure 7.11   Potential GDP effects of jointly implemented structural reforms closing performance gaps

short-term effects of deflationary supply-side reforms at the ZLB are smaller due to various mitigating factors: the impact of reforms on the profitability of investment, the disposable income of liquidity-constrained households and the competitiveness effect in external trade. The adverse real interest rate effect also depends on the short-term deflationary impact of the reform, which can be smaller depending on the type of reform measures. Structural reforms are thus crucial to boost potential growth rates in the EU and to mitigate the impact of the ungoing deleveraging process.

NOTES

1. The views expressed here are those of the authors and should not be attributed to the European Commission.
2. For references to QUEST model publications, see http://ec.europa.eu/economy_finance/research/macroeconomic_models_en.htm.
3. For example, Christiano et al. (2011), Coenen et al. (2012) and Roeger and in 't Veld (2010); and empirical evidence in, for example, Auerbach and Gorodnichenko (2012) and Almunia et al. (2010).
4. The finding of large negative output effects and significant negative spillovers of course does not imply that fiscal consolidations should have been avoided. Highly indebted countries faced pressure from financial markets, or in some cases had completely lost access to markets, and a slower pace of consolidation could have raised general fears of sovereign default. Such expectations of default could lead to worse growth outcomes than consolidations per se (Corsetti et al., 2010; Roeger and in 't Veld, 2013).
5. It should be pointed out that the simulations focused on the demand shortfalls associated with private and public sector deleveraging. Not considered in these simulations were negative demand effects from the counterfactual with rising sovereign risk premia in the absence of fiscal consolidation.
6. In fact, the reaction of the central bank in a simulation in which the monetary policy restriction is removed is so strong as to make the impact of deleveraging slightly less negative compared to the baseline scenario.
7. Against this background the Commission has launched a €300 billion investment initiative to unblock much-needed investment in key areas such as infrastructure, education, research and innovation, renewable energy and in small and medium-sized enterprises development.

REFERENCES

Almunia, M., A. Benetrix, B. Eichengreen, K. O'Rourke and G. Rua (2010), 'From Great Depression to Great Credit Crisis: Similarities, Differences and Lessons', *Economic Policy*, 62, 219–65.

Auerbach, A. and Y. Gorodnichenko (2012), 'Measuring the Output Responses to Fiscal Policy', *American Economic Journal, Economic Policy*, 4, 1–27.

Christiano, L., M. Eichenbaum and S. Rebelo (2011), 'When Is the Government Spending Multiplier Large?', *Journal of Political Economy*, 119, 78–121.

Coenen, G., C. Erceg, C. Freedman, D. Furceri, M. Kumhof, R. Lalonde, D. Laxton, J. Linde, A. Mourougane, D. Muir, S. Mursula, C. de Resende,

J. Roberts, W. Roeger, S. Snudden. M. Trabandt and J. in 't Veld (2012), 'Effects of Fiscal Stimulus in Structural Models', *American Economic Journal, Macroeconomics*, 4 (1), 22–68.

Corsetti, G., K. Kuester, A. Meier and G. Muller (2010), 'Debt Consolidation and Fiscal Stabilization of Deep Recessions', *American Economic Review, Papers and Proceedings*, 100, 41–5.

Cuerpo, C., I. Drumond, J. Lendvai, P. Pontuch and R. Raciborski (2015), 'Private Sector Deleveraging in Europe', *Economic Modelling*, 44 (January), 372–83.

European Commission (2013), 'The Euro Area's Growth Prospects over the Coming Decade', *Quarterly Report of the Euro Area*, 12 (4), 7–16.

European Commission (2014), 'Private Sector Deleveraging: Outlook and Implication for the Forecast', in European Commission, 'European Economic Forecast Autumn 2014', *European Economy* 2014(7), 44–8.

Iacoviello, M. (2005), 'House Prices, Collateral Constraints and Monetary Policy in the Business Cycle', *American Economic Review*, 95 (3), 739–64.

in 't Veld, J. (2013), 'Fiscal Consolidations and Spillovers in the Euro Area Periphery and Core', European Economic Papers no. 506, Brussels: European Commission.

Kiyotaki, N. and J. Moore (1997), 'Credit Cycles', *Journal of Political Economy*, 105 (2), 211–48.

Koo, R. (2011), 'The World in Balance Sheet Recession: Causes, Cure, and Politics', *Real-World Economics Review*, 58, 19–37.

Reinhart, C.M. and K.S. Rogoff (2009), 'The Aftermath of Financial Crises', *American Economic Review*, 99 (2), 466–72.

Roeger, W. and J. in 't Veld (2010), 'Fiscal Stimulus and Exit Strategies in the EU: A Model-based Analysis', European Economy Economic Papers no. 426, Brussels: European Commission.

Roeger, W. and J. in 't Veld (2013), 'Expected Sovereign Defaults and Fiscal Consolidations', European Economy Economic Papers no. 479, Brussels: European Commission.

Varga, J. and J. in 't Veld (2014), 'The Potential Growth Impact of Structural Reforms in the EU: A Benchmarking Exercise', European Economy Economic Papers no. 541, Brussels: European Commission.

Vogel, L. (2014), 'Structural Reforms at the Zero Bound', European Economy Economic Papers no. 537, Brussels: European Commission.

PART III

Macroeconomic adjustments and economic inequality

8. External rebalancing: is it cyclical or structural?

Daniel Gros

The credit boom of the early 2000s led to an unprecedented widening of current account 'imbalances' globally, but particularly within the European Union (EU) and the euro area. While the euro area maintained a balanced current account overall, large differences arose between its members, with Germany running increasingly large current account surpluses and some countries in the periphery running increasingly large deficits. In the cases of Greece and Portugal, these deficits went above 10 per cent of gross domestic product (GDP). Very large deficits arose also throughout Central and Eastern Europe (CEE). A number of the EU member countries in this region were running current account deficits in excess of 20 per cent of GDP for some years.

These deficits were financed by equally large capital inflows. When these inflows stopped suddenly, the deficits could no longer be financed and a quick adjustment became inevitable. The adjustment in the CEE regions was quickest with current account improvements of more than 10 per cent of GDP within less than two years. The adjustment within the euro area was generally slower. On average (unweighted) across EU member countries one observes an improvement of the current account between 2007 and 2013 of 6.3 per cent of GDP.

Somewhat surprisingly, there is no strong correlation between the size and sign of the initial 'imbalance' and subsequent change. This is partially due to the fact that the adjustment was largely asymmetric: the deficit countries reduced their deficits (or turned them into surpluses), whereas the countries which had a surplus already in 2007/2008 did not reduce their surpluses. This applies not only to the largest surplus country, Germany, but also to almost all other countries north of the Alps. Current account balances are largely determined by the balance of trade in goods and services, but other payment flows can at times become important as well. Reduced factor payments and EU funds make a substantial difference for most CEE countries (savings on factor payments) helping the adjustment.

At the end, one is left with the question of whether non-cyclical is the same as structural.

8.1 CYCLICAL OR STRUCTURAL?

The key question now is whether these current account adjustments are cyclical or structural. If they were merely cyclical – that is, a result only of import compression because of a fall in domestic demand – a recovery in output would lead to renewed deficits of an unsustainable size. Fortunately, a recent study of the European Commission (http://ec.europa.eu/economy_finance/eu/forecasts/2014_winter/box2_en.pdf) has calculated the 'cyclically adjusted change in current account imbalance'. (A competing view is provided by Timbeau et al., 2014.)

8.1.1 Was it Just Import Compression?

A first result is that the actual and cyclically adjusted current account balances go together across countries. As Figure 8.1 shows, the correlation between the two is rather high (close to 90 per cent). The countries with the largest actual improvement in the current account are also estimated to have had the largest improvement in the cyclically adjusted balance. It is interesting that a similar result was found at the global level. Haltmaier (2014) concludes that 'The main result is that the bulk of the reduction in the global current account imbalance since 2006 appears to have been structural.' Turning back to Europe, one finds that, as one would expect, the cyclically adjusted change is generally smaller than the actual one (6.3 per cent of GDP actual, versus 4.1 cyclically adjusted), but not by a large margin.

The current account balance can be decomposed into the balance on trade in goods and services and other flows such as factor payments and EU funds. The latter two make a substantial difference in some cases and for most CEE countries. The correlation between the trade balance and the overall current account balance is surprisingly low, as shown in Figure 8.2.

The sometimes large differences between the current account balance and the trade balance are important, because the former is key for the sustainability of the foreign indebtedness position whereas the trade balance is more important for domestic employment. Higher exports lead to more employment. Yet savings on factor payments, for example, might improve the current account, but do not generate domestic employment.

On average the difference between the current account and the trade balance is small (about 1 per cent of GDP). But for many CEE countries

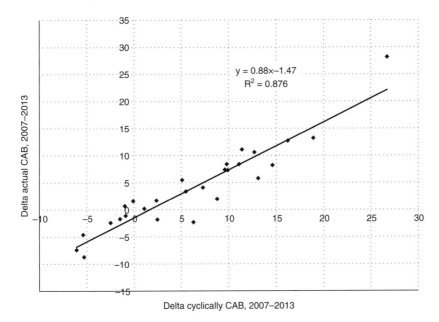

Note:　CAB = cyclically adjusted balance.

Source:　European Commission (2014).

Figure 8.1　*Actual current account balance and cyclically adjusted current account balance*

(and Greece) this difference between the current account and the trade balance is large, often several times larger than the average. Greece constitutes again an outlier, with a gain worth 5 per cent of GDP through lower factor payments, which in turn were the result of the haircut on its foreign debt combined with the very low interest rates Greece pays on its official debt (and now reinforced by lower interest rates in general in the euro area). The overall impression is that trade flows did adjust, but current accounts often improved much more than the trade balance with a substantial support from lower interest rates.

8.1.2　What Drives the (Cyclically Adjusted) Trade Balance?

A key question for policy makers is: What factors explain the large differences across countries in (cyclically adjusted) trade balances (good and services)? The main variable which should help in producing an

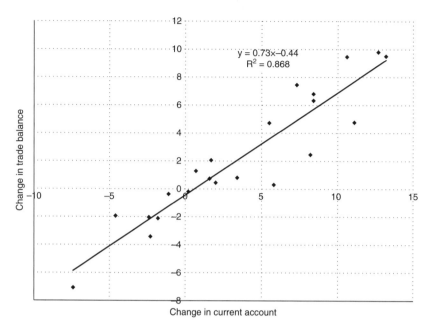

Source: European Commission (2014).

Figure 8.2   Current account balance and trade balance

improvement in the trade balance which is not just cyclical should be the real exchange rate. Strong growth in foreign markets should also help, but this factor will be analysed separately.

It is often argued that membership in the common currency area makes the adjustment more difficult because a large downward adjustment in domestic prices is much more costly than a simple devaluation of the exchange rate. If this were the case, one should see little change in the real exchange rate and only a weak correlation between the trade balance adjustment and the exchange rate within the euro area. However, this is not quite the case.

Figure 8.3 shows for the euro area countries the relationship between the change in the real effective exchange rate and the change in the cyclically adjusted trade balance (both over the time period 2008–2013). The correlation coefficient, at close to 50 per cent, is surprisingly high. But it is also apparent that Greece constitutes an outlier as it had a large improvement in its competitiveness, but a relatively small improvement in its cyclically adjusted trade balance.

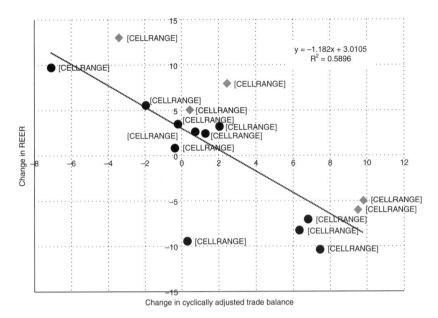

y = −1.182x + 3.0105
R² = 0.5896

Note: REER = real effective exchange rate.

Source: European Commission (2014).

Figure 8.3   *Real effective exchange rates and cyclically adjusted trade balances in the euro area*

Figure 8.3 also shows that the CEE countries, indicated by diamonds, are somewhat special in the sense that almost all of these dots lie above the trend line. This implies that their adjustment was larger than one would expect given the link between the trade balance and the real effective exchange rate for euro area countries on average (see also Belke et al., 2013). This result does not change if Greece is eliminated from the picture. But without Greece the correlation between the change in the real effective exchange rate (REER) and the cyclically adjusted trade balance increases to close to 70 per cent.

Changes in competitiveness have thus played an important role within the euro area. Surprisingly, competitiveness seems to have played a less important role outside the euro area. The correlation between changes in competitiveness and the trade balance is much lower among the EU member countries which are not part of the euro area (see Figure 8.4). The case of the United Kingdom (UK) is here particularly important given the emphasis of the UK authorities on the benefits of its floating exchange

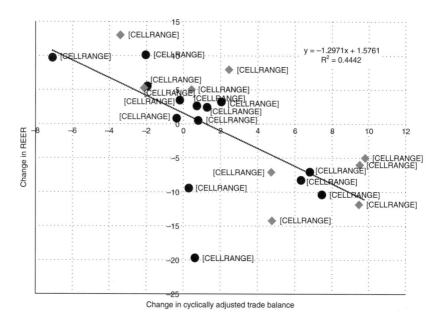

Change in REER

Change in cyclically adjusted trade balance

$y = -1.2971x + 1.5761$
$R^2 = 0.4442$

Note: REER = real effective exchange rate.

Source: European Commission (2014).

Figure 8.4   Real effective exchange rates and the cyclically adjusted trade balances across the EU

rate. The UK is an outlier even more than Greece, because its trade balance has not improved despite a large gain in competitiveness.

8.2   DETERMINANTS OF THE CYCLICALLY ADJUSTED TRADE BALANCE

Another factor in an external rebalancing should be the strength of foreign demand. Strong growth in a country's export market should make it easier to achieve an improvement in the trade balance by increasing exports, rather than lowering imports. One could thus ask: 'What matters more for cyclically adjusted trade balance: real exchange rate or export market growth?'

An answer to this question cannot be obtained by just looking at the simple correlation between these two variables and the trade balance. Instead one needs to look at their joint influence. This can be done by a simple cross-section regression in which the change in the trade balance is explained by changes in the real effective exchange rate and the change in the growth of export markets (see, e.g., Bobeicay et al., 2014, Belke and Dreger, 2013). However, the results from the simple exercise performed here are interesting because they are somewhat surprising:

$$Trade\ balance = 7.3 - 0.4\ REER - 0.4\ EXMg - 7.0\ dummy\ CEE$$

where *EXMg* stands for export market growth, defined as the difference between the actual export growth rate and the change in market shares. The surprising result here is that the contribution of foreign market growth to the adjustment in the trade balance has been on average negative, as one can see from the fact that the sign on this variable is negative. More work remains to be done to elucidate this puzzle.[1]

This negative relationship is exemplified by two outliers. At one extreme one finds Finland, whose export performance was lacklustre although one of its main export markets (Russia) was growing strongly, at least until 2013. But this positive element was overshadowed by the decline of Nokia, whose market share had risen strongly during the early 2000s and then fell dramatically from 2008 to 2013. Portugal is at the other extreme, with a good growth rate in exports despite low growth in its main export markets. Portuguese exporters were apparently able to switch to emerging markets, especially booming Angola, to such a large extent that this outweighed the collapse of demand in the nearest large market, namely Spain. What remains, however, beyond these extreme special cases, is that (changes in) the real exchange rate (that is, competitiveness) seem to matter more for the trade balance than the growth in foreign markets.

8.3 CONCLUSIONS

The financial crisis led to a large, but asymmetric rebalancing after 2007: a large improvement in current account balances can be observed for the countries which had been running large deficits during the preceding boom years, but the countries which had surpluses during the boom years continued with surpluses after the boom ended. This result is compatible with a 'sudden stop' episode; that is, large deficits had been financed by large capital inflows which stopped suddenly when risk materialized and risk aversion returned. The sudden stop seems to have operated both in the euro area and in Central and Eastern Europe, but it occurred about one to two years earlier in the CEE countries.

Most of the observed improvement of the current accounts was due to an improvement in the balance of trade in goods and services, but a reduction in interest payments played an important role in CEE. This should be surprising because the external debt of the deficit countries had increased considerably during the boom years. But the drop in interest rates, which materialized after an initial spike in risk premia, was more important than the increase in the net debt due to the current accounts accumulated prior to 2008.

The difference between the trade balance and the current account is important for the political economy of the adjustment since the trade balance is key for domestic job creation, whereas the current account is key for external sustainability. An improvement in the trade balance via higher exports implies job creation, but this would not be the case for an improvement in the current account via lower interest payments.

There is a high correlation between the actual and cyclically adjusted trade balances, and changes in competitiveness explain most of the variation in the improvement in cyclically adjusted trade balances across euro area member countries. This suggests that the adjustment which did occur was not just due to import compression.

Somewhat surprisingly the link between competitiveness and the improvement in the trade balance was less strong outside the euro area. This implies that membership of the euro area did not impede the necessary adjustment in real exchange rates. The two most important outliers in the relationship between competitiveness and the trade balance are Greece and the UK.

It is tempting to consider the adjustment in the trade balance which is non-cyclical as structural. But this would be mistaken since any improvement in the trade balance based on lower domestic wages and prices could be undone by either domestic inflation or an appreciation of the exchange rate. One should consider as 'structural' only the part of the non-cyclical change in the trade balance which is not due to relative costs. Looked at in this way, one finds much less 'structural' improvement.

NOTE

1. Preliminary research indicates that the puzzle remains even if one relates foreign demand to export growth.

REFERENCES

Belke, A. and C. Dreger (2013), 'Current Account Imbalances in the Euro Area: Does Catching Up Explain the Development?', *Review of International Economics*, 21(1), 6–17.

Belke, A., G. Schnabl and H. Zemanek (2013), 'Real Convergence, Capital Flows, and Competitiveness in Central and Eastern Europe', *Review of International Economics*, 21(5), 886–900.

Bobeicay, E., P. Soares, A. Estevesz and K. Staehr (2014), 'Exports and domestic demand pressure: a dynamic panel data model for the euro area countries', ECB, manuscript.

European Commission (2014), 'Autumn Economic Forecast'.

Haltmaier, J. (2014), 'Cyclically Adjusted Current Account Balances', Board of Governors, International Finance Discussion Paper 1126, available at http://www.federalreserve.gov/econresdata/ifdp/2014/files/ifdp1126.pdf.

Timbeau, X. et al. (2014), 'Independent Annual Growth Survey (IAGS) 2015', Third Report, 11 December, available at http://www.iags-project.org/documents/iags_report2015.pdf.

9. Macroeconomic imbalances and economic inequality in CESEE

Mario Holzner

Milanovic and Ersado (2010) indicate that research on inequality in transition is constrained by very little theory explaining the changes of inequality during transition and only a limited number of rigorous empirical studies available. However, early explanations and descriptions were offered and summarized in the seminal work of this topic's doyen, Branko Milanovic (1998, 1999). The aim of this chapter is to statistically take into account the whole period since the beginning of transition, including the more recent boom-and-bust period, and to shed light on the specific relationship of macroeconomic imbalances and economic inequality in Central, Eastern and South-Eastern Europe (CESEE), which is an important but under-researched issue since the early transition crisis. This descriptive analysis is based on related findings of almost a decade of empirical inequality in transition research at the Vienna Institute for International Economic Studies (wiiw).[1] The overall research question is: in what way was the general development of inequality in transition as well as the marked differences in levels of inequality between the transition countries affected by macroeconomic imbalances, or in what way did they have an impact on the building up of these imbalances?

9.1 THE DEVELOPMENT OF HOUSEHOLD INCOME INEQUALITY IN TRANSITION

The general development of disposable household income inequality as indicated by the Gini index (see Figure 9.1) during transition was characterized by a strong increase of inequality in the early years of transition and throughout most of the 1990s. Inequality stabilized in the early boom period and even started to fall in some cases in the mid-2000s. It appears that inequality has again stabilized in the wake of the global financial crisis.

Thus there is no evidence for an inverted U-shaped development, as suggested by the Kuznets curve theory, of first rising and later falling

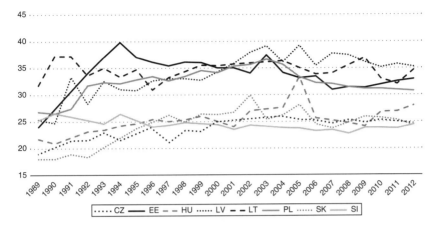

Notes:
CZ = Czech Republic, EE = Estonia, HU = Hungary, LV = Latvia, LT = Lithuania,
SK = Slovakia, SI = Slovenia.
UNU-WIDER WIID = United Nations University Wider Income Inequality Database;
V3.0b refers to September 2014.
TransMonEE = A database capturing a vast range of information on social and economic
issues relevant to the situation and well-being of children, adolescents and women in 28
CEE, CIS and EU countries.
WDI = World Development Indicators.

Source: UNU-WIDER WIID V3.0b, Eurostat, TransMonEE, WDI, interpolations.

Figure 9.1   *Gini index for disposable household income in Central and*
            Eastern Europe, 1989–2012

inequality for countries in development. Data for the economies from
Central and Eastern Europe (CEE) are the most comparable. Figure 9.1
depicts a similar development for most of these countries but also marked
differences in the level of income inequality. The Baltics and also Poland
show income inequality levels higher than the European Union (EU)
average of a Gini coefficient of about 30. The Central European economies of the Czech Republic, Slovakia and Slovenia, and by and large also
Hungary, display an inequality level of below the EU average.

In the case of countries from South-Eastern Europe (SEE) inequality
appears to be ever increasing throughout the whole period of analysis,
given data availability (see Figure 9.2). However for this group of economies comparison within and between countries is rather limited due to
many breaks in the data series as well as different concepts of inequality measurement. Also some of the data relates to consumption and not
to income. The quality of data is even worse for the Commonwealth of

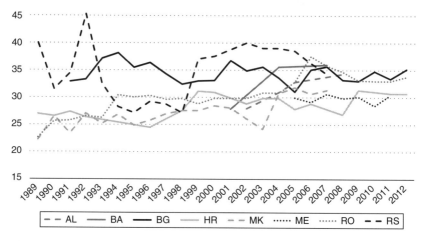

Figure 9.2   *Gini index for income/consumption in South-Eastern Europe,*
              1989–2012

Independent States (CIS) in Eastern Europe. Given the data available for
this group of economies we can observe in Figure 9.3 since the mid-2000s
a moderate reversal from very high levels of inequality. However, especially
Georgia and Russia still have extremely high inequality levels, similar to
those found in developing economies from Africa.

9.2   TRANSITION CRISIS, BUMPY RECOVERY AND MACROECONOMIC IMBALANCES

The transition crisis was characterized by a huge output loss that coincided with increasing levels of income inequality. A strong reduction in
formal (public) employment as well as an increasing wage inequality in

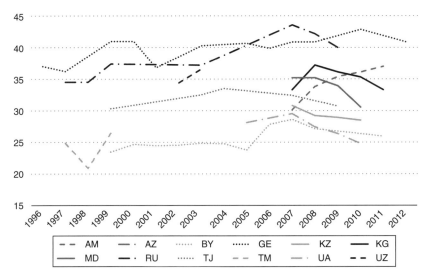

Notes:
AM = Armenia, AZ = Azerbaijan, BY = Belarus, GE = Georgia, KZ = Kazakhstan,
KG = Kyrgyzstan, MD = Republic of Moldova, RU = Russia, TJ = Tajikistan,
TM = Turkmenistan, UA = Ukraine, UZ = Uzbekistan.
UNU-WIDER WIID = United Nations University Wider Income Inequality Database;
V3.0b refers to September 2014.
TransMonEE = A database capturing a vast range of information on social and economic
issues relevant to the situation and well-being of children, adolescents and women in 28
CEE, CIS and EU countries.
WDI = World Development Indicators.

Source: UNU-WIDER WIID V3.0b, Eurostat, TransMonEE, WDI, interpolations.

*Figure 9.3   Gini index for income/consumption in the Commonwealth of
Independent States, 1996–2012*

the growing private sector were at the core of rising income inequality
in that period (Leitner and Holzner, 2008).[2] Comparable data for the
new EU member states for this early period of transition in Figure 9.4
suggests a strong negative relationship between average growth of gross
domestic product (GDP) and the average Gini index level[3] (both averages
are according to data availability). In particular, the Baltic states suffered
a heavy output loss in the wake of the collapse of the Soviet Union. This
is also true for Croatia due to the war after the break-up of Yugoslavia.
These countries together with Bulgaria and Poland had the highest levels
of income inequality (among the new EU member states) in the early transition period.

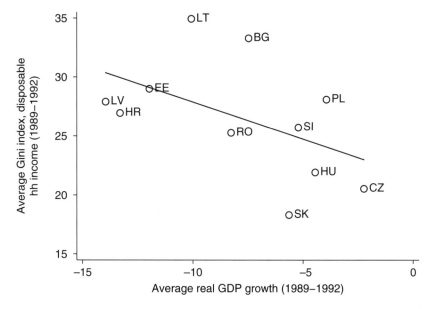

Notes:
Averages due to data availability.
BG = Bulgaria, CZ = Czech Republic, EE = Estonia, HR = Croatia, HU = Hungary,
LV = Latvia, LT = Lithuania, PL = Poland, RO = Romania, SK = Slovakia,
SI = Slovenia.
wiiw = The Vienna Institute for International Economic Studies.
UNU-WIDER WIID = United Nations University Wider Income Inequality Database;
V3.0b refers to September 2014.
TransMonEE = A database capturing a vast range of information on social and economic
issues relevant to the situation and well-being of children, adolescents and women in 28
CEE, CIS and EU countries.
WDI = World Development Indicators.

Source: wiiw, UNU-WIDER WIID Vb3.0B, Eurostat, TransMonEE, interpolations.

*Figure 9.4   Average Gini index and growth of gross domestic product,
1989–1992*

The decay and the large scale privatization of formerly state-owned enterprises as well as the loss and reorientation of international trade flows had
a lagged effect on unemployment rates. Consequently the period of bumpy
recovery throughout the 1990s (culminating in the banking crises of the
late 1990s) saw double-digit unemployment rates in most of the new EU
member states. In the mid-1990s inequality levels were the highest where
unemployment was vast (see Figure 9.5). Again, this group of countries
comprises most of the Baltic states, Bulgaria and also Poland. But what

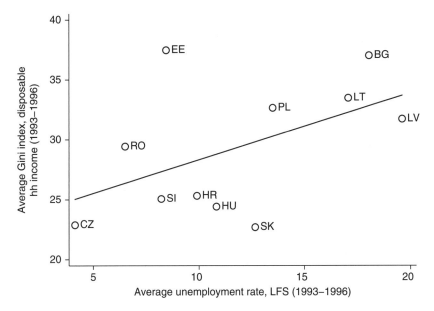

Notes:
Averages due to data availability.
LFS = Labor Force Survey.
BG = Bulgaria, CZ = Czech Republic, EE = Estonia, HR = Croatia, HU = Hungary,
LV = Latvia, LT = Lithuania, PL = Poland, RO = Romania, SK = Slovakia,
SI = Slovenia.
wiiw = The Vienna Institute for International Economic Studies.
UNU-WIDER WIID = United Nations University Wider Income Inequality Database;
V3.0b refers to September 2014.
TransMonEE = A database capturing a vast range of information on social and economic
issues relevant to the situation and well-being of children, adolescents and women in 28
CEE, CIS and EU countries.
WDI = World Development Indicators.

Source: wiiw, UNU-WIDER WIID V3.0b, Eurostat, TransMonEE, interpolations.

Figure 9.5   Average Gini index and unemployment rate, 1993–1996

was the relationship between inequality and the macroeconomic imbalances (as measured by the current account balance) of that era? If at all, the mid-1990s saw a somewhat U-shaped relationship (see Figure 9.6) between the Gini index and the current account balance as a share in GDP. Interestingly, countries with higher levels of inequality were rather out of macroeconomic balance. Levels of inequality similar to those in the Nordic countries were found only in the Czech and the Slovak Republics. They also had a fairly balanced current account.

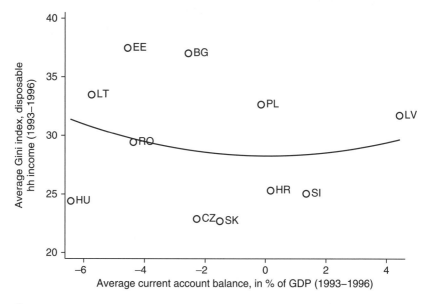

Notes:
Averages due to data availability.
BG = Bulgaria, CZ = Czech Republic, EE = Estonia, HR= Croatia, HU = Hungary,
LV = Latvia, LT = Lithuania, PL = Poland, RO = Romania, SK = Slovakia, SI = Slovenia.
wiiw = The Vienna Institute for International Economic Studies.
UNU-WIDER WIID = United Nations University Wider Income Inequality Database;
V3.0b refers to September 2014.
TransMonEE = A database capturing a vast range of information on social and economic
issues relevant to the situation and well-being of children, adolescents and women in 28
CEE, CIS and EU countries.
WDI = World Development Indicators.

Source: wiiw, UNU-WIDER WIID V3.0b, Eurostat, TransMonEE, interpolations.

*Figure 9.6   Average Gini index and current account (% of GDP),
1993–1996*

9.3   EXCURSUS: PERSONAL/SECTORAL INCOME INEQUALITY IN THE NEW EU MEMBER STATES

In order to better study the change of income inequality in transition between the boom and the bust period of the 2000s with more data points, I have calculated a Gini index for income inequality based on detailed sectoral data on average gross wages and employment, unemployment

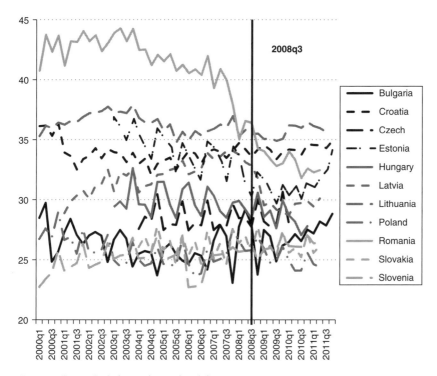

Source: Own calculations using national data.

Figure 9.7   Quarterly Gini coefficients based on wage, pension and unemployment benefits data

benefits and unemployment benefit receivers, as well as average pensions and number of pensioners. For a more detailed description of the data as well as subsequent econometric analysis, see Holzner (2013).

The overall picture in Figure 9.7 appears to be rather inconclusive. It can be seen that for a number of countries the development of income inequality appears to be rather flat and the global financial crisis did not seem to have a major impact.

In this respect it is also interesting to have a look at income inequality development, excluding those sectors that are directly and predominantly influenced by the state. Therefore I have repeated my Gini calculations for a sample without gross wages for the sectors of public administration, education, human health and social work activities as well as pensions and unemployment benefits. Figure 9.8 shows the results of this exercise. In contrast to the previous results, most of the

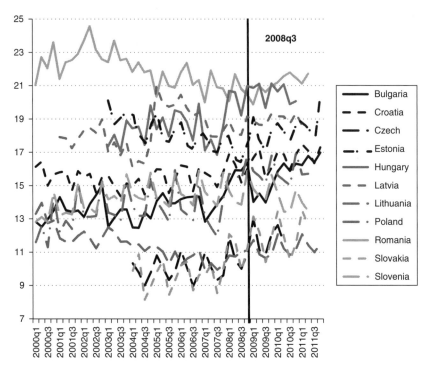

Source: Own calculations using national data.

Figure 9.8   Quarterly Gini coefficients based on wage data without public sector

'private' Gini coefficients experienced an increase of inequality throughout most of the analysed period and especially after the outbreak of the global financial crisis in the third quarter of 2008. An econometric analysis shows the following. While in the private sector wage dispersion further continued to increase during the boom just as during the economic breakdown, the public sector was inequality-reducing both in the period of plenty as well as in the age of austerity. In the earlier period this was *inter alia* due to social protection expenditures (see also Holzner, 2010) while in the latter period counter-intuitive 'progressive' austerity measures such as cuts in the top public wages were inequality-reducing.

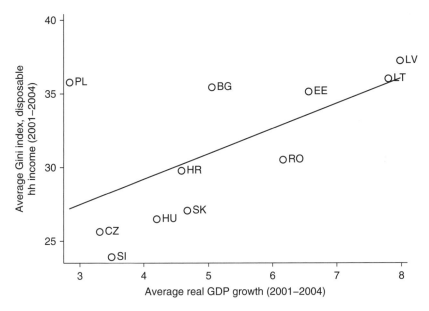

Notes:
Averages due to data availability.
BG = Bulgaria, CZ = Czech Republic, EE = Estonia, HR = Croatia, HU = Hungary,
LV = Latvia, LT = Lithuania, PL = Poland, RO = Romania, SK = Slovakia, SI = Slovenia.
wiiw = The Vienna Institute for International Economic Studies.
UNU-WIDER WIID = United Nations University Wider Income Inequality Database;
V3.0b refers to September 2014.
TransMonEE = A database capturing a vast range of information on social and economic
issues relevant to the situation and well-being of children, adolescents and women in 28
CEE, CIS and EU countries.
WDI = World Development Indicators.

Source: wiiw, UNU-WIDER WIID V.3.0B, Eurostat, TransMonEE, interpolations.

Figure 9.9 Average Gini index and GDP growth, 2001–2004

9.4 EARLY BOOM PHASE INEQUALITY AND BUBBLES

In the early boom phase in the first half of the 2000s it appears that
the new EU member states with the highest levels of household income
inequality experienced the largest GDP growth rates (see Figure 9.9).
Anecdotal evidence from the Baltic states suggests that especially better-
earning private sector employees were triggering a construction boom.
Hence in these countries high levels of inequality might have reinforced the

build-up of bubbles (not necessarily only in real estate) and corresponding macroeconomic imbalances.

9.5   EXCURSUS: HOUSEHOLD WEALTH AND DEBT DISTRIBUTION

New comparable data from the Eurosystem's Household Finance and Consumption Survey (HFCS)[4] allows us to look in more detail at wealth and debt distribution. However, so far, Slovakia and Slovenia are the only new EU member states for which data are available. Compared to the Baltic countries, these two countries did not experience too much of a housing bubble.

Both have very high shares of real estate holdings throughout the income distribution (see Figure 9.10), comparable to the situation in Spain, but very different from the situation in Austria where half of the population lives in rented flats, cooperative and social housing. The

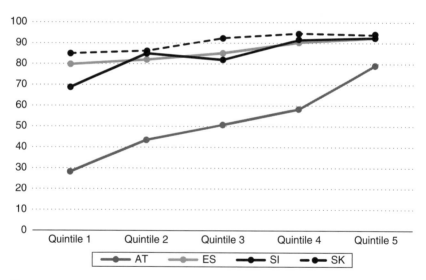

Notes:
Data collected 2008–2011.
AT = Austria, ES = Spain, SI = Slovenia, SK = Slovakia.

Source: Household Finance and Consumption Survey, first survey.

Figure 9.10   Share of households holding real estate by gross income quintiles (%)

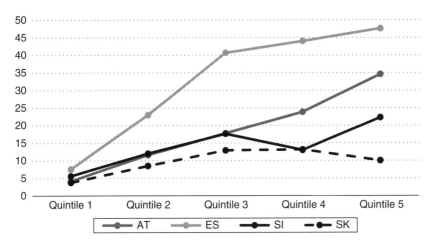

Notes:
Data collected 2008–2011.
AT = Austria, ES = Spain, SI = Slovenia, SK = Slovakia.

Source: Household Finance and Consumption Survey, first survey.

*Figure 9.11   Share of households holding mortgage debt by gross income
quintiles (%)*

mortgage debt distribution over the household gross income quintiles
provides a somewhat different picture (see Figure 9.11). While Spanish
households are heavily indebted, Austrian households are not, and
households from Slovakia and Slovenia are even less so. This is mainly
due to the fact that in most transition economies public housing was
privatized to the population for largely symbolic prices and hence mortgage debt is only a more recent phenomenon among younger households
seeking private housing.

9.6   BOOM PEAK, THE GREAT RECESSION AND
MACROECONOMIC IMBALANCES

At the peak of the boom in the late 2000s the relationship between inequality and the current account balance in percentage of GDP becomes
perfectly linear (see Figure 9.12) as all the new member states (NMS)
run current account deficits in this period. Again countries with the
highest levels of household disposable income inequality also run the

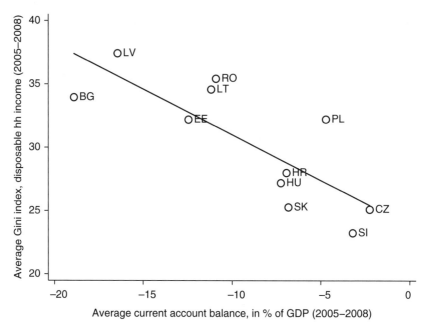

Notes:
BG = Bulgaria, CZ = Czech Republic, EE = Estonia, HR= Croatia, HU = Hungary,
LV = Latvia, LT = Lithuania, PL = Poland, RO = Romania, SK = Slovakia, SI = Slovenia.
wiiw = The Vienna Institute for International Economic Studies.
UNU-WIDER WIID = United Nations University Wider Income Inequality Database;
V3.0b refers to September 2014.
TransMonEE = A database capturing a vast range of information on social and economic
issues relevant to the situation and well-being of children, adolescents and women in 28
CEE, CIS and EU countries.
WDI = World Development Indicators.

Source: wiiw, UNU-WIDER WIID V3.0b, Eurostat, TransMonEE, interpolations.

Figure 9.12   *Average Gini index and current account (% of GDP),*
              2005–2008

largest current account deficits (that is, Bulgaria and the Baltic states).
Interestingly enough, these are also the economies that chose a fixed
exchange rate regime and hence had only limited possibilities to counter
the huge foreign capital inflows of that time.

This relationship changes strongly in the period of the Great Recession
and its dry-up of international capital flows, when the U-shaped pattern
of the transition crisis re-emerges (see Figure 9.13). While a few of the
high-inequality countries still run debt-increasing current account deficits,

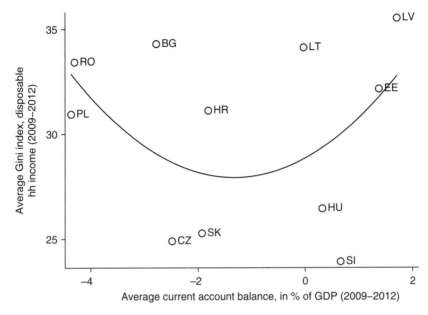

Notes:
BG = Bulgaria, CZ = Czech Republic, EE = Estonia, HR = Croatia, HU = Hungary,
LV = Latvia, LT = Lithuania, PL = Poland, RO = Romania, SK = Slovakia, SI = Slovenia.
wiiw = The Vienna Institute for International Economic Studies.
UNU-WIDER WIID = United Nations University Wider Income Inequality Database;
V3.0b refers to September 2014.
TransMonEE = A database capturing a vast range of information on social and economic
issues relevant to the situation and well-being of children, adolescents and women in 28
CEE, CIS and EU countries.
WDI = World Development Indicators.

Source: wiiw, UNU-WIDER WIID V3.0b, Eurostat, TransMonEE, interpolations.

*Figure 9.13   Average Gini index and current account (% of GDP),
2009–2012*

others (especially the Baltic states) were forced to run surpluses due to
massive consumption (and hence import) contraction. Those countries
(the Czech Republic, Slovakia, Slovenia and Hungary) that do not lack
competitiveness, and that had sustainable growth rates and a fairly balanced current account throughout most of the transition, are also preserving the lowest levels of inequality.

While many of the analysed scatter plots change shape depending on the
period analysed there is one factor that remains extremely stable throughout transition. This is the relationship between the share of manufacturing

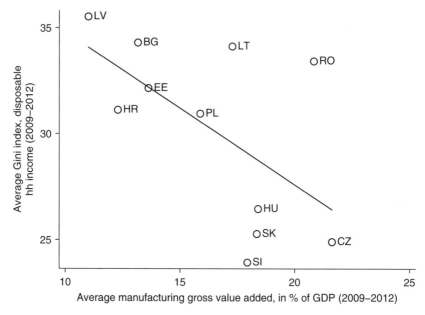

Notes:
BG = Bulgaria, CZ = Czech Republic, EE = Estonia, HR = Croatia, HU = Hungary,
LV = Latvia, LT = Lithuania, PL = Poland, RO = Romania, SK = Slovakia, SI =
Slovenia.
wiiw = The Vienna Institute for International Economic Studies.
UNU-WIDER WIID = United Nations University Wider Income Inequality Database;
V3.0b refers to September 2014.
TransMonEE = A database capturing a vast range of information on social and economic
issues relevant to the situation and well-being of children, adolescents and women in 28
CEE, CIS and EU countries.
WDI = World Development Indicators.

Source: wiiw, UNU-WIDER WIID V3.0b, Eurostat, TransMonEE, interpolations.

*Figure 9.14   Average Gini index and manufacturing share in GDP,
2009–2012*

gross value added in GDP and the Gini index (see Figure 9.14 for the latest
period). The core countries among the new EU member states display a
large manufacturing sector and low levels of inequality, while the opposite holds true for the new member states at the EU periphery. Several
structural elements are related to this. The economies with a large manufacturing sector and low inequality also have larger collective bargaining coverage rates (see Figure 9.15) that allow for a more equitable and

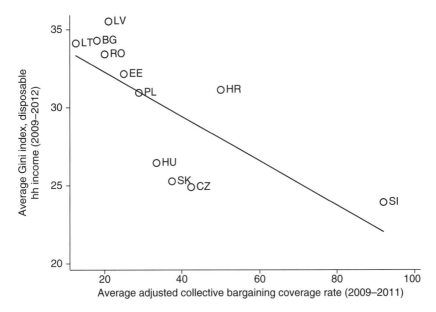

Notes:
Averages due to data availability.
BG = Bulgaria, CZ = Czech Republic, EE = Estonia, HR = Croatia, HU = Hungary,
LV = Latvia, LT = Lithuania, PL = Poland, RO = Romania, SK = Slovakia, SI = Slovenia.
ICTWSS = Database on Institutional Characteristics, of Trade Unions, Wage Setting, State
Intervention and Social Pacts in 34 countries between 1960 and 2012.
ILO = International Labour Organization.
UNU-WIDER WIID = United Nations University Wider Income Inequality Database;
V3.0b refers to September 2014.
TransMonEE = A database capturing a vast range of information on social and economic
issues relevant to the situation and well-being of children, adolescents and women in 28
CEE, CIS and EU countries.
WDI = World Development Indicators.

Source: ICTWSS, ILO, UNU-WIDER WIID V3.0b, Eurostat, TransMonEE,
interpolations.

*Figure 9.15   Average Gini index and collective bargaining coverage,
2009–2012*

coordinated incomes policy. Consequently these are also the economies
with higher income levels as measured by the GDP per capita at purchasing power parity (see Figure 9.16).

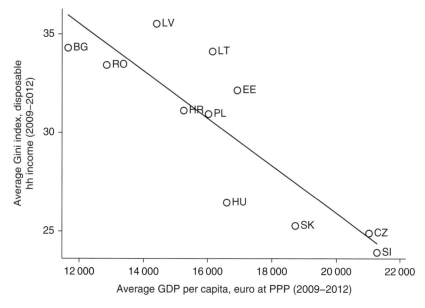

Notes:
PPP = purchasing power parity.
BG = Bulgaria, CZ = Czech Republic, EE = Estonia, HR = Croatia, HU = Hungary,
LV = Latvia, LT = Lithuania, PL = Poland, RO = Romania, SK = Slovakia, SI = Slovenia.
wiiw = The Vienna Institute for International Economic Studies.
UNU-WIDER WIID = United Nations University Wider Income Inequality Database;
V3.0b refers to September 2014.
TransMonEE = A database capturing a vast range of information on social and economic
issues relevant to the situation and well-being of children, adolescents and women in 28
CEE, CIS and EU countries.
WDI = World Development Indicators.

Source: wiiw, UNU-WIDER WIID V3.0b, Eurostat, TransMonEE, interpolations.

Figure 9.16   Average Gini index and GDP per capita, 2009–2012

9.7   CONCLUSIONS

In most countries from Central, Eastern and South-Eastern Europe disposable household income inequality as measured by the Gini index increased strongly during the transition crisis in the early 1990s, and to a certain extent also throughout the bumpy recovery period in the late 1990s with its banking and exchange rate crises. Inequality stabilized throughout the boom period in the early 2000s and even started to decline a little during the peak of the boom in the second half of the 2000s. Since the outbreak of the Great Recession inequality has stabilized again. While private sector wage inequality increased in both the boom as well as the bust period, the state had a stabilizing function, intervening in the field of public wages as well as in pensions and transfers. Overall core CEE countries have inequality levels below the EU average, while the others have inequality levels above the EU average.

In what way was the general development of inequality as well as the marked differences in levels of inequality between the countries affected by macroeconomic imbalances, or in what way did they have an impact on the building up of these imbalances? The initial rise in inequality during the transition crisis was strongly influenced by huge output and employment losses. Macroeconomic imbalances indicated both by large current account deficits (build-up of debt) and surpluses (often reflecting consumption and hence import contraction) could be observed among the countries hit the most and longest by the crisis. These were predominantly economies with an ailing export sector and fixed exchange rates. Appreciated real exchange rates and higher levels of inequality in these countries have likely fuelled the development of credit bubbles during the subsequent boom period and have thereby reinforced macro-imbalances in the form of massive current account deficits (and thus capital inflows), such as in the Baltic states. With the outbreak of the Great Recession and the drying up of international capital flows the most exposed and unequal economies had to face a sudden stop and a forced shift from current account deficit to surplus.

The core economies from CEE have managed to develop in a more stable way with less extreme growth rates and fairly balanced current accounts. These countries have secured low levels of inequality. The common denominator is a large share of manufacturing industry providing for goods exports that can cover imports, offering high incomes to many who – in poorer countries with a less stable industrial sector – otherwise have to live by subsistence farming or petty trade. A large manufacturing sector also allows for a better organization of social partnership (wage bargaining) arrangements, which has again favourable repercussions on the balanced and equitable development of the economy.

Policy recommendations for unbalanced and unequal economies without a substantial manufacturing sector comprise measures of industrial policy including public infrastructure investment as well as the development of a cooperative social partnership system that has the potential to coordinate income distribution as well as real exchange rate policy under the premises of a fixed nominal exchange rate regime. This in turn would also help to reduce macro-imbalances.

NOTES

1. Over the past decade inequality research at the Vienna Institute for International Economic Studies (wiiw) was *inter alia* supported by the Anniversary Fund of the Oesterreichische Nationalbank (OeNB), the Austrian Federal Ministry of Finance (BMF), the Global Development Network (GDN) and the Austrian Chamber of Labour (AK)
2. A reprint of that article (Leitner and Holzner, 2012) was later published in Milanovic (2012).
3. Comparing data in levels yields some insights, while the comparison of first differences does not yield strong relationships of the variables analysed in this context.
4. The following results stem from a forthcoming wealth and debt inequality report comparing euro area HFCS data for the Austrian Chamber of Labour (AK).

REFERENCES

Holzner, M. (2010), 'Inequality, Growth and Public Spending in Central, East and Southeast Europe', wiiw Working Papers, No. 71.

Holzner, M. (2013), 'Inequality and the Crisis: A Causal Inference Analysis Quantitative Research on New Quarterly Income Inequality Data for CESEE', The wiiw Balkan Observatory Working Papers, No. 110.

Leitner, S. and M. Holzner (2008), 'Economic Inequality in Central, East and Southeast Europe', *Intervention: European Journal of Economics and Economic Policies*, 5(1), 155–88.

Leitner, S. and M. Holzner (2012), 'Economic Inequality in Central, East and Southeast Europe', in Branko Milanovic (ed.), *Globalization and Inequality*, Cheltenham, UK and Northampton, MA, USA, Edward Elgar Publishing, pp. 138–71.

Milanovic, B. (1998), 'Income, Inequality, and Poverty during the Transition from Planned to Market Economy', Washington, DC, World Bank.

Milanovic, B. (1999), 'Explaining the Increase in Inequality during Transition', *Economics of Transition*, 7(2), 299–341.

Milanovic, B. (ed.) (2012), *Globalization and Inequality*, Cheltenham, UK and Northampton, MA, USA, Edward Elgar Publishing.

Milanovic, B. and L. Ersado (2010), 'Reform and Inequality during the Transition', UNU-WIDER Working Paper, No. 201-0/62.

10. Inequality, the crisis and stagnation

Till van Treeck

The inequality of income and wealth is one of the defining issues of our time, in terms of both its social and its macroeconomic implications. In this chapter, I focus on the macroeconomic implications of inequality. In particular, it is possible to identify four themes on which there seems to be growing consensus among many economists especially in the various heterodox traditions, but also increasingly in the mainstream of the economics profession.

The first theme on which there is growing consensus is the notion that the rise in inequality has contributed in an important way to the unsustainable rise in household debt in the United States and ultimately to the financial and economic crisis starting in 2007 (e.g. Palley, 1994; Dutt, 2006; Frank, 2007; Cynamon and Fazzari, 2013; Fitoussi and Stiglitz, 2009; Rajan, 2010; Kumhof and Rancière, 2010; Mian and Sufi, 2014).

Secondly, there is the by now widely held view that rising inequality at the international level has contributed to the so-called global imbalances in terms of national current account positions (e.g. Kumhof et al., 2012; van Treeck and Sturn, 2012; Hein and Truger, 2012; Stockhammer, 2013; Behringer and van Treeck, 2013; Belabed et al., 2013).

Thirdly, there has recently been a shift of the focus of attention from merely looking at income inequality to analysing the longer-term implications of income inequality for wealth inequality (e.g. Piketty, 2014; Saez and Zucman, 2014). And fourthly, the argument has been made that a high level of inequality can, generally speaking, be a cause of low economic growth, or even secular stagnation (e.g. Dutt, 2006; Palley, 2012; Ostry et al., 2014; Cingano, 2014).

While it would be beyond the scope of this chapter to go into the details of each of these important issues, I will try to give a broad and non-technical overview on how these issues can be seen to be linked.[1] Section 10.1 discusses the link between income inequality and the United States (US) household debt crisis. Section 10.2 discusses the link between changes in income distribution and the current account surplus of Germany. Section 10.3 looks at the relation between income distribution and current account imbalances for a panel of 20 industrialized countries. Section 10.4 then goes on to discuss the implications of the empirical findings for the evolution of wealth inequality. Finally, section 10.5 concludes by arguing that inequality may indeed turn out to be one of the main causes of secular demand stagnation.

10.1   THE INEQUALITY–CRISIS NEXUS IN THE UNITED STATES

Figure 10.1 shows the spectacular rise in the share of total pre-tax household income going to the top of income distribution in the United States, which started in the early 1980s. Figure 10.2 shows the equally spectacular decrease in the private household saving rate, also starting in the early 1980s, to near 0 per cent just before the crisis. It also shows that households' debt-to-income ratio increased very strongly in the United States over the same period.

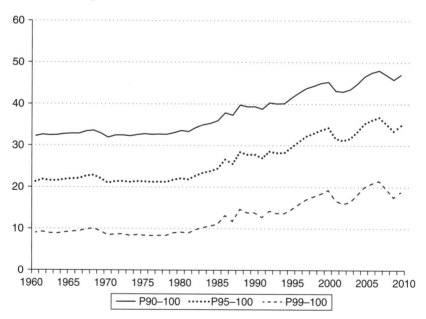

Source: Piketty and Saez (1998, updated), http://eml.berkeley.edu/~saez/.

Figure 10.1   *Top 1%, 5%, and 10% household incomes as a percentage of total pre-tax household income (including capital gains), United States, 1960–2010*

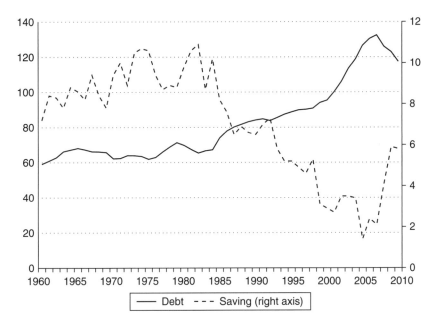

Source: Bureau of Economic Analysis, Federal Reserve.

Figure 10.2   Debt and saving as a percentage of household disposable income, United States, 1960–2010

These macroeconomic trends are intriguing, not least from a traditional Keynesian point of view. In fact, simple Keynesian models would predict that higher income inequality leads to a higher aggregate saving rate, because rich households have a lower marginal propensity to spend than poor households. On the other hand, models with upward-looking status comparisons, like some variants of the relative income hypothesis, predict a negative link between inequality and the aggregate saving rate (Frank, 2005). According to this view, households just below the top of the distribution in the United States, which could be called 'upper middle class', have reduced their saving in order to try and keep up with the spending patterns of households at the top. This, in turn, may also have increased the pressure on the lower-middle and lower classes to increase spending relative to their incomes. Ultimately, therefore, the rising standard of living at the top of the distribution has affected the consumption norms of the entire income distribution ('expenditure cascades'; see Frank et al., 2010).

It is important to emphasize that this explanation of the fall in the saving rate is not primarily about the saving behaviour of poor households. By definition, poor households receive only a small share of total incomes, and hence the effect of the saving behaviour of poor households on the aggregate saving rate is rather limited. By contrast, the relative income hypothesis in the US context highlights the difficulties faced by the middle and upper-middle class in providing for what they perceive as basic needs in the face of rising inequality at the top of the distribution. Typical middle-class needs include the aspiration to send their children to relatively good schools or universities, to live in relatively decent neighbourhoods, or to achieve a relatively high standard of health care.

All of these goods can be qualified as positional goods: what matters for the career prospects of one's children, for example, is the relative quality of their education rather than its absolute quality. Clearly, not everybody can attend better than average schools, and even though today's relatively bad schools may be better than in the past, career prospects strongly depend on the quality of one's education relative to others of their generation. Similarly, social status depends not so much on the absolute size or price of one's home, but rather on its relative price. Again, not everyone can live in a more expensive home or neighbourhood than the average person would aspire to. But the relative decency of a neighbourhood also determines the relative quality of the infrastructure and social networks that are important for households to strive economically.

Now, when people just above a given family in the income distribution scale begin to spend much more money on education, simply because their incomes increase, but at the same time that given family's own income is stagnant, then that family either has to accept that the relative quality of their children's education decreases, or it can reduce their saving and go into debt. And this seems to be what many US middle-class households have done; that is, they have traded off their retirement savings for the purchasing of positional goods such as education, housing or health care. Clearly, and importantly in this context, the institutional environment in the United States, where most of these basic needs have to be paid for privately, puts enormous pressure on households to save less and go into debt, as their relative incomes decrease. Moreover, given the uncertainties surrounding future income prospects and the dependence of future income on the current consumption of positional goods, it is not clear if households' decision to 'live beyond their means' can be qualified as 'irrational', at least from the perspective of any given individual household.

Evidence in favour of the above explanation of the decrease in the US household saving rate can be provided based on micro data. As shown by Saez and Zucman (2014), it was the bottom 99 per cent of the wealth distribution who strongly reduced their saving rates starting in the early 1980s, whereas the saving rate of the top 1 per cent remained roughly stable.

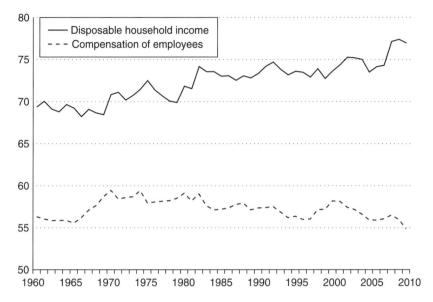

Source: Bureau of Economic Analysis, Federal Reserve.

Figure 10.3 *Disposable household income and compensation of employees as a percentage of GDP, United States, 1960–2010*

Meanwhile, the rise in the debt-to-net worth and the debt-to-income ratios took place within the bottom 95 per cent of the distribution, and not at all at the top (Kumhof and Rancière, 2010; Cynamon and Fazzari, 2013).

Finally, it may be important to emphasize the fact that the functional distribution of income (the distribution of the national income between wages and profits, or between household and corporate income), has been much more stable in the United States since the 1980s, compared to the personal distribution of income (the distribution of income between households). As Figure 10.3 shows, even though the wage share has decreased somewhat over the two or three decades preceding the crisis, the total share of household income in national income has actually remained rather stable.

In my view, these very powerful macroeconomic trends have a number of implications for economic theory. Firstly, models focusing exclusively on the functional income distribution (as is the case in many post-Keynesian and other heterodox models) may miss an important part of the inequality–crisis nexus for the United States.[2]

Secondly, mainstream theories of consumption are unable to explain the decline in the household saving rate and the rise in household debt in the United States. In fact, the permanent income or life-cycle theories of consumption see no link between any given household's saving rate and its (permanent) relative income. Rather, some variants of these theories try to explain the decrease in the aggregate saving rate in the United States by referring to the so-called wealth effect. But the wealth effect cannot explain why the saving rate of the top 1 per cent, where most of the increase in wealth took place, has actually remained stable. Moreover, much of the increase in the net worth-to-income ratio of the bottom 95 per cent of the income distribution before the crisis was due to the rising prices of owner-occupied houses. Yet, as argued by Cynamon and Fazzari (2013), in most cases an owner-occupied house merely signals an intention to consume future housing services. Since few households actually decide to sell their house, an owner-occupied house should not generally be considered as an asset in which households park wealth that they intend to use later to pay down debt. Thirdly, the current renaissance of the long-neglected relative income hypothesis of consumption is in my view highly warranted.

10.2   INCOME DISTRIBUTION AND MACROECONOMIC INSTABILITY IN GERMANY

At first sight, the rise in inequality in Germany has been similar to that in the United States, at least when looking at the Gini coefficient of equivalized household disposable income, which is still the most routinely considered indicator of income inequality. However, when looking at top household income shares, no major shifts can be observed for Germany over the past decades, especially for the top 1 per cent household income share. This is also why, according to Piketty and Saez (2006), Germany can be qualified as an L-shape country, whereas the United States and other Anglo Saxon countries have been qualified as U-shape countries (cf. Figure 10.1).

It is problematic, however, to directly compare trends in top household income shares across countries without also looking at trends within the corporate sector, which is essentially owned by rich households. In Germany, the corporate sector has been a persistent net saver since 2002 (Figure 10.4), due to a large extent to the rise in retained profits. Therefore, to the extent that retained corporate profits are not counted as household income, top household income shares à la Piketty may underestimate the rise of top-end inequality in Germany.

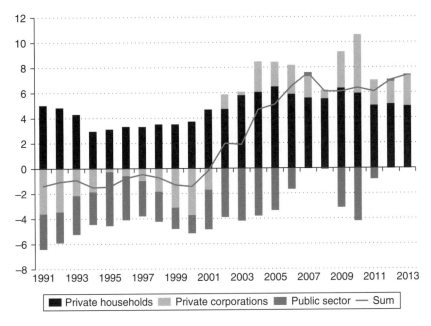

Source: Eurostat.

Figure 10.4   *Top household incomes and retained corporate earnings as a percentage of private pre-tax income, Germany, 1995–2007*

Figure 10.5 shows the rise in capital, or profit income as a percentage of national income in Germany since the early 2000s, as well as the rise in corporate retained earnings as a share of disposable private income over the same period. Based on these trends, Figure 10.6 puts in perspective the development of top household income shares by taking into account the profits retained by corporations between 1995 and 2007.

Of course, it would be excessive to argue that all retained earnings should simply be counted as top household income. But Figure 10.6 can be thought of as a simple thought experiment, in that it shows what would have happened to personal income inequality if the German corporate sector had behaved more like the US corporate sector, which has passed rising returns on to top managers and shareholders, and thereby to the household sector.

The very different behaviour of German corporations is, of course, linked to the rather different institutional environment in Germany, where the shareholder value orientation of firms is much weaker compared to the

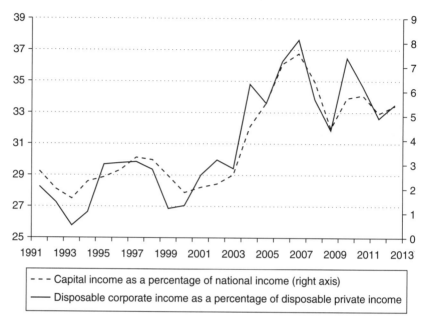

Source: Eurostat.

Figure 10.5   Sectoral financial balances as a percentage of GDP, Germany, 1991–2013

United States, and where many firms are small and medium-sized enterprises which are often family-owned. Clearly, the main objective of many German firms does not seem to be to pay maximum salaries and dividends to their managements and shareholders, but rather to accumulate wealth within firms, in many cases with a view to passing this corporate wealth on to the next generation as inheritances.

In conclusion, it can be argued that the 'corporate veil' in Germany hides the true rise in inequality between households, when focusing only on measures of personal income distribution. But the rise in retained corporate profits also restrains domestic demand to the extent that the investment spending of firms has not increased proportionally to the rise in retained profits. Finally, and perhaps paradoxically, the rise in corporate saving has limited the pressure for the middle class to engage in debt-financed consumption, because rich households (which can be seen as the reference group for the middle class) have not increased their spending in proportion with the rise in incomes, but rather have increased their saving rate indirectly through corporate net saving. In this context, it should also

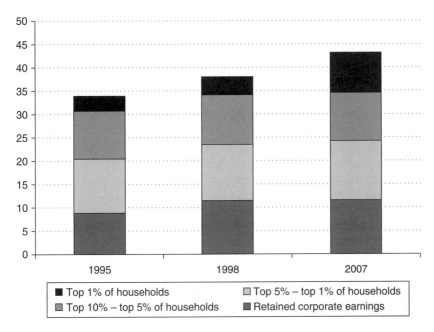

Source: Statistisches Bundesamt.

Figure 10.6 *Capital income and disposable corporate income, Germany,*
1991–2013

be noted that the ability of the middle class in Germany to engage in debt-financed consumption is restricted in Germany by more conservative bank lending practices compared to the United States. Similarly, the much more extensive provision of public goods, compared to the United States, also limits the room for positional 'arms races'.

Figure 10.4 places the financial balance of the German corporate sector in a broader macroeconomic context. Since both the private household sector and the public sector have also been in or near financial surplus in recent years, the current account surplus of the German economy has become structural. In sum, the weakness of domestic demand, caused in part by the shift in functional income distribution and corporate saving behaviour, has contributed to macroeconomic instability at the international level in terms of the global current account imbalances.

Some observers (OECD, 2010, 2012) have argued that the current account surplus of Germany was due especially to weak investment spending, and they have concluded from this that Germany should deregulate its product and labour markets further, in order to give a boost to investment. However, the weak overall investment demand in Germany was due primarily to the weakness of public investment and construction investment, whereas business equipment investment, which in theory should be most sensitive to corporate profitability and regulations, has not been especially weak (van Treeck and Sturn, 2012). Note also that net foreign direct investments account only for a small part of the rise in the corporate financial balance.

Koo (see Chapter 5 in this volume) argues that Germany was in balance sheet recession at the beginning of the 2000s, and that many corporations had to consolidate their balance sheets following the rise in corporate debt during the economic upswing and stock market boom of the late 1990s. However, the net flow of credit to the German corporate sector in the aggregate was negative for only two years, 2003 and 2004 (see also Koo, Chapter 5 in this volume, Figures 5.5, 5.7). It is therefore questionable whether the concept of balance sheet recession, whereby the corporate sector would 'minimize debt', actually applies for Germany for more than only a short period of time.

I would conclude that the main reason for the structural current account surpluses and the weak domestic demand should be seen in the weakness of private household spending, caused in part by the shift in the functional distribution of income.

10.3 FUNCTIONAL AND PERSONAL INCOME DISTRIBUTION AND CURRENT ACCOUNT IMBALANCES

The purpose of this section is to take a somewhat more systematic look at the relationship across countries between changes in top household income shares and the functional distribution of income on the one hand, and their implications for national current account positions on the other. Figure 10.7 relates changes in top household income shares to changes in the corporate financial balances as a percentage of gross domestic product (GDP) for the Group of Seven (G-7) countries and China for the period of the mid-1980s to just before the crisis. Interestingly, top household income shares have increased most in those countries where the corporate financial balance has increased less (the United States and United Kingdom). A similar relationship exists for the change in top household income shares and the change in the share of wages in national income. In a sense, top management salaries and profits paid out to shareholders have stabilized wages and household income in the Anglo Saxon countries, while in

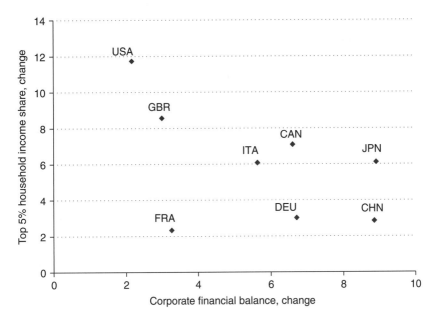

Note: The figure shows the change in, respectively, the corporate financial balance in % of GDP (horizontal axis) against the change in the top 5% household income share (vertical axis). For the United Kingdom changes are shown for the periods 1984/7–2003/7. For China changes are shown for the periods 1992/5–2000/3. For all other countries, changes are calculated for the period1980/3–2004/7 or for the longest available time span within this period.

Sources: World Top Incomes Database, Eurostat. See Behringer and van Treeck (2013).

Figure 10.7   *Change in top household income shares against change in corporate financial balance as a percentage of GDP, G7 countries and China, mid-1980s to mid-2000s*

countries such as Germany, Japan and China, the rise in profits and corporate net savings is actually hiding the 'true' rise in income inequality.

Behringer and van Treeck (2013) estimated standard current account equations on the basis of a macro panel including 20 countries for the period 1972–2007. The estimations include measures of the personal and functional income distribution as explanatory variables, while controlling for more standard determinants of current account positions such as the initial net foreign asset position, the fiscal balance, relative per capita income, the old age dependency ratio, population growth and private credit. An important result is that an increase in top income shares was linked to a decrease of the current account, while an increase in corporate net saving (or a decrease in the wage share) was linked to an increase of the current account. Also, taken together, the effects of changes in the personal and functional distribution could explain a considerable part of the current account imbalances before the crisis.

As an overall conclusion, it can be argued that rising inequality generally tends to increase macroeconomic instability, but it depends crucially on the country-specific nature of inequality (as well as on country-specific institutions), whether instability materializes in the form of rising household indebtedness and current account deficits, or in the form of weak domestic demand and excessive current account surpluses.

10.4   INCOME AND WEALTH INEQUALITY

In his international bestseller *Capital in the Twenty-First Century*, Thomas Piketty (2014) has formulated a simple, but much-debated, model which can be used to analyse the link between income and wealth inequality. According to Piketty, the model consists of two 'fundamental laws of capitalism', even though the 'first law' is merely a definition, and the 'second law' is a simple arithmetic truism.[3] More precisely, the first law defines the share of capital income in the national income, α, as the rate of return on capital, r, times the wealth-to-income ratio, β. The 'second law' states that in long-term equilibrium the wealth-to-income ratio, β, converges to the saving rate, s, divided by the nominal growth rate of the national income, g. Besides, Piketty argues that throughout the history of capitalism, there has been a tendency of the rate of return on capital, r, to exceed the growth rate, g. Piketty also shows that if the gap between r and g is large enough, then it can be expected that wealth will rise faster than income and income and wealth inequality will rise indefinitely.

The crucial condition for the inequality $r > g$ to imply an indefinitely rising wealth and income inequality is that the saving rates of high-income groups significantly exceed the saving rates of lower-income groups. Because if the saving rate were independent of relative income, $r > g$ would have no effect whatsoever on equilibrium income and wealth inequality, which would then be identical to wage inequality (that is, the traditional focus of attention in mainstream economics).

However, as we have seen above for the examples of the United States and Germany, the discrepancy between top-end and average saving rates has increased strongly in both countries, albeit in rather different ways: in the United States, lower-income groups have lowered their saving rates, presumably in an attempt to keep up with the spending patterns of the rich; whereas in Germany, rich households have increased their saving rates through corporate retained earnings. This means that, even independently of the precise relationship between *r* and *g*, the increased gap between saving rates implies a tendency for the inequality of income and wealth to rise further.

While recent evidence documents the substantial rise in wealth inequality in recent decades for the United States (Saez and Zucman, 2014), reliable data do not exist for Germany. The available data based on household surveys suggest that although income inequality has increased, wealth inequality has remained roughly stable since 2002 (Grabka and Westermeier, 2014). But these findings are called into question by the observations made above about recent trends in income distribution and saving rates in Germany.

10.5   INEQUALITY AND DEMAND STAGNATION

In this short chapter, I have argued that inequality was an important cause of the global financial crisis, which has materialized in some countries (for example, the United States) in the form of overindebted households, and in others (for example, Germany) in the form of excessive current account surpluses which are linked to the overindebtedness of the trading partners. Clearly, this inequality-induced 'debt overhang' directly adds to the now much-debated risk of 'secular stagnation'.

Some economists argue that further structural reforms (that is, deregulation) in the product and labour markets are now needed to give a boost to investment. But a more fundamental question is how consumption demand, which after all makes up 60–70 per cent of GDP, can recover, given current levels of inequality and household debt. Generally speaking, for demand growth to recover in a sustainable way, middle- and lower-class incomes would have to move at least in parallel with average trend productivity. In fact, it would seem that some rather massive redistribution of income will be necessary to overcome the unsustainable debt-led and export-led models that we have seen before the crisis.

Economists should further improve their understanding of the links between the distribution of income and macroeconomic development. Because the nature and macroeconomic implications of rising inequality can vary substantially across countries, theoretical and empirical research should systematically include both the functional and the personal distribution of income.

144   *The challenge of economic rebalancing in Europe*

NOTES

1. This chapter draws on van Treeck and Sturn (2012) and Behringer et al. (2013, 2014). A version of this chapter is published in the *European Journal of Economics and Economic Policies* (forthcoming).
2. In particular, this casts some doubt about the suitability of the so-called 'Bhaduri–Marglin model' for empirical investigations into the 'wage-led' or 'profit-led' nature of economic growth in different countries. The original model by Bhaduri and Marglin (1990, p.77, footnote 1) assumes that the total income going to households (wages and distributed profits, if any) are consumed, and that a positive fraction of profits is saved. Given the stability of the share of total household income in the national income in the United States (Figure 10.3), it would seem difficult to argue that shifts to the distribution of income between the household and corporate sectors played a major role in affecting overall macroeconomic trends in the United States during the decades prior to the crisis of 2007.
3. For an interesting critique of Piketty's interpretation of the model, see Bernardo et al. (2014).

REFERENCES

Behringer, J., C. Belabed, T. Theobald and T. van Treeck (2013), 'Einkommensverteilung, Finanzialisierung und makroökonomische Ungleichgewichte', *Vierteljahreshefte zur Wirtschaftsforschung – Nachhaltige europäische Konsolidierungspolitik: Chancen und Herausforderungen*, 82(4), 203–21.
Behringer, J., T. Theobald and T. van Treeck (2014), 'Einkommens- und Vermögensverteilung in Deutschland: Eine makroökonomische Sicht', Institut für Makroökonomie und Konjunkturforschung (IMK), IMK Report Nr. 99.
Behringer, J. and T. van Treeck (2013), 'Income distribution and the current account: a sectoral perspective', Institute for New Economic Thinking (INET), INET Research Notes 35.
Belabed, C., T. Theobald and T. van Treeck (2013), 'Income distribution and current account imbalances', Institute for New Economic Thinking (INET), INET Research Notes 36.
Bernardo, J., F. Martinez and E. Stockhammer (2014), 'A post-Keynesian response to Piketty's "Fundamental Contradiction of Capitalism"', Post Keynesian Economics Study Group Working Paper 1411.
Bhaduri, A. and S. Marglin (1990), 'Unemployment and the real wage: the economic basis for contesting political ideologies', *Cambridge Journal of Economics*, 14(4), 375–93.
Cingano, F. (2014), 'Trend in income inequality and its impact on economic growth', OECD Social, Employment and Migration Working Papers, No. 163.
Cynamon, B. and S. Fazzari (2013), 'Inequality, the Great Recession, and slow recovery', available at http://papers.ssrn.com/sol3/papers.cfm?abstract_id=2205524.
Dutt, A.K. (2006), 'Maturity, stagnation and consumer debt: a Steindlian approach', *Metroeconomica*, 57 (3), 339–64.
Fitoussi, J.-P. and J.E. Stiglitz (2009), 'The ways out of the crisis and the building of a more cohesive world', Observatoire français des conjonctures économiques Document de Travail, 2009 (17).

Frank, R.H. (2005), 'Positional externalities cause large and preventable welfare losses', *American Economic Review, AEA Papers and Proceedings*, 95(2), 137–41.

Frank, R.H. (2007), *Falling Behind: How Rising Inequality Harms the Middle Class*, Berkeley, CA: University of California Press.

Frank, R.H., A.S. Levine and O. Dijk (2010), 'Expenditure cascades', available at http://papers.ssrn.com/sol3/papers.cfm?abstract_id=1690612.

Grabka, M. and C. Westermeier (2014), 'Anhaltend hohe Vermögensungleichheit in Deutschland', *DIW Wochenbericht*, 81(9), 151–64.

Hein, E. and A. Truger (2012), 'Finance-dominated capitalism in crisis: the case for a global Keynesian New Deal', *Journal of Post Keynesian Economics*, 35(2), 183–210.

Kumhof, M., C. Lebarz, R. Rancière, A.W. Richter and N.A. Throckmorton (2012), 'Income inequality and current account imbalances', International Monetary Fund (IMF), Working Paper 12/08.

Kumhof, M. and R. Rancière (2010), 'Inequality, leverage and crises', International Monetary Fund (IMF), Working Paper 10/268.

Mian, A. and A. Sufi (2014), *House of Debt: How They (and You) Caused the Great Recession, and How We Can Prevent It From Happening Again*, Chicago, IL: University of Chicago Press.

OECD (2010), *OECD Economic Surveys: Germany 2010*, Paris: OECD Publishing.

OECD (2012), *OECD Economic Surveys: Germany 2012*, Paris: OECD Publishing.

Ostry, J.D., A. Berg and C.G. Tsangarides (2014), 'Redistribution, inequality, and growth', International Monetary Fund (IMF), IMF Staff Discussion Notes 14/02.

Palley, T.I. (1994), 'Debt, aggregate demand, and the business cycle: an analysis in the spirit of Kaldor and Minsky', *Journal of Post Keynesian Economics*, 16(3), 371–90.

Palley, T.I. (2012), *From Financial Crisis to Stagnation: The Destruction of Shared Prosperity and the Role of Economics*, Cambridge: Cambridge University Press.

Piketty, T. (2014), *Capital in the Twenty-First Century*, Cambridge, MA: Harvard University Press.

Piketty, T. and E. Saez (2006), 'The evolution of top incomes: a historical and international perspective', *American Economic Review*, 96(2), 200–205.

Rajan, R. (2010), *Fault Lines: How Hidden Fractures still Threaten the World Economy*, Princeton, NJ: Princeton University Press.

Saez, E. and G. Zucman (2014), 'Wealth inequality in the United States since 1918: evidence from capitalized income tax data', National Bureau of Economic Research (NBER), Working Paper 20625.

Stockhammer, E. (2013), 'Rising inequality as a cause of the present crisis', *Cambridge Journal of Economics*, DOI: 10.1093/cje/bet052.

Van Treeck, T. and S. Sturn (2012), 'Income inequality as a cause of the Great Recession? A survey of current debates', International Labour Organization (ILO), Conditions of Work and Employment Series 39.

PART IV

The future of (central) banking in Europe

11. The ECB, the banks and the sovereigns

Lucrezia Reichlin

On the bright side, the euro area economy seems finally to be on the path of a recovery at the time of writing in early 2015; and, after much hesitation, the European Central Bank (ECB) has announced a programme of sovereign bonds purchases to undertake quantitative easing (QE) which has been less divisive than what could have been expected just a few months ago. Although the programme is designed so as to decentralize the bulk of credit risk at the level of national central banks, markets have reacted positively to the announcement and, with the exception of Greece, we have seen further compression of spreads. On the dark side, however, the problem of debt overhang is likely to weigh on the euro area economies for the years to come since a low growth, low inflation environment is likely to persist even under the brightest scenario. In this context, and without a realistic prospect of further fiscal integration amongst the members of the European Union (EU), there is a risk that the European Central Bank will be overburdened by excessive responsibilities. To avoid this path, a new grand bargain between monetary policy authorities, governments and euro area institutions has to be achieved.

To understand the dilemma that the ECB is likely to face if such a bargain is not achieved, it is useful to look back and analyse monetary policy in the euro area since the 2008 crisis. This is what I will do in the next section where, by heavily borrowing from my paper with Pill (Pill and Reichlin, 2014) I will present a brief critical narrative of ECB policy since 2009. My effort is to analyse the particular challenge faced by the ECB as a central bank operating in a Union without federal budgetary responsibility and in the context of a large debt overhang, partly legacy of the crisis. I will claim that, gradually since 2012, the institution has started building the intellectual architecture of a new bargain but that both the nature of that bargain and the ability to achieve it are still very unclear.

The following section will address one specific issue: the home bias in the government bond market which emerged as a response to the risks associated to the crisis and which has generated a dangerous correlation between sovereign and bank risk (the so-called 'diabolic loop'). This problem is very much related to the central theme of my narrative since is one of the consequence of the problem of debt overhang. The 'diabolic loop' has been discussed extensively by Brunnermeier et al. (2011). The aim of the section is to introduce a proposal, designed with Luis Garicano (Garicano and Reichlin, 2014) which provides a solution to this problem. The proposal has both a regulatory and a monetary policy aspect. It aims at disincentivating banks to cumulate excess asset concentration in their 'own' government bonds while, at the same time, establishing the conditions for the market-driven creation of euro area safe assets that could be targeted by the ECB's QE measures.

11.1 THE ECB AND THE CRISIS: A SHORT NARRATIVE[1]

In the immediate aftermath of the Lehman collapse, the ECB was praised for the speediness and effectiveness of its intervention. In the period since, the ECB has had more mixed reviews, as it has sometimes struggled to maintain the initiative and to convince the markets of the credibility of its policy objectives. Although the scope of its mandate has expanded considerably, with the addition in particular of unified responsibility for banking supervision within the euro zone, the ECB has been forced at times to address problems outside its natural domain – problems of bank and sovereign solvency – for which it had neither appropriate tools nor a clear mandate. This, I will argue, was the natural consequence of conducting monetary policy in a period of large debt overhang, partly accumulated before the crisis and partly resulting as its legacy. The ECB was not the only central bank facing this problem but the difficulties in the euro area have been compounded by the lack of fiscal responsibilities at the federal level and by inadequate crises management tools in the design of the Treaty on the Functioning of the European Union.

How should we interpret and assess the ECB's record over this period of history? As suggested in Pill and Reichlin (2014), it is useful to divide the seven years since the crisis into three phases: (1) a banking crisis (2007–2009), where the immediate focus was on liquidity problems within the financial sector; (2) a sovereign crisis (2010–2012), in which the central issue came to be the inter-related solvency problems of public sector and bank balance sheets in a number of countries within the euro zone; and finally (3) an attempt to establish a new, more workable framework for the governance of the euro area (2012 to date), which started with ECB President Mario Draghi's commitment to do 'whatever it takes' to sustain the euro, taking institutional form in the announcement of the ECB's Outright Monetary Transactions (OMT) programme.

In the first phase, although the policy tools used were non-standard, the objective was clearly within the central bank's normal remit: responding to a liquidity crisis by acting as lender of last resort. In the immediate aftermath of the fall of Lehman the ECB intervened directly with banks, effectively replacing the interbank market, which had ceased to function after Lehman, as a source of wholesale funding. This was wholly successful. As Tommaso Padoa Schioppa correctly anticipated (Padoa-Schioppa, 2004), it was possible for the ECB to act effectively as lender of last resort via the market operations of the euro system (Reichlin, 2014).

Furthermore, the ECB's intervention appears successful if judged in terms of its effects on both the real economy and on inflation. Several attempts to measure the macroeconomic impact of the ECB's non-standard measures in this phase (see Lenza et al., 2010; Giannone et al., 2012; Peersman, 2011) have reached similar conclusions: by preventing a more severe interruption in the flow of credit, the ECB's actions in this phase had a positive impact on real economic activity. Other studies (see Giannone et al., 2012; Pill and Smets, 2013) show that the path of the interbank rate – three-month Euribor – was lower than it would have been had the ECB not intervened as it did. Both studies show that the ECB managed to maintain an accommodative stance and that the zero lower bound constraint on the interest rate was not bounding during this first phase. The reason that the ECB's policy was effective in this way was due to the fact that inflation rates in the euro area rose to levels above 2 per cent by the end of this period, while unemployment rate did not rise immediately as a consequence of the recession.

Although the ECB in this phase can therefore rightly be judged successful by the standard criteria that we might use to assess monetary policy, it did nothing to address the structural problems underlying the crisis. Specifically, nothing was done to force the necessary recapitalization and restructuring of the banks. Of course, the ECB's actions were not intended to address these issues, which were left to those responsible: national governments and regulators. In some cases those national authorities did act to rescue failing banks (for example, in Germany), but in others, where the size of the problem was larger than the fiscal resources of the national government, the problem was simply put off. And in this context the ECB's accommodative liquidity provision may even have exacerbated the problem, as it reduced the urgency of resolution.

Procrastination may have been inevitable because in many euro area countries the balance sheets of the banks were larger than the national GDP. However, this points to the absence – at the euro area level – of tools or institutions to enable the necessary risk-sharing to resolve bank solvency problems. As a result, and also because of the increasingly close entanglement between solvency and liquidity issues for the banks, the ECB was called upon to address solvency problems despite the fact that they fell outside its natural remit. There was no one else to play this role. The absence of tools and institutions for risk-sharing at the euro area level, and the consequent pressure on the ECB to act beyond its mandate, is at the heart of the problem with which the ECB was grappling during this phase, and with which it has continued to grapple ever since.

The second phase starts in the spring of 2010 when, following the election of a new Greek government and the consequent restatement of the Greek fiscal position, that country's insolvency was laid bare. Soon Greece was unable to raise funds on the market.

Following the logic of the Treaty would have meant allowing the market to find its own solution: that is, allowing Greece to default. However, this could also have led to Greece's exit from the euro and possibly, via a process of contagion, to the exit of other weak countries too. There was also the risk of financial contagion, as banks across the euro area had significant holdings of Greek government bonds. The ECB therefore saw some kind of bailout solution for Greece as fundamental to its own mandate: to protect the euro and the euro system.

The ECB itself lacked the tools to implement a bailout; indeed it was and is expressly forbidden from providing government finance. This had to be done by national governments and some bilateral deals with Greece were struck before eventually the European Financial Stability Facility (EFSF) and subsequently the European Stability Mechanism were established, under the auspices of the 'troika', comprising the European Commission, the ECB and the IMF.

Unfortunately, this approach failed to convince the markets. This was partly because private sector bondholders were concerned that their own holdings were being subordinated to bailout loans. So Greek government bond spreads continued to rise and contagion to other government bond markets increased.

If it was to act, the ECB continued to face the same choice between two unpalatable options: either buying Greek government bonds directly, thereby assuming the credit risk itself and thereby violating the Treaty, or imposing losses ('haircuts') on private sector bondholders and thereby fanning the flames of contagion.

Pragmatically, the ECB found a middle way. It announced the Securities Markets Programme (SMP), which involved purchasing bonds issued by Greek and other peripheral countries' governments on the secondary market. Widening yield spreads on peripheral governments' bonds effectively obstructed the transmission of a unified monetary policy from the ECB in Frankfurt. So the SMP was justified as necessary to maintain effective monetary policy transmission within the euro area, and to prevent the fragmentation of the euro area financial system along national lines. Whatever the stated aim, the positive effect of the SMP was to buy time for the implementation of the troika-led adjustment programme, and to ease the way towards a partial restructuring of Greek government debt in which private sector bondholders did, eventually, accept write-downs. The ECB also used the troika programme as a pretext to relax its requirements for the use of sovereign debt as collateral, further reducing pressure on Greek government bond yields.

The ECB's intervention bought time but, notwithstanding the fact that it did lead to a partial restructuring, it did not address the underlying solvency issues. Nor did it completely defuse the threat of contagion: shortly afterwards both Ireland (in November 2010) and Portugal (in June 2011) went into troika programmes in order to avail themselves of external support.

In the first half of 2011 it briefly looked as though the euro area economy was emerging from its post-crisis malaise. Both gross domestic product (GDP) and inflation were seen to be recovering. The ECB decided to raise its policy interest rate in April and again in July. In retrospect, the ECB may have misjudged the state of the recovery or it may have played excessively tough on inflation in order to gain support on its action with respect to weak banks and governments, driven by financial stability concerns. The second recession, into which the euro area economy fell in the second half of 2011, came as a surprise and, *ex post*, shows that the dynamics of the real economy was affected by the uncertainty about the way in which financial instability caused by the debt problem was going to be addressed.

This downturn helped to reignite concerns about contagion to the larger European economies, specifically Italy and Spain. In Italy the crisis focused new attention on long-standing weakness in public finances. In Spain, despite going into the crisis with a relatively low level of debt, the government's standing in the bond markets was weakened both by the depth of the recession and by its implicit guarantee of the financial sector, which had been badly hit by the collapse of the property boom.

If either of these states needed a bailout, it was doubtful whether the European Stability Mechanism (ESM) would be credible to provide it; the size of these countries' outstanding debts was far larger than the funds committed to the ESM. And recent private sector involvement in the restructuring of Greek debt (the haircuts) set a bad precedent, despite protestations that this was a one-off, exceptional event.

Two further problems loomed over the market's appreciation of these risks. Firstly, the ECB's own actions in relation to Greece and the other peripheral countries were controversial. They sailed close to the wind in terms of providing monetary finance to governments. And they also had distributional consequences: transferring risks from private sector balance sheets to the balance sheet of the central bank. These considerations made it harder to see how the ECB would react to a solvency problem on a larger scale.

Secondly, the crisis acted as a catalyst in the emergence of the 'diabolic loop' of interdependence between the credit risks of sovereigns and their banks. In peripheral countries in particular, banks held large quantities of their own governments' bonds on their balance sheets, which meant that concerns over sovereigns' solvency put the banks' balance sheets under pressure. At the same time, sovereigns' implicit guarantees of the banks domiciled in their countries dragged down the creditworthiness of those governments. These were the preconditions for a vicious spiral of deteriorating creditworthiness. And they were exacerbated by the emergence of a perceived danger of exit from the euro area.

Assets in vulnerable countries began to incorporate a 'redenomination' risk premium for fear of depreciation following euro exit (see Battistini et al., 2014, amongst others). This risk premium pushed up yields and bank funding costs, to the detriment of medium-term sustainability of sovereign and bank balance sheets as well as developments in the real economy, which in turn made exit more likely.

This vicious cycle, whereby rising redenomination risk became self-fulfilling, was an example of a multiple equilibria situation akin to developing countries' debt crises. In such circumstances, as it has been forcefully argued by De Grauwe (2012), drawing a hard distinction between liquidity and solvency issues may not be possible.

The ECB's initial response to these widening difficulties was to return to its response to the crisis in the periphery a year earlier, extending the SMP to Italian and Spanish bonds in August 2011. This initiative failed, for reasons directly related to the awkwardness of the ECB's position. Because of sensitivities about the ECB over-reaching its remit and providing monetary finance to governments, the purchases of Italian and Spanish bonds under the SMP were said to be limited and temporary, thereby undermining any possibility that this initiative might have had a strong demonstration effect in the market. For the same reason the ECB said that this intervention would be conditional on policy commitments from the (Italian) national government, which prompted a reaction in Italy (including from the Italian government) against external interference, which in turn further undermined the credibility of the ECB's intervention. And of course, worries about the subordination of private sector creditors resurfaced.

The immediate threat of a banking crisis only subsided when, at the end of 2011, the ECB (under its newly appointed President, Mario Draghi) announced a programme of longer-term refinancing operations (LTROs), providing bank funding at unusually long (three-year) terms, and using a fixed rate, full allotment (FRFA) tender process. The significance of this initiative was that it allowed the banks to profit from a safe carry trade on holdings of their own governments' bonds, thereby both bolstering the financial position of the banks themselves and indirectly supporting vulnerable sovereigns.

Once again, however, the ECB's pragmatic response to the crisis had averted danger in the short term, but the underlying problems – bank and sovereign solvency – were not addressed. This of course was not a responsibility of the Ecse problems. In this vacuum, the ECB's intervention (the LTROs) had the effect of entrenching the interdependence between bank and sovereign balance sheets.

So again, we can characterize the ECB's approach as 'muddling through'. Facing the difficult choice between sticking to the old rules of the Maastricht set-up (and risking financial and macroeconomic instability) and acting in a pragmatic manner (and risking hitting the institutional and political constraints that Maastricht had set out to manage), the ECB, for understandable reasons, adopted the latter strategy. A major financial crisis was avoided but the incentives for the necessary fundamental changes were not created, and since the strategy lacked credibility, it was eventually tested by the market in the summer of 2011 when contagion spread to Italy and Spain.

Beside the lack of credibility, the strategy failed for two additional reasons. First, it was based on the miscalculation that provision of liquidity, fiscal austerity and an emphasis on supply-side reforms would have led to the stabilization of debt in Greece, Ireland and Portugal, especially in a context in which exchange rate devaluation could not be used in the adjustment. Second, the costs for the real economy of allowing undercapitalized banks to carry on, rather than forcing a recapitalization (as in the United States), was underestimated. The volume of loans to non-financial corporations dropped sharply in this period, much more sharply than in 2008–2009 if you adjust for the relative decline in industrial production (see Colangelo et al., 2014; Reichlin, 2014). Eventually, uncertainty about the repartition of responsibility between the different agencies – the central bank, the governments and the European federal authorities – led to a fragmentation of the financial markets, a credit crunch and a second recession.

The third phase in this history (see Pill and Reichlin, 2014) starts in the summer of 2012 when Mr Draghi committed to do 'whatever it takes' to save the euro, and it continues to the present day. This phase includes a number of specific initiatives, including the announcement of the Outright Monetary Transactions (OMT) programme (at the same time as the 'whatever it takes' speech) and the asset quality review (AQR) which concluded late in 2014. As important, perhaps, are a number of speeches in which Mr Draghi seems to have been attempting to create the basis for a new 'grand bargain', based on commitments to reform by national governments, engendering trust that such adjustment and reform will limit future exposures, and thereby making some sharing of legacy burdens politically feasible. Some such risk-sharing for legacy debt will be necessary to stabilize the euro area and to create conditions conducive to economic growth, without which the euro area will continue to be fiscally and financially unstable. Among the significant comments made by Mr Draghi during this phase were his speech in London in June 2014 in which he called for a euro area framework to coordinate and monitor structural reforms, and his Jackson Hole speech in August 2014 in which he argued for greater coordination of monetary and fiscal policy at the euro area level.

Pill and Reichlin (2014) characterize ECB policy in this phase as:

> an attempt to find a balance between two extreme positions: one emphasizing a strict interpretation of the 'no monetary financing' prohibition; and another calling on the ECB to act as a backstop in a debt crisis (De Grauwe, 2012; Krugman, forthcoming), disregarding moral hazard problems or concerns about the potential fiscal consequences of this action.

We argue that the promise of potentially unlimited liquidity support subject to conditionality under the OMT can be seen as steering a middle way:

> recognition that a bad equilibrium resulting from self-fulfilling crisis is possible, but also containing moral hazard so as to avoid unsustainability and insolvency. In turn, this acts as a mechanism to manage a tradeoff between risks to price stability (stemming from the moral hazard and threat to central bank credibility) and risks to financial instability (stemming from destabilizing self-fulfilling market dynamics). (Pill and Reichlin, 2014)

Concluding this narrative, we can say that, overall, the ECB was effective in the initial phase because – and to the extent that – it was required to address liquidity issues, which clearly fell within its natural remit. But since the related problems of solvency, of both sovereigns and banks, were not addressed at the national level, the ECB was progressively drawn to act beyond its natural remit. This was the main story during the second phase of this history, the darkest period. Through this phase the ECB tried, pragmatically, to steer a middle path between on the one hand the 'monetary dominance' enshrined in the Maastricht Treaty, under which default would have been the solution to fiscal unsustainability, and on the other hand, 'fiscal dominance' which would have required it to finance national governments as necessary. But pursuit of the pragmatic middle way has had negative consequences itself, particularly by postponing necessary adjustment. The ECB's actions in the most recent phase of the story can be interpreted – positively – as an attempt to regain the initiative and orchestrate a collective response to the euro area's more fundamental problems. For the euro area to prosper, this will need to include a 'grand bargain' to deal with the debt overhang left by the financial crisis. Without that, the euro itself will remain vulnerable.

11.2 A SAFE ASSET FOR THE EURO ZONE: THE GARICANO–REICHLIN PROPOSAL

The euro area experience of the financial crisis has two distinct phases which mimic the two distinct ('double-dip') recessions in economic activity (Reichlin, 2014). Financial fragmentation is central to both phases, but takes different forms. The initial sudden stop following the failure of Lehman was associated with bank wholesale liabilities becoming overwhelmingly domestic, as cross-border wholesale transactions dried up. But it was only in the second sovereign phase of the crisis from late 2010 that governments were (in some cases) called upon to support banks, while domestic banks increased their holdings of domestic sovereign debt as foreign investors withdrew. Indeed one of the fundamental lessons of the crisis is that, in a monetary union without common fiscal authority, financial fragmentation along national lines emerges as a response to risk. As I have discussed in the previous section, this has been the cause of a dangerous correlation between sovereign and bank risk.

This feature is the consequence of the fact that public finances are a national responsibility. Under these conditions, the sovereign–bank correlation imparts a national character to any resulting market segmentation. Although many of the problems leading to the crisis have been fixed over the last few years (in particular, with the establishment of the Banking Union and the single supervisor) and the recapitalization effort of banks is now well under way, the 'diabolic loop' between banks and sovereigns has not disappeared. On the contrary, given the current regulatory framework on treatment of government bonds for liquidity and capital purposes, and the ECB collateral policy, banks have an incentive to acquire their own sovereign bonds and use them as collateral to obtain ECB liquidity.

Recently, Luis Garicano and I (Garicano and Reichlin, 2014) have made a proposal to help address this problem while providing an option for QE purchases which has some advantages with respect to the scheme recently announced by the ECB. The proposal has two complementary aspects, related to regulatory and supervisory policy and to monetary policy.

From the regulatory side we propose that the ECB and the Single Supervisory Mechanism (SSM) would announce that only the senior tranche of the security so produced would be counted as risk-free for the purposes of the risk weighting and liquidity coverage ratio calculations. Alternatively, the ECB/SSM would impose a risk concentration limit on own sovereign debt and exempt these senior bonds from such limitations.[2]

As for monetary policy, we suggest that the ECB announce that for its QE operations it would target a bond formed by the senior 60 per cent tranche of a synthetic bond formed of debt of euro area countries in fixed proportions to GDP. The ECB would not be involved in the tranching, but instead simply announce that this is the instrument used. We conjecture that the market would have an incentive to create such asset.

There are several desirable features of this proposal. Firstly, it would most likely reduce the geographic bias in the flight to safety, as the safe asset is (regulatorily) a Europe-wide one. Secondly, it would eliminate the moral hazard induced by the expectation that, in case of crisis, the ECB would intervene to guarantee the debt (see the previous section). Indeed, governments can default in this world, as the banks are protected from the fallout; markets will thus monitor the governments instead of second-guessing the (bailout) intentions of the ECB. Thirdly, it would eliminate the 'diabolic loop', since a sovereign in trouble would not jeopardize its own banks, and it would reduce the geographic segmentation of the euro zone markets. An additional advantage of the proposal is that this would be the first step towards the creation of a large safe asset since it would generate a large euro area-wide security. Such an asset would be a natural target for QE purchases since it would not carry any fiscal risk. Indeed, it is the junior tranches that would harness market discipline by pricing sovereign default risk.

We believe that targeting this asset is a better solution to the problem of risk-sharing within the euro area than buying composite bonds and decentralizing the bulk of the risk at the national central banks level, as is envisaged by the recent ECB QE proposal. Decentralization carries the danger that, under stress, the market could price a lack of commitment to the euro from the ECB.

Let us emphasize that this synthetic debt would not involve any risk-sharing among different governments or any debt mutualization. Each government would continue to issue its own debt and face its own interest rates in the market, and the junior tranches would reflect default risk.

11.3 CONCLUDING REMARKS

After more than six years of crisis the euro area has gone a long way in strengthening its own governance institutions and, although it has paid a high price in terms of growth and unemployment, it has escaped implosion. This should be no case for complacency. The economy is still weak and a large stock of debt – both private and public – is threatening the recovery and possibly creating problems for financial stability in the future.

In section 11.1 of this chapter I have focused on the challenges faced by the ECB during the crisis. I have argued that ECB policy during the crisis has been dominated by the problem of financial stability posed by the legacy debt in a context in which liquidity and solvency issues have been tightly related. Since 2008, but in particular since the debt crisis of spring 2010, the European Central Bank found itself in uncharted territory, having to implement monetary policy in a situation where the high debt overhang involving almost all member states called for action at several levels: debt restructuring, recapitalization of banks, and coordination of monetary and fiscal policy. In the absence of credible federal institutions other than the central bank, and given the flaws in the euro area-level tools for crisis management, the ECB found itself being overburdened by the need to implement policies which were required for financial stability but had controversial fiscal implications. The evolution of these policies, eventually leading to the recent decision to embark on quantitative easing, cannot be understood without an appreciation of the parallel evolution of the euro area governance at the broader level which eventually saw the establishment of the European Stability Mechanism (ESM), the banking union and the comprehensive review of the asset quality of the systematically important banks. In this context, I have argued that, at least since late 2012, the ECB has strived for a new 'grand bargain' involving different responsibilities for monetary and budgetary authorities. The nature of this bargain and its credibility, however, are still very much uncertain.

Looking ahead, at the heart of the matter is the issue of whether (and, if so, how) the ECB should manage legacy debt problems – which cannot simply be wished away – by taking fiscal and banking risk onto its own balance sheet. In the recently announced QE programme the ECB has opted for a scheme which is based on national decentralization of risk associated to sovereign bonds purchases. This has been a pragmatic solution to the fact that an open-ended QE, if prolonged, would imply warehousing a large part of the legacy debt with significant cross-country distributional effects (since the legacy problems are of different magnitude in different euro area countries). But of course, in this case, the meaning of risk decentralization will be tested by the market.

In section 11.2 of this chapter I have argued for an alternative to such decentralization, consisting in purchases of the senior tranche of a composite asset. This proposal, I have argued, would have to be coupled with changes in the treatment of sovereign bonds for capital and liquidity charges, and with measures which incentivize a geographical diversification of sovereign holdings by financial institutions.

As I have concluded in my paper with Huw Pill, upon which this chapter is based:

> At the end of the matter, however, the ECB and the other parties involved in the euro area economic governance will have to deal with a time consistency problem. The key question is how to enforce commitment to longer-term adjustment while relieving the burden of legacy problems in the short run. The traditional answer to this question is to build economic institutions that underpin the credibility of reform and discipline over the medium term, and thereby give confidence that legacy problems can be addressed without creating moral hazard and/or threats to the credibility of the ECB in its pursuit of price stability. Mr Draghi's Jackson Hole initiative, complementing the creation of the banking union, should be seen in this light. At this stage, whether his efforts will be successful remains an open question. (Pill and Reichlin, 2014)

NOTES

1. This section borrows heavily from Pill and Reichlin (2014) and relies on research published in various papers with Colangelo, Giannone and Lenza.
2. Unlike in the Brunnermeier et al. (2011) proposal, no European debt agency or any other intermediary need be involved. Instead, a (small) ECB office would declare senior synthetic bonds as 'conforming euro-safe bonds' when they fulfil these criteria, similar to the Fannie Mae and Freddie Mac role in the US in declaring some mortgages with certain loan-to-value ratios, ratings, and so on as conforming.

REFERENCES

Battistini, N., M. Pagano and S. Simonelli (2014), 'Systemic risk, sovereign yields and bank exposures in the euro crisis', *Economic Policy*, 29, pp. 203–51.
Brunnermeier, M.K., L. Garicano, P.R. Lane, M. Pagano, R. Reis, T. Santos, S. Van Nieuwerburgh and D. Vayanos (2011), 'European Safe Bonds: ESBies', Euro-nomics.com, manuscript.

Colangelo, A., D. Giannone, M. Lenza, H. Pill and L. Reichlin (2014), 'Cross-border transactions in the euro area and the financial crisis', mimeo, June.

Garicano, L. and L. Reichlin (2014), 'A safe asset for Eurozone QE: a proposal', *Vox*, 14 November.

Giannone, D., M. Lenza, H. Pill and L. Reichlin (2012), 'The ECB and the inter-bank market', *Economic Journal*, 122, pp. 467–86.

De Grauwe, P. (2012), 'The governance of a fragile eurozone', *Australian Economic Review*, 45(3), pp. 255–68.

Krugman, P. (forthcoming), 'Currency regimes, capital flows and crises', *IMF Economic Review*.

Lenza, M., H. Pill and L. Reichlin (2010), 'Monetary policy in exceptional times', *Economic Policy*, 62, pp. 295–339.

Padoa-Schioppa, T. (2004), *Regulating Finance: Balancing Freedom and Risk*, Oxford: Oxford University Press.

Peersman, G. (2011), Macroeconomic Effects of Unconventional Monetary Policy in the Euro Area, ECB Working Paper Series, No 1397.

Pill, H. and L. Reichlin (2014), 'Exceptional policies for exceptional times: the ECB response to the rolling crises of the euro area and how it has brought us towards a new grand bargain', CEPR Working Paper 10193, October.

Pill, H. and F. Smets (2013), 'Monetary policy frameworks after the great financial crisis', in J. Baude, Z. Eckstein, S. Fischer and K. Flug (eds), *The Great Recession: Lessons for Central Bankers*, Cambridge, MA: MIT Press, pp. 21–50.

Reichlin, L. (2014), 'Monetary policy and banks in the euro area: the tale of two crises', *Journal of Macroeconomics*, 39(PB), pp. 387–400.

12. Europe's banking union: glass half full or glass half empty?

Thorsten Beck

The European debt crisis united European Union (EU) policy-makers in the goal of centralizing bank supervision and crisis management in the event of bank failures, with a view to ending taxpayer bailouts and taking key decisions out of national hands through the creation of a banking union. The banking union was to consist of three pillars, the first of which – the Single Supervisory Mechanism (SSM) – was established when the European Central Bank (ECB) took over responsibility for bank supervision (directly for the largest banks, indirectly for all banks) in the euro zone in late 2014, following a year-long 'comprehensive assessment' effort to assess capital positions across the largest banks in the euro zone and to apply stress tests to these capital positions to establish their resilience. By that time, European authorities had agreed on the second pillar of the banking union, the Single Resolution Mechanism (SRM), to come into effect in 2016. The SRM will be a coordination mechanism on top of national resolution mechanisms that also involves the European Commission, the European Council, the ECB and national resolution authorities. A third pillar, a joint deposit insurance funding scheme, has been quietly dropped.

These events are important steps for the euro zone and the EU towards the recovery of a sound and stable banking system and the single European market in banking. But it is important to put these steps into the broader perspective of crisis resolution and the future of banking in Europe. In previous years, economists had put forward many suggestions to address the crisis, including the establishment of a banking union, only a few of which have moved towards actual implementation. In this chapter I will ask (and hope to answer) several questions in this context: (1) Where does Europe stand in terms of regulatory integration? (2) Will these recent achievements help us to overcome the crisis? (3) Will the crisis help us to get back to a single European banking market? (4) And what else is there to do? A sneak preview of the four tentative responses: (1) at the very beginning; (2) no; (3) it might eventually; and (4) a lot.

In the following, I will discuss the need for a banking union, based both on theoretical arguments and on experiences from the recent crisis. I will also provide a comparison between the United States (US) and the euro zone to introduce a benchmark for crisis resolution. I will then propose different elements for an 'ideal' banking union, before comparing this to the structure currently in place or envisaged.

12.1   WHY DO WE NEED A BANKING UNION?

While the need for a full-fledged banking union in Europe may be asserted with many theoretical arguments, the recent crisis experience may illustrate best where a banking union might have helped to better address the crisis.[1] This discussion is based on the assumption that having a single market in banking brings large benefits for the EU, especially for the euro zone, in terms of higher competition and better risk diversification.[2] Alternatively, one can see the disintegration of the single market in banking after the onset of the euro zone crisis in 2009 as hurting optimal resource allocation and economic recovery, often supported by regulatory ring-fencing actions. The fragility of banking systems in many euro zone economies has also been at the core of the broken transmission channel for monetary policy decisions by the ECB.

First, the crisis has shown that bank supervisors focus on national stability interests and do not take into account externalities that arise from bank failures for stakeholders and economies outside their regulatory perimeter. This is consistent with theory and empirical evidence during the global financial crisis (Beck et al., 2013). Given the importance of banks and the close political connections between the banking sectors and governments, there is also a tendency to protect national champions. During the recent crisis, this led to a more lenient approach of regulators vis-à-vis their own banks, including regulatory forbearance and delayed intervention. Cross-border banks in which supervisors intervened were often split along national borders rather than business lines, with consequent efficiency losses, most prominently in the case of Fortis Bank.

The comprehensive assessment of 2013–2014 has provided evidence for this tendency towards regulatory forbearance by national supervisors. For example, more than 20 per cent of the reviewed debtors were reclassified as non-performing in Greece, Malta and Estonia. Slovenia even saw a 32 per cent reclassification, with one bank hitting 43 per cent. The large variation in loan reclassification across countries and the rather high number in some countries suggests that this is not simply due to different national loan classification regimes but rather to a high degree of regulatory forbearance, if not regulatory capture.

Second, resolution mechanisms that focus on maintaining as much of the failing bank's franchise value as possible, rather than liquidating the entire institution, face limitations in small financial systems, where the options to merge a failing bank with a healthy bank are often few. In addition, in smaller financial systems banks are more likely to co-vary in their performance, so that one failure rarely comes alone. And even if possible, such a merger might have negative repercussions for competition in a small market. If resolution is limited to the national level, this therefore leaves recapitalization and nationalization, or liquidation, with most European countries with failing banks having opted for the former. Being able to resolve banks on a supra-national level thus provides more opportunities for efficient resolution.

Third, the limitations of resolving a failing bank are even worse in countries with a weak fiscal position, exacerbated where banks concentrate a large share of their government bond holdings in claims on their own sovereign. This phenomenon is often referred to as the deadly embrace of sovereigns and banks and has been documented especially for banks in several periphery countries of the euro zone. The Irish and Spanish governments' fiscal positions both came under the pressure during the crisis, partly due to resources used for bank bailouts. Greek banks needed a bailout when Greek government bonds were restructured in 2011. A more recent example is the failure of the Portuguese Banco Espirito Santo: the Portuguese government had to rely on 'troika' (European Commission, ECB and International Monetary Fund) funding to resolve the bank, in light of its own precarious fiscal position.

Fourth, deposit insurance has developed into an integral part of the financial safety net across all EU member states, partly fostered by harmonization pressure exerted by Brussels. However, the experience of Cyprus has shown that a deposit insurance scheme is only as good as the sovereign backing it. During the negotiations on European support for Cyprus the idea was floated to make all depositors, even insured ones, participate in the losses of Cypriot banks. Ultimately, this idea of depositor contribution, masked as a tax, was dropped due to political pressure. However, the lack of a sovereign being able to stand behind its banks and the deposit insurance scheme forced Cyprus to impose capital controls to prevent further bank runs.

Fifth, the protracted resolution process of Cyprus showed that in addition to a banking, sovereign, macroeconomic and currency crisis, the euro zone faces a broader governance crisis. Decisions are taken jointly by national authorities who each represent the interest of their respective country (and taxpayers), without taking into account the externalities of national decisions arising on the euro zone level. It is in the interest of every member government with fragile banks to 'share the burden' with the other members, for example through the ECB's liquidity support. This is in absence of a proper financial safety net on the euro zone level that can internalize these problems.

Sixth, the limited institutional and fiscal capacity to resolve failing banks have incentivized many national supervisors into actively pushing their banks into ring-fencing, which ultimately undermines the single European market in banking. Specifically, as described by Gros (2012a), in some cases supervisors in core countries have de facto prevented the local subsidiaries of cross-border banks from funding their headquarters located in periphery countries.[3] This implies that the savings surpluses of countries such as Germany or the Netherlands can no longer be recycled to countries with a current account deficit, and even the existing stocks of cross-border liabilities cannot be rolled over in the market.

This 'tragedy of commons' character of the euro zone does not only apply to the area of banking, but is much broader as it also relates to policy coordination in other areas, including fiscal policy but also geographically tainted arguments over monetary policy. While recognizing the general problem of policy coordination, in the following I will focus exclusively on banking.

12.2 A TRANSATLANTIC COMPARISON

Gros (2012b) offers a very useful comparison to underline the benefits of not just a banking but a broader economic union for states subject to a large economic shock, such as a housing bust. Specifically, he compares two political units of similar size: Ireland and Nevada. These two economies of similar size both experienced a housing and credit boom-and-bust cycle in the 2000s. Both are part of a currency union, based on the euro and the US dollar, respectively. The critical difference between the two is that Ireland is an independent country while Nevada forms part of a fiscal, banking and political union. Ireland suffered from a major financial crisis, while Nevada did not suffer from a local financial crisis (though it did, obviously, suffer from the US financial crisis). While banks in both Nevada and Ireland failed, bank failures turned into a systemic banking crisis only in Ireland. The US Federal Deposit Insurance Corporation (FDIC) intervened and transferred the operations to other, stronger banks, often outside Nevada. While the total costs of these resolutions amounted to 30 per cent of Nevada's gross domestic product (GDP), the state government's fiscal position was not affected to that extent, as the losses were borne on the federal level; unlike in Ireland, where losses were transferred to the government. In addition, in Nevada a lot of the losses accumulated on the balance sheets of banks headquartered outside the state; unlike in Ireland, where most mortgage lending was provided by local banks. And given Ireland's lack of monetary policy authority as part of a currency union, there was no way to monetize the bank bailouts, which ultimately forced the Irish government into a troika programme. While this clearly shows the advantages of a banking union, the US banking union comes with a fiscal and a political union, both of which do not exist as yet in the euro zone. Finally, this type of union has taken 200 years to develop in the US and is still work in progress.

On a broader level, the different structures in the euro zone and the US also explain the approaches to crisis resolution on the two sides of the Atlantic. In the US an early recognition of losses through stress tests and forced recapitalization was at the core of crisis resolution, while in Europe most governments shied away from both transparency and hard choices after the initial round of bailouts in 2008. The response was rather a 'bunker' approach where nations focused purely on their own banks' fragility and the attempts to 'share the burden' through liquidity support from the ECB. The state aid examinations by the Directorate General (DG) Competition of the European Commission – intended to ensure that competition was not being distorted by bailouts and that these were undertaken only as emergency measures with the overarching aim of financial stability – were the only indirect coordination mechanism across the EU. This also imposed a higher burden on the ECB and the network of national central banks to provide liquidity support, even where the health of banks was clearly in doubt, as in the case of the Cypriot banks.

12.3   BANKING UNION: THE IDEAL

Based on the analysis so far and the crisis experience, what would the ideal banking union look like? A complete financial safety net on the national level consists of an effective regulatory and supervisory framework, and an effective resolution framework that minimizes both the moral hazard risk of bailing out and the negative effects of bank closure for the rest of the banking system and the real economy. If a deposit insurance scheme is in place, then it should be linked to the resolution framework and have sufficient funding arrangements in place, either *ex ante* or *ex post*, and with public backstop funding (Beck and Laeven, 2008).

A financial safety net on the supra-national level, such as planned in the form of a banking union for the euro zone, should therefore contain similar components. This has been referred to as the three pillars of a banking union, with a single supervisor, a single resolution framework and a joint deposit insurance fund. Importantly, the deposit insurance fund would have to have access to public backstop funding on the supra-national level. This last issue points already to the political sensitivities involved, especially in the absence of a full fiscal union in the euro zone.

The equivalent to a national financial safety net also implies that a banking union that complements the currency union should focus not only on cross-border banks, but on all banks. It does not imply that supervision is centralized in one institution; rather it means that the ultimate responsibility lies at the supra-national level – the buck stops at the European level. Most importantly, the establishment of a supra-national supervisory authority alone is not sufficient. Rather, and in line with the arguments above, bank resolution – that is, both the power and the resources to be able to intervene in failing banks – is critical for the success of such a banking union, as also argued by Schoenmaker (2012) and others. The critical issue is that powers and resources to intervene in failing banks have to go hand in hand. Independence of the institution from both the political sphere and the regulated entities is critical.

12.4   WHAT HAS BEEN ACCOMPLISHED?

There are two ways to look at this, corresponding to the 'glass half full' and 'glass half empty' attitudes. On the one hand, the fact that some basic elements of a European financial safety net have been put in place is a success. It can be considered a great success, given the political and legal reluctance against any form of centralizing the financial safety on the European level in the wake of the 2008 crisis. While in the wake of the crisis it was often argued that any centralization of bank regulation or supervision would require treaty changes, ultimately all these reforms have been undertaken in the context of the existing treaties.[4] It can also be considered a great success given the general political sensitivities of bank regulation, already discussed above. On the other hand, this compromise is far from the financial safety net that an integrated European banking market would need, and a half-baked banking union might actually backfire. In the following, I will discuss the different components put in place and compare them with the ideal.

12.4.1 The Comprehensive Assessment and the Single Supervisory Mechanism

The Single Supervisory Mechanism (SSM) established at the ECB is an important step forward. Such a single supervisor can internalize cross-border externalities as discussed above, and reduce distortions in the supervisory process by matching the perimeter of banks with the regulatory perimeter. And given the risk of political capture of regulators that we could observe across Europe (in both the core and the periphery), delegating supervision to the supra-national level is also progress. Given how politically sensitive banking has been across Europe, this is indeed a big step for the euro zone. The comprehensive assessment as the entry point into the SSM has fulfilled its function of providing a level playing field across banks in the euro zone, and opening the closet somewhat to catch a glimpse of some of the skeletons.

The comprehensive assessment and the implementation of the Single Supervisory Mechanism might already have had some positive effects on the return of market discipline. Several banks that are close to the minimum capital requirements went to the market in 2014 to raise additional equity, supposedly before being forced to do so by the ECB after the conclusion of asset quality review and stress tests. More specifically, 12 of the 25 banks that the comprehensive assessment showed had a capital shortfall as of 31 December 2013 did not have one at the time of publication of the comprehensive assessment, due to capital raised during the year. This could very well be interpreted as the return of market discipline. In addition, recent bank failures have seen junior creditors being bailed in rather than bailed out (SNS Reaal and Cyprus), even though the bail-in rule, established under the Bank Recovery and Resolution Directive (BRRD) formally kicks in only after 2016. It remains to be seen how far this renewal of market discipline carries when more systemic shocks hit, and countries are affected that are more closely linked to the rest of the European financial system.

However, doubts about the exercise persist, including about why a sovereign default was not part of the adverse scenarios and why deflation was not modelled as a stress scenario. In addition, the leverage ratio – that is, the unweighted capital–asset ratio – was not taken into account. While, on average, banks have a leverage ratio above the required 3 per cent, there are 14 banks below it, even before applying the asset quality review (AQR), and once the AQR is taken into account 17 fail to pass muster. Including the repercussions of the stress increases this number even further. More importantly, and as shown by Acharya and Steffen (2014), using the unweighted rather than the weighted capital–asset ratio provides a very different ranking of weak banks, with several French and German banks (all of which passed the comprehensive assessment) being in need of capital, in line with a market-based assessment of bank fragility. Given that the leverage ratio will become part of the regulatory rulebook under Basel 3, as adopted under the Capital Requirements Regulation (CRR) and Capital Requirements Directive (CRD) IV, additional capital will therefore have to be raised. And considering unweighted capital–asset rather than weighted capital–asset ratios is important not only given the changing rulebook, but also given empirical findings that unweighted capital–asset ratios are better at predicting bank failure than weighted capital–asset ratios (e.g. Demirguc-Kunt et al., 2013).

Importantly, these stress tests are just the beginning of the supervisory process by the ECB, with markets still to be convinced that there are no further skeletons hidden in the closets of the 130 banks that were screened, or any of the other smaller banks. Only time will show whether this stress test is more credible than previous rounds, which lost credibility almost immediately after giving clean bills of health to institutions such as Dexia and Bankia, which shortly afterwards failed.

Important institutional questions remain. What are the relative roles of the European Banking Authority and the European Central Bank? What will happen to the banks with a net capital shortfall, given that the Single Resolution Mechanism (SRM) discussed below will not enter into effect until 2016, and the necessary funding by the Single Resolution Fund (SRF) will only become available over time? What is the role of the SSM in macroprudential regulation and its relationship with the European Systemic Risk Board (ESRB), which covers the whole EU and not just SSM members? While the SSM can use macroprudential tools covered under the CRR and CRD IV, it cannot use other macroprudential tools, which will remain exclusively under national authority (Sapir, 2014). Given that not only micro- but also macroprudential decisions have externalities beyond national borders (Schoenmaker, 2014), this seems to be another gap in the banking union. The ESRB, which does not have any formal powers beyond issuing warnings and recommendations, cannot completely fill this gap. Finally, what is the relationship with non-euro countries, both those that will join the SSM and those that will not? The critical difference for non-euro members of the SSM would be an asymmetry in their financial safety net, with lender of last resort and resolution funding strictly on the national level, although solutions such as access to liquidity lines might be considered (Zettelmeyer et al., 2012). Cooperation with the Bank of England, which will stay out of the SSM for the near future, will be critical, given the importance of London as a financial centre. Ultimately, tailor-made solutions are necessary for arrangements with European countries outside the euro zone (Beck and Wagner, 2015).

Going forward, many challenges remain for the ECB as bank supervisor. It has to work with different national banking acts and different accounting and auditing standards, which might not only throw sand into the wheels of its own procedures but also hamper the development of a level playing field in regulation and supervision. Further, there could be arbitrage possibilities when it comes to monitoring banks that are directly supervised by the ECB and those that are not. In addition, the question of the regulatory perimeter will arise for the SSM as much as for other bank regulators, and thus the challenge of potentially expanding regulation and supervision towards non-bank segments of the financial system closely interconnected with banks. It remains to be seen how easy it will be for the SSM legally and politically to redefine its regulatory perimeter.

The major concerns, however, lie less with the SSM – the first pillar of the banking union – and more with the other two pillars: resolution and deposit insurance. These both remain unresolved.

12.4.2   The Single Resolution Mechanism: A Political Compromise

Resolution frameworks across Europe are being strengthened, on the national level, but also – with the bail-in clause introduced under the bank recovery and resolution directive (BRRD) – on the European level. The SRM, with all the caveats stated below, is an important first step. In its current form, however, it is still mainly a country-based framework, with supra-national support only kicking in at a second stage. In addition, it is a rather complicated coordination mechanism, which involves several players, especially for the case of larger financial institutions. Specifically, while the Single Resolution Board (SRB), with representatives of European and national institutions, proposes action, the European Commission takes the decision and national resolution authorities are to execute it. Ultimately, the name (Single Resolution Board) points to the main construction flaw: it being a network or college construction rather than a single decision-taker. The risk is again that decisions will reflect the sum of national interests rather than those of the euro zone. In addition, the fact that the UK is outside the SRM will critically hamper its effectiveness, given the importance of London as an international financial centre and many European banks having substantial parts of their operation in London. In addition, the target size of the resolution fund of €55 billion would not cover any major bank failure, which leaves the problem of 'too big to fail' unresolved in Europe. Even in the presence of much more rigorous bail-in rules introduced under the BRRD, interim funding might be necessary as large banks are unlikely to be resolved over a weekend. Finally, and even more important than the limited self-funding, there is no public backstop funding mechanism in place, which reduces the effectiveness of the resolution framework. Ultimately, this again leaves the failure of any large financial institution outside the formal financial safety net, and subject to political ad hoc weekend negotiations. It also does not allow for a clear severance of the sovereign–bank embrace as resolution funding is not completely on the supra-national level.

The third pillar, a common deposit insurance fund, has been quietly dropped, for the same reason that no public backstop has been established for the SRM. Political resistance to loss-sharing across countries was simply too great.

Even in a world with high confidence in the competence, independence and integrity of the supervisory institution and process, the shortcomings of these other two pillars will affect the SSM. How credible can a supervisor be in threatening to close a bank if there is no watertight resolution process in place? Over the past years, we have seen several occasions when intervention and the resolution of weak and failing banks was delayed because the necessary tools and resources were lacking; the Cypriot banks being the most prominent example.

In summary, several important elements of a fully functioning banking union have been missed, including a European bank resolution mechanism that deserves the name, and a proper funding mechanism. Critically, a public backstop is missing. The ECB would have to play a significant role in such a public backstop mechanism (either directly or indirectly by serving as backstop to, for example, the European Stability Mechanism). The fact that the ECB is being pushed indirectly into such a role, by taking on a greater role in crisis management beyond monetary policy, under the headline 'whatever it takes', is rather ironic and politically counterproductive.

12.4.3 The Sovereign–Bank Deadly Embrace Continues

Beyond institutional reforms to construct a European financial safety net, there are other important impediments, including zero risk weights for government bonds, which increase incentives to hold government papers and facilitate the 'Sarkozy carry trade', named after the former French President who suggested that banks use cheap ECB funding to buy government bonds of their home-country sovereign to thus ease fiscal pressures. Obviously, this leads to an exacerbation of the sovereign–bank embrace discussed above. An additional regulatory constraint is the lack of any concentration limit for government bonds, unlike for private sector lending. Recent statements by ECB officials, however, suggest that this might be addressed soon.

Not cutting the link between banks and sovereigns also implies that a different asymmetry can arise, where fiscally strong governments can bail out their banks, while fiscally weak governments cannot, undermining the single European market in banking further by preventing a level playing field (Hellwig, 2014).

Most importantly, the banking union just agreed on is a forward-looking structure, designed for the next crisis, but not supposed to address the current crisis. Beck and Trebesch (2013) and others have suggested shorter-term solutions involving a euro zone-level bad bank to address the legacy problems. Specifically, a Eurozone Restructuring Agency (ERA) can take charge of coordinating the restructuring and recapitalization of viable and liquidating non-viable banks throughout the euro zone. Such an agency should be a temporary vehicle, with a clear sunset clause, so that it ends its duty after the banking union is completed. By now it has become clear, however, that euro zone authorities have opted for the flow solution, hoping that banks will recover capital cushions through profits rather than going for an aggressive recapitalization exercise as in the US. Based on past crisis experiences, this seems a rather optimistic approach.

12.5   ARE WE THERE YET?

Earlier in 2014, there was an increasing sentiment that the euro zone is about to exit the crisis. With both Ireland and Portugal having exited or being close to exiting the Troika programmes, Greece showing signs of economic recovery and the crisis in Cyprus being less deep than feared, there were understandable hopes the worst might be behind us. On the other hand, there are serious doubts about whether many of the over-indebted sovereigns in the euro zone will be able to accumulate sufficient primary surpluses to get out of the crisis by themselves (Eichengreen and Panizza, 2015). In spite of (currently) quiet and seemingly complacent markets, the sovereign fragility in the euro zone is not gone.

In the short term, there are substantial risks for the euro zone. There is a substantial political risk that elections, especially in crisis countries such as Greece in early 2015 and Spain later in 2015, will produce governments that deviate from previous agreements and might substantially worsen the fiscal positions of their countries. Recent events following the Greek elections have confirmed this conjecture. At the same time, the reluctance to make further deals to redistribute the costs of the crisis in some of the core countries might become politically too strong to push such deals through.

Political uncertainty related to the snap elections in Greece again raises the scary scenario of a sovereign debt crisis. And the biggest risk might not be such a crisis in Greece, but rather that similar scenarios become more likely for other periphery countries, or are perceived as becoming more likely by the markets. With this background, it now seems a clear mistake that important policy reforms addressing sovereign debt fragility, be they a crisis resolution approach as a European Redemption Pact (see, e.g., Buch and Weigert, 2012) or a longer-term attempt at institutionalizing a sovereign bankruptcy regime, have been put on ice. Ultimately, a reappearance of sovereign fragility will have repercussions for bank fragility, at a time when the banking union structures are still being put in place and a euro zone crisis management framework is far from ready.

While on the upside there might be the chance of a 'grand bargain', on the downside there might be attempts by populist government to break loose from the 'Berlin–Brussels diktat'. Such political shocks could again bring turmoil to the euro zone. While the ECB has so far successfully managed such shocks with its 'whatever it takes' approach, its reputation has come increasingly under stress in several core countries, most critically in Germany.

Focusing more on the long-term perspectives, the discussion on the banking union is also related to a broader question about the role of the banking system in European finance. As pointed out by many observers, European financial systems are heavily bank-based, with a limited role for non-bank financial providers and capital markets (Langfeld and Pagano, 2015). This exacerbates the link between governments and banks, as there are a limited number of non-bank buyers of government papers. It makes financial systems more concentrated and results not only in larger banks, but also in a stronger reliance of economies on large banks.

Both the short-term risks and the long-term structural deficiencies suggest that the reform efforts so far are important advances, but that we are really at the early stages of the overall reform process, at the end of which will hopefully stand a single European market in banking matched by a European financial safety net. The road towards that objective, however, still seems rather long. It will encompass not only further reforms to the newly created banking union, but also structural reforms that reduce the importance of banks while increasing the role of non-bank providers in the European financial system. By reducing banking nationalism within the European Union, carefully designed regulatory reforms in banking can thus also contribute to the recently advocated Capital Markets Union. Ultimately, however, the banking union will not be able to stand alone without further integration along other policy dimensions, most prominently fiscal policy. From an optimistic viewpoint, banking union might open the door to such reforms; from a pessimistic viewpoint, further reforms might be prevented by the lack of a fiscal union.

12.6   IN CONCLUSION

The successful completion of the comprehensive assessment is a necessary, though far from sufficient, measure to set the stage for a recovery of lending in the euro zone. A well-capitalized banking system will have more confidence in lending to the private sector.

All that said, there are other significant barriers to a euro zone recovery, including the lack of consumer demand and the threat of deflation. A similar exercise to the comprehensive assessment undertaken a few years ago, and a more rapid (and more complete) introduction of the banking union might have resulted in a different economic situation today, but obviously there is no counterfactual for that. The national political interests that postponed the undertaking of the comprehensive assessment and the establishment of the SSM for so long also constrain a comprehensive economic policy approach to the current crisis. This would have to be a sensible mix of supply-side structural reforms, fiscal easing and more aggressive monetary easing in the form of quantitative easing (QE), all of which would involve far greater political consensus across the EU than is presently forthcoming. The compromises so far of half-baked reforms and policy packages (be they banking union, monetary easing or public investment packages), however, have not helped, and might make things even worse, as they are not sufficient to foster economic recovery but increase political resistance to further necessary reforms.

In a nutshell, the euro zone has made a big step forward, both in harmonization and centralization of bank regulation, but a long agenda remains. Short-term risks are still there and are set to stay for a long time. Most importantly, there is the risk of complacency and regulatory reform fatigue. The euro zone is not prepared for the next shock and crisis. There is a lot more to do.

NOTES

1. For a discussion of different arguments in favour of a banking union, see the different contributions in Beck (2012).
2. See Allen et al. (2011) for a general discussion on benefits and risks of cross-border banking.
3. One such an example is the restrictions that the German supervisory authority BaFin imposed on the German subsidiary of the Italian Unicredit (Hellwig, 2014).

4. Specifically, the SSM was created by a Regulation of the European Council under Art. 127 (6) of the Treaty on the Functioning of the European Union (TFEU). The SRM was created under Art. 114 of TFEU, and the Single Resolution Fund will be created on the basis of an intergovernmental agreement by 26 EU governments.

REFERENCES

Acharya, V. and S. Steffen (2014), 'Benchmarking European Central bank's asset quality review and stress test: a tale of two leverage ratios', VoxEU, 21 November, http://www.voxeu.org/article/benchmarking-aqr-tale-two-leverage-ratios.

Allen, F., T. Beck, E. Carletti, P. Lane, D. Schoenmaker and W. Wagner (2011), 'Cross-border banking in Europe: what's next?' London: CEPR.

Beck, T. (ed.) (2012), *Banking Union for Europe – Risks and Challenges*, VoxEU, e-book, http://www.voxeu.org/sites/default/files/file/Banking_Union.pdf.

Beck, T. and L. Laeven (2008), 'Resolution of failed banks by deposit insurers: cross-country evidence', in A. Demirguc-Kunt, E. Kane and L. Laeven (eds), *Deposit Insurance around the World, Issues of Design and Implementation*, Cambridge, MA: MIT Press.

Beck, T., R. Todorov and W. Wagner (2013), 'Supervising cross-border banks: theory, evidence and policy', *Economic Policy*, 73, 5–44.

Beck, T. and C. Trebesch (2013), 'Benchmarking the European Central bank's asset quality review and stress test: a tale of two leverage ratios', VoxEU, 18 November, http://www.voxeu.org/article/eurozone-bank-restructuring-agency.

Beck, T. and W. Wagner (2015), 'Supranational supervision: how much and for whom?', *International Journal of Central Banking*, forthcoming.

Buch, C. and B. Weigert (2012), 'Legacy problems in transition to a banking union', in T. Beck (ed.), *Banking Union for Europe – Risks and Challenges*, VoxEU, e-book, http://www.voxeu.org/sites/default/files/file/Banking_Union.pdf.

Demirguc-Kunt, A., E. Detragiache and O. Merrouche (2013), 'Bank capital: lessons from the crisis', *Journal of Money, Credit and Banking*, 45, 1147–64.

Eichengreen, B. and U. Panizza (2015), 'A surplus of ambition: can Europe rely on large primary surpluses to solve its debt problem?', *Economic Policy,* forthcoming.

Gros, D. (2012a), 'Banking union: Ireland vs. Nevada, an illustration of the importance of an integrated banking system', CEPS Commentary.

Gros, D. (2012b), 'The single European market in banking in decline – ECB to the rescue?', in T. Beck (ed.), *Banking Union for Europe – Risks and Challenges*, VoxEU, e-book, http://www.voxeu.org/sites/default/files/file/Banking_Union.pdf.

Hellwig, M. (2014), 'Yes, Virginia, there is a European banking union! But it may not make your wishes come true', available at http://www.oenb.at/Publikationen/Volkswirtschaft/Volkswirtschaftliche-Tagung/2014/Volkswirtschaftliche-Tagung-2014.html.

Langfeld, S. and M. Pagano (2015), 'Bank bias in Europe: effects on growth and systemic risk', *Economic Policy*, forthcoming.

Sapir, A. (2014), 'Europe's Macroprudential policy framework in light of the banking union', in Dirk Schoenmaker (ed.), *Macroprudentialism*, VoxEU, e-book, http://www.voxeu.org/article/macroprudentialism-new-vox-ebook.

Schoenmaker, D. (2012), 'Banking union: Where we're going wrong?' in T. Beck (ed.), *Banking Union for Europe – Risks and Challenges*, VoxEU, e-book, http://www.voxeu.org/sites/default/files/file/Banking_Union.pdf.

Schoenmaker, D. (ed.) (2014), 'Macroprudential spillovers: The role of organisational structure', VoxEU e-book, http://www.voxeu.org/article/macroprudential-spillovers-and-organisational-structure.

Zettelmeyer, J., E. Berglöf and R. De Haas (2012), 'Banking Union: The View from Emerging Europe', in T. Beck (ed.), *Banking Union for Europe – Risks and Challenges*, VoxEU, e-book, http://www.voxeu.org/sites/default/files/file/Banking_Union.pdf.

13. What can monetary policy achieve, and what is the relation between monetary policy and financial stability?

Lars E.O. Svensson

In this chapter, I will discuss two questions. First, what can – and cannot – monetary policy achieve? Second, what is the relation between monetary policy and financial stability, and how can, if necessary, monetary policy and financial stability policy be coordinated?

13.1 WHAT CAN – AND CANNOT – MONETARY POLICY ACHIEVE?

Monetary policy can stabilize inflation around a given inflation target and resource utilization around its estimated long-run sustainable rate. Since the inflation rate over the longer run is primarily determined by monetary policy, it is possible to select a fixed target for the inflation rate and for the monetary policy to achieve an average inflation rate over a longer period in line with the target.

In contrast, the long-run sustainable rate of resource utilization (measured by, for instance, potential output or the minimum long-run sustainable unemployment rate) is largely determined not by monetary policy but by non-monetary factors that affect the structure and working of the economy. These factors may change over time and may not be directly observable and measurable. This means that it is not appropriate to set a fixed monetary policy target for the long-run rate of resource utilization. Instead the long-run rate of resource utilization must be estimated, and such estimates are necessarily uncertain and subject to revision.

Thus, monetary policy cannot improve the long-run sustainable rate of resource utilization; for that, structural policies must be used. Generally, monetary policy cannot solve structural problems.

13.1.1   Monetary Policy Cannot Achieve Financial Stability

Furthermore, monetary policy cannot achieve financial stability; this requires financial stability policy (micro- and macroprudential policy). For instance, 'leaning against the wind' cannot solve debt problems.

The Riksbank provides a clear example, having applied an aggressive leaning-against-the-wind policy starting in the summer of 2010 in order to limit household indebtedness. This policy has led to zero or even negative inflation and an unemployment rate much above its long-run sustainable rate. Using the Riksbank's own estimates, the potential benefit of this policy, in the form of a better expected future macroeconomic outcome because of a lower probability of a future financial crisis, and a less deep crisis if it should occur, can be shown to be miniscule compared to the cost, in the form of a worse macroeconomic outcome in the near future. Expressed in terms of the unemployment rate, the benefit in terms of a lower expected future unemployment rate turns out to be only about 0.4 per cent of the cost in terms of higher unemployment rate in the next few years. The benefit should obviously have been more than 100 per cent of the cost to justify the policy. (See Svensson, 2015 for details.)

Furthermore, the Riksbank experience points to an inherent flaw in a policy of leaning against the wind to limit indebtedness, a policy supported, for instance, in the 2014 *Annual Report* of the Bank for International Settlements (2014). Leaning against the wind means a policy that is tighter than justified by stabilizing inflation around the inflation target, and resource utilization around its long-run sustainable rate. It thus means running inflation on average below the inflation target. But inflation targets have in many economies become credible, in the sense of inflation expectations being anchored to the targets. This means that inflation below the inflation target also means inflation below inflation expectations. This will tend to increase households' and other agents' real debt burden. It will also increase unemployment, and reduce employment and incomes, which will in turn reduce the debt-service capacity of indebted agents. The conclusion is that leaning against the wind is generally likely to be counterproductive as a way of managing debt problems.

In particular, in Sweden, since actual inflation was running much below the inflation target and households' expectations from the end of 2011 to the end of 2014, the real value of a given nominal debt held at the end of 2011 became about 6 per cent higher at the end of 2014 than what households had expected and planned for (Svensson, 2015). This is a substantial increase in households' real debt burden.

13.2   WHAT IS THE RELATION BETWEEN MONETARY POLICY AND FINANCIAL STABILITY?

In order to answer this question, it is necessary to distinguish between monetary policy and financial stability policy.[1]

13.2.1   How to Distinguish between Different Economic Policies?

In general, when we discuss different economic policies, we distinguish policies according to their objectives, their instruments and the authorities that control the instruments and are responsible for achieving the objectives. For instance, fiscal policy and monetary policy have distinct and different objectives, instruments and responsible authorities. Still, there is considerable interaction between the policies, in that the objectives of fiscal policy are affected by monetary policy and vice versa. Therefore, good fiscal policy has to take into account the effects of monetary policy on the fiscal policy objectives, and vice versa. But the policies are clearly separate. Similarly, financial stability policy and monetary policy are separate policies, although with some interaction, sometimes considerable.

Regarding monetary policy, for flexible inflation targeting, the objective is price stability and real stability. More concretely, the objective is to stabilize inflation around an inflation target and resource utilization around its long-run sustainable rate. In normal times, the instruments are the policy rate and communication. The latter includes publishing forecasts of the target variables, such as inflation and unemployment, and possible forward guidance, such as publishing a policy rate path, a forecast for the policy rate. In crisis times, the set of instruments include balance sheet policies, such as asset purchases (quantitative easing), fixed-rate lending at longer maturities, and foreign exchange interventions and exchange rate floors. The authority controlling the instruments and responsible for achieving the objectives is the central bank.

Regarding financial stability policy, the objective is financial stability. The definition of financial stability is not as clear and obvious as the definition of price stability. A definition that I prefer is that the financial system can fulfil its three main functions – transforming saving into financing, providing risk management and transmitting payments – with sufficient resilience to disturbances that threaten these functions. The crucial part of the definition is 'sufficient resilience'. In the future there will unavoidably be disturbances and shocks to the financial system, very likely from unexpected directions and of unexpected kinds. The crucial thing is that there is sufficient resilience to disturbances.

In normal times, the instruments of financial stability policy are supervision, regulation and communication, including capital and liquidity requirements, loan-to-value caps, banking resolution requirements, financial stability reports, and so on. In crisis times, further instruments include lending of last resort, variable-rate lending at longer maturities (credit easing), guarantees, bank resolution, capital injections, asset purchases, and so on. The authority or authorities controlling the instruments vary across countries and may include the financial supervisory authority, the central bank, the ministry of finance, the national debt office, a separate bank resolution authority, and so on.

13.2.2 Monetary Policy and Financial Stability are Different and Distinct and Normally Best Conducted Independently

Clearly, from the above perspective, monetary policy and financial policy are different and distinct policies. This is also the case when the same institution, the central bank, is in charge of both policies.

Importantly, price stability does not imply financial stability. Monetary policy can achieve price stability, but it cannot achieve financial stability. There is no way in which monetary policy can achieve sufficient resilience of the financial system; there is, for instance, obviously no way in which monetary policy can ensure that there are sufficient capital and liquidity buffers in the financial system.

Furthermore, financial stability policy cannot achieve price stability. Financial stability policy can achieve financial stability, but it cannot stabilize inflation around the inflation target and unemployment around its long-run sustainable rate. Thus, both policies are needed to achieve both monetary policy objectives and financial stability objectives.

Still, there is interaction between the two policies. Financial stability policy affects financial markets, spreads between different interest rates and lending by banks. This way it indirectly affects inflation and resource utilization. Monetary policy affects resource utilization, credit losses and assets prices. This way it indirectly affects balance sheets and leverage. Thus, there is interaction between the two policies, as there is interaction between fiscal policy and monetary policy.

My view is that, in normal times, it is best to conduct monetary policy and financial stability policy independently, with each policy taking the conduct of the other policy into account in order to best achieve its objectives. This is similar to how monetary policy and fiscal policy are conducted. In game-theory terms, it corresponds to a non-cooperative Nash equilibrium rather than a cooperative equilibrium. This is best for two reasons. First, monetary policy is much more effective than financial stability in stabilizing inflation around the inflation target and resource utilization around its long-run sustainable rate, whereas financial stability policy is much more effective than monetary policy in achieving financial stability. Second, it clarifies the accountability of the authority responsible for each policy. Bean (2014) provides a thorough discussion of why and how monetary policy and financial stability policy can achieve a good outcome by each policy focusing on its objective.

In crisis times, full cooperation and coordinated policies by the relevant authorities are warranted. These authorities may include the financial supervisory authority or authorities, the central bank, the ministry of finance, the bank resolution authority, and so on.

13.3 WHAT IF MONETARY POLICY POSED A THREAT TO FINANCIAL STABILITY?

There could on rare occasions arise situations when monetary policy might pose a threat to financial stability even when it fulfils the monetary policy objectives. Normally, the financial stability authority should be able to contain such threats with its available instruments. But how should a situation be handled when such a threat cannot easily be contained?

The August 2013 forward guidance by the Bank of England's Monetary Policy Committee (MPC) provides an example of how to handle such a situation (Bank of England, 2013). The MPC agreed its intention not to raise the policy rate until the unemployment rate had fallen to a threshold of 7 per cent, subject to three 'knockouts' not being breached. The third knockout is the Financial Policy Committee (FPC) judging that the stance of monetary policy poses a significant threat to financial stability that cannot be contained by the substantial range of mitigating policy actions available to the FPC, the Financial Conduct Authority and the Prudential Regulation Authority in a way consistent with their objectives.

Thus, according to this example, the financial stability authority should warn the monetary policy authority if monetary policy poses a threat to financial stability that the financial stability authority cannot contain with its available policy instruments. Then the monetary policy authority may choose to adjust monetary policy, either tightening (leaning against the wind) or loosening, depending on the situation. This clarifies the responsibility of each authority and makes it possible to hold them accountable.

So, is there any role at all for monetary policy in maintaining financial stability? If financial policy is ineffective or inappropriate, monetary policy may have to be adjusted (to be tighter or looser, depending on the situation). This means using monetary policy as a last line of defence, when the first line of defence, financial stability policy, is failing. But only in very rare situations would that defence be needed. And even then such defence would be justified only if the expected benefits exceed the costs.

13.3.1   The Best Contribution of Monetary Policy to Financial Stability

The best contribution to financial stability by monetary policy, except in very special circumstances, is certainly to just fulfil its objectives and stabilize inflation around the inflation target and resource utilization around its long-run sustainable rate. Suppose that the inflation target is 2 per cent and that average inflation equals the inflation target. Furthermore, assume that average resource utilization equals the long-run sustainable rate, and that this is consistent with an average real growth rate of, say, 3 per cent. This would then result in an average growth rate of nominal gross domestic product (GDP) and disposable income of 5 per cent per year. We may then also expect nominal asset prices, including housing prices, to grow on average by 5 per cent per year. This means that the debt-to-income, debt service-to-income, and loan-to-value ratios for a given nominal debt would on average halve in about 14 years. This is a pretty rapid fall of these ratios and a considerable contribution to any required balance sheet repair.

13.4   CONCLUSION

My conclusion is that we should not ask too much from monetary policy. Monetary policy can really at best just stabilize inflation around a given inflation target and resource utilization around its estimated long-run sustainable rate and in this way keep average inflation on target and average resource utilization equal to its long-run sustainable rate. In particular, monetary policy cannot achieve financial stability; a separate financial stability policy is needed for that. Leaning against the wind is an inherently flawed policy to manage debt problems, since running inflation below credible inflation targets and restricting the growth of nominal incomes will increase the real debt burden and reduce agents' debt service capacity.

Furthermore, monetary policy and financial stability policy are distinct and very different policies, and normally best conducted independently, but with each policy fully informed about and taking into account the conduct of the other. On rare occasions, the monetary policy may pose a threat to financial stability that cannot be contained by the instruments of the financial stability policy. The authority judging whether such a situation has occurred should be the authority responsible for financial stability. That authority should then warn the monetary policy authority about the threat. This clarifies the responsibility and makes it possible to hold each authority accountable. Monetary policy should only be the very last line of defence of financial stability and therefore only very rarely be used for that purpose. Also in such cases, the use of monetary policy is justified only if the expected benefits exceed the costs. Normally, the best contribution of monetary policy to financial stability is just to stabilize inflation around the inflation target and resource utilization around its long-run sustainable rate and in this way contribute to a healthy and sustainable growth of nominal GDP, disposable incomes and asset prices.

NOTE

1. This section builds on Svensson (2014).

REFERENCES

Bank for International Settlements (2014), '84th Annual Report: 1 April 2013–31 March 2014', available at www.bis.org.
Bank of England (2013), 'Monetary Policy Trade-offs and Forward Guidance', August, available at www.bankofengland.co.uk.
Bean, Charles (2014), 'The Future of Monetary Policy', speech in London, 20 May, available at www.bankofengland.co.uk.
Svensson, Lars E.O. (2014), 'Monetary Policy and Financial Stability Policy are Different and Normally Best Conducted Independently', in *Monetary Policy in a Changing Financial Landscape*, ECB Forum on Central Banking, Sintra, Portugal, 25–27 May 2014, pp. 81–9, available at www.larseosvensson.se.
Svensson, Lars E.O. (2015), 'Inflation Targeting and Leaning Against the Wind', in South African Reserve Bank (2015), *Fourteen Years of Inflation Targeting in South Africa and the Challenges of a Changing Mandate: South African Reserve Bank Conference Proceedings 2014*, Pretoria: South African Reserve Bank, available at www.larseosvensson.se.

PART V

Regional perspectives on monetary policy
issues: dilemmas and trade-offs

14. Policy trade-offs in CESEE and elsewhere

Raimondas Kuodis

Rather than focusing only on monetary policy trade-offs, I will address possible changes in the overall policy mix in this chapter, taking into account two aspects: (1) macroeconomic policy failures in the developed world since the mid-1980s; and (2) what is often overlooked, distributional effects of various policies. In my view, the conventional policy mix has clearly reached its limits, and we should be looking for the (old or new) ideas in the unorthodox economic theory which, unjustifiably, have received too little attention so far among central bankers.

14.1 MONETARY VERSUS MACROPRUDENTIAL

First, I would like to offer some thoughts on the division of burden between monetary and macroprudential policies. For more than two decades from the late 1990s onward, developed economies lived happily in the illusionary era of the so-called 'Great Moderation', but then, seemingly out of the blue, the lesser depression struck.

The 'moderation' period was characterized by relatively stable real growth rates and consumer price inflation, but was also accompanied by a very rapid expansion of credit and debt, widening income inequality and recurrent asset price bubbles. According to the unorthodox economists, these three phenomena are clearly related, and unorthodox economists moreover call the period in question not the 'Great Moderation', but 'financialization' – the epoch of the domination of financial industry interests in the economy and economic policy. They claim that financialization is a particular form of neoliberalism and that it represents the most recent stage of capitalism (Palley, 2013; Epstein, 2006; Hein, 2013).

What economic policies could have helped the developed economies to avoid this roller-coaster ride with unprecedented accumulation of debt? Unfortunately, most of the central banks have focused mainly on moving along the credit demand curves[1] (by changing policy rates[2]), but failed to control the process of rapid shifting-out of these curves. Since more and more private credit had been flowing to the real estate sector (Borio, 2012), this did not have the first-order impact on the central banks' target: consumer price indices, which, conveniently for central banks, exclude investment goods such as newly built houses.

Therefore, in the future, central banks should shift most of the burden from monetary policy (that is, moving along stationary credit demand curves) to the much more important game in town: runaway shifting out of the credit demand curves.[3] And the policy which should be assigned this larger role is macroprudential policy.

14.2   ASSET-BASED RESERVE REQUIREMENTS

Monetary policy can also be improved. For decades, some unorthodox economists have been advocating the use of so-called asset-based reserve requirements, a system whereby banks would hold reserves against their assets, not liabilities, as at present (Palley, 2000). The reserve requirement for each asset category would be set at the discretion of the central bank, and that can drive a wedge of any size between the official policy rate and the interest rate on the particular asset class, for example mortgage loans.

This policy innovation could have helped, for example, Sweden, when experiencing a state of lowflation while having to deal with a property boom at the very same time. Asset-based reserve requirements can spare monetary authorities from the dilemma of whether or not to increase official policy rate in such situations, thus harming not only the bubbly sector but the rest of the economy as well and increasing, rather than decreasing, the real debt of households (as pointed out by Lars E.O. Svensson in Chapter 13 in this volume).

14.3   DISTRIBUTIONAL EFFECTS

Let me now turn to the issue which, regretfully, has received relatively little attention in mainstream economic theory: the distributional effects of monetary policy. This topic is clearly related to the policy's burden-sharing problem discussed above.

The argument that the official interest rate should be downgraded as the main tool for dealing with the financial cycle can also be supported by the distributional dimension, which has finally gained deserved public attention with the publication of Thomas Piketty's (2014) *Capital in the Twenty-First Century*. As was demonstrated by, for example, Willem Thorbecke (1997) in the paper 'The Distributional Effects of Disinflationary Monetary Policy', relatively large real interest rate increases (as, for example, suggested by the Taylor principle) without the support of macroprudential policies, have strong asymmetric effects on: (1) certain economic sectors such as construction and durables manufacturing; (2) low-income worker groups; and (3) borrowers (as opposed to lenders).

Real wage stagnation and financial industry incentives have led to an unprecedented increase of private debt in many developed economies; instead of consuming from earned income, households were allowed, as Raghuram Rajan (2011) put it, 'to eat credit', and banks gladly filled that structural demand gap, with the gains from that process going mostly to the so-called '1 per cent', which includes most of the financiers.

Paraphrasing Robert E. Lucas, who said about the United States' fiscal stimulus that 'there's nothing to apply a multiplier to',[4] most of poor people do not have savings 'to apply a compound interest rate to'; indeed, relatively high real interest rates in the past have been one of the channels of growing income disparities. In the context of growing inequality, the unfortunate representative–agent set-up, used by many central banks, has allowed them to disregard an important socio-economic cost that higher real interest rates bring upon societies, if monetary policy alone is used to deal with the excesses of the financial cycle.

14.4   FAIR REAL INTEREST RATE

What level of real interest rate is fair? Post-Keynesians argue that it should be slightly above 0 per cent, mainly because 'profit, not interest, is the reward for enterprise' (Smithin, 2006). To quote John Smithin:

> The real value of existing sums of money, representing past effort in the form of work and enterprise, would be preserved, but there would be no increase in their value arising from the mere possession of money. Further accumulation would only be possible by contributing further work or enterprise, or assuming further risk. This state of affairs would not, however, really constitute the 'euthanasia of the rentier' (Keynes, 1936), as it is not the nominal interest rate that is set at zero but the real rate. Accumulated financial capital at least retains its original real value. (Smithin, 2006)

14.5   CONSENSUS

As a result of the recent global financial and economic crisis, the right consensus seems to be emerging that business cycles, which have been

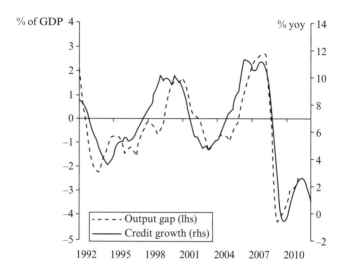

Source: Mayer (2012) – data were from OECD, ECB, Deutsche Bank Research.

Figure 14.1   Euro area output gap and credit growth

predominantly caused by credit growth accelerations (Mayer, 2012; see, for example, Figure 14.1, taken from Mayer, 2012), should be addressed with both monetary and macroprudential policies. To borrow Andrew G. Haldane's (2014) term, macroeconomic policy should be two-handed or ambidextrous; and I would add that the macroprudential policy arm should be much stronger than the monetary policy arm due to its superior distributional effects and its effectiveness.

14.6   INCOMES POLICY

In addition, central banks, in their pursuit of consumer price stability, could reconsider the place of the long-forgotten incomes policy in the overall policy mix. Since excessive inflation or deflation is frequently the outcome of the conflict between labur and capital, it should be dealt with using the instrument which directly moderates the conflicting claims on income.

This approach would also take some pressure off monetary policy or help in the environment of lowflation/deflation. For example, in July 2014, the Bundesbank was reported to welcome above-inflation wage increases in some sectors in Germany, despite the fact that the Bundesbank has historically been a strong advocate of wage restraint.[5]

14.7   FISCAL POLICY

Space constraints allow only a brief mentioning of the role of fiscal policy. The main unorthodox fiscal policy doctrine was outlined by Abba Lerner in 1943, and it is called 'functional finance'. What is meant by 'functional', and what are the main principles of this doctrine? Let me quote the original paper here (Lerner, 1943):

> The central idea is that government fiscal policy, its spending and taxing, its borrowing and repayment of loans, its issue of new money and its withdrawal of money, shall be undertaken with an eye only to the results of these actions on the economy and not to any established traditional doctrine about what is sound or unsound.
>
> Functional Finance . . . prescribes . . . the adjustment of total spending . . . to eliminate both unemployment and inflation . . . the adjustment of public holdings of money and of government bonds . . . to achieve the rate of interest which results in the most desirable level of investment . . . the printing, hoarding, or destruction of money as needed . . .
>
> [The] result might be a continually increasing national debt . . . [This] possibility presented no danger . . . so long as Functional Finance maintained the proper level of total demand for current output; and . . . there is an automatic tendency for the budget to be balanced in the long run as a result of the application of Functional Finance, even if there is no place for the principle of balancing the budget

More and more economists now believe that it is primarily the euro area which should be the first to reconsider open-mindedly its fiscal orthodoxy, taboos and Treaty-imposed constraints on what is allowed or not under the fiscal rules. Even the smartest unconventional monetary policy cannot replace a well-functioning fiscal framework as a way to achieve full employment, not to mention the distributional aspect that unconventional monetary measures help 'The Wall Streets' first, before the effects trickle down (or not) to 'The Main Streets'. And, judging by the results that are really important for ordinary people, such as unemployment levels, the euro area's fiscal policy has been far from being 'functional' in A. Lerner's sense.

14.8   CONCLUSIONS

To conclude: in my humble opinion, the authorities of the developed countries need a major reconsideration of the relative roles of various economic policies in order to unburden the societies not only from the new waves of financialization (with the resulting mountains of debt), but also from the policy recommendations to avoid the prospect of secular stagnation with even larger doses of financialization. Unfortunately, many of the policy-makers are not free to start with a clean (intellectual and institutional) slate.

First, mainstream macroeconomic textbooks continue contaminating the minds of generations of current and future policy-makers by getting so many things wrong: starting from the money creation process and the role of banks, and ending with the disregard of distributional aspects of various policies, to name a few. Second, many countries do not enjoy full monetary sovereignty. Notably, the euro area countries are users, not issuers of the euro. In such a set-up, financial markets, which are generally prone to producing multiple equilibria, play a leading role in shaping the borrowing conditions and consequently the macro outcomes, not the sovereigns. To quote Randall Wray (2003) from his paper 'Is Euroland The Next Argentina?':

> The ability of a sovereign government with a floating currency to make payments is not revenue-constrained, and it can issue securities at any rate it desires. In contrast, a non-sovereign government must obtain dollars/Euros before it can spend them, and it cannot exogenously set the interest rate. Rather, market forces determine the interest rate at which it borrows.

Therefore, while the major reassessment of the policy configuration is needed, I fear that the world will have to wait for another major crisis until this finally happens.

NOTES

1. Reflecting the inverse relationship between the level of interest rates and the volume of credit demand.
2. How responsive investment is, for example, to interest rate changes is an empirical issue. For a pessimistic view see Goodhart and Erfurth (2014): 'the empirical evidence shows capital expenditure to be notably interest-insensitive'; or *The Economist* (2014).
3. Or shifting in of the credit demand curves, during the crisis years in the euro area.
4. http://delong.typepad.com/sdj/2011/09/department-of-huh-no-department-of-wtf-robert-lucas-edition.html.
5. http://uk.reuters.com/article/2014/07/30/uk-germany-wages-weidmann-idUKKBN0FZ03U20140730.

REFERENCES

Borio, Claudio (2012), 'The Financial Cycle and Macroeconomics: What Have We Learnt?', BIS Working Paper No 395.

The Economist (2014), 'Monetary Policy: Tight, Loose, Irrelevant', available at http://www.economist.com/news/finance-and-economics/21625875-interest-rates-do-not-seem-affect-investment-economists-assume-tight-loose?fsrc=scn%2Ftw_ec%2Ftight_loose_irrelevant.

Epstein, Gerald A. (2006), *Financialization and the World Economy*, Cheltenham, UK and Northampton, MA, USA: Edward Elgar Publishing.

Goodhart, Charles A.E. and Philipp Erfurth (2014), 'Monetary Policy and Long-Term Trends', available at http://www.voxeu.org/article/monetary-policy-and-long-term-trends.

Haldane, Andrew G. (2014), 'Ambidexterity', Speech at the American Economic Association Annual Meeting, 3 January, available at http://www.bankofengland.co.uk/publications/Documents/speeches/2014/speech713.pdf.

Hein, Eckhard (2013), *The Macroeconomics of Finance-Dominated Capitalism – and Its Crisis*, Cheltenham, UK and Northampton, MA, USA: Edward Elgar Publishing.

Lerner, Abba (1943), 'Functional Finance and the Federal Debt', *Social Research*, 10(1), February, 38–51.

Mayer, Thomas (2012), *Europe's Unfinished Currency*, London: Anthem Press.

Palley, Thomas I. (2000), 'Stabilizing Finance: The Case for Asset-Based Reserve Requirements', report issued by the Financial Markets Center, Philomont, VA, available at http://www.thomaspalley.com/docs/articles/macro_policy/stabilizing_finance.pdf.

Palley, Thomas I. (2013), *Financialization: the Economics of Finance Capital Domination*, London: Palgrave.

Piketty, T. (2014), *Capital in the Twenty-First Century*, transl. A. Goldhammer, Cambridge, MA: Belknap Press.

Rajan, Raghuram (2011), *Fault Lines: How Hidden Fractures Still Threaten the World Economy*, Princeton, NJ: Princeton University Press.

Smithin, John (2006), 'The Theory of Interest Rates', in Philip Arestis and Malcolm Sawyer (eds), *A Handbook of Alternative Monetary Economics*, Cheltenham, UK and Northampton, MA, USA: Edward Elgar Publishing.

Thorbecke, Willem (1997), 'The Distributional Effects of Disinflationary Monetary Policy', Jerome Levy Economics Institute Working Paper No. 144, available at http://ssrn.com/abstract=70816 or http://dx.doi.org/10.2139/ssrn.70816.

Wray, R. (2003), 'Is Euroland The Next Argentina?', available at http://www.cfeps.org/pubs/wp-pdf/WP23-Wray.pdf.

15. A central bank's dilemmas in highly uncertain times: a Romanian view

Daniel Daianu

This chapter looks at policy dilemmas faced by the National Bank of Romania (NBR) over the years, framing the analysis in a European and historical context. These dilemmas include older concerns, such as massive capital inflows and outflows as well as a very burdensome legacy of resource misallocation and entrenched expectations of high inflation. They also include newer concerns that arose or intensified during the Great Recession, namely corrections of large macroeconomic imbalances under very unfavourable international circumstances and in a highly uncertain European environment. While the NBR's monetary policy arrangements ('light' inflation targeting) have provided leeway for undertaking the correction of imbalances, high euroization has dented their efficacy, given the wealth effect and the balancesheet impact of exchange rate depreciation. Moreover, the spectre of stagnation in the euro area, financial deleveraging, unconventional policies pursued by key central banks, the ongoing reform of banking regulation and supervision, the growth of shadow banking, and so on have created a range of big challenges for the central banks of the newer European Union (EU) member states.

15.1 ROMANIA: HUGE CORRECTION OF IMBALANCES IN A HIGHLY UNFAVOURABLE ENVIRONMENT

The Romanian economy cannot extricate itself from the the goods and bads of the EU economies. Like other economies that had boomed owing to massive credit expansion and external borrowing, it was severely hit by the financial crisis. The freeze of financial markets compelled Romanian policy-makers to ask for external assistance in order to fend off the prospects of a liquidity crisis turning into a solvency crisis, in spite of rather low public debt. The correction of external and domestic imbalances which has been achieved is quite remarkable and matches similar adjustment processes in

Table 15.1   Current account balance (% of GDP), 2007–2014

	2007	2008	2009	2010	2011	2012	2013	2014E	2015F
Romania	−13.4	−11.5	−4.5	−4.6	−4.6	−4.5	−0.8	−0.6	−1.2
Bulgaria	−24.3	−22.4	−8.6	−1.5	0.1	−0.8	2.6	2.1	2.3
Poland	−6.1	−6.5	−3.9	−5.0	−5.2	−3.5	−1.3	−2.0	−2.4
Hungary	−7.2	−7.0	−0.8	0.3	0.8	1.9	4.1	4.3	4.3

Notes:
The data for Romania and Poland (2011–2015) are based on the methodology of the 6th edition of the *Balance of Payments Manual* of the International Monetary Fund (BMP6). The data for Hungarian GDP are based on the European System of Accounts (ESA) as updated in 2010.
E = estimated, F = forecast.

Source: Eurostat, European Commission, autumn forecast 2014.

other newer EU member states. But while the Baltic economies had to undertake internal devaluation (because of their currency boards), Romania was able to use the exchange rate, too, as an adjustment tool. It is worthy to note that the external borrowing made during 2005–2008 was primarily done by the private sector and driven by foreign banks' operations in Romania. The current account deficit went down to 0.8 per cent of gross domestic product (GDP) in 2013, from a double-digit level during 2007–2008 (Table 15.1). This turnaround can be explained by the upsurge of exports and the freeze of financial markets, with the ensuing forced compression of imports. The deficit for 2014 is estimated to be close to 0.6 per cent of GDP.

The period 2010–2013 moreover saw a massive correction of the fiscal imbalance (Figure 15.1), enabled by agreements with the EU and international financial institutions (IFIs). Notwithstanding the negative, procyclical, fiscal impulse driven by the need to correct major structural budget deficits, and the fact that interest rates did not ease as some might have expected, the economy bounced back into positive territory in 2011. Inflation stood at 1.6 per cent at the end of 2013, dropping further to about 0.8 per cent in 2014. Economic growth is estimated at about 2.8 per cent in 2014, down from 3.5 per cent in 2013 (Figure 15.2).

Public debt trebled, but stabilized at around 40 per cent of GDP (Figure 15.3). The United States Federal Reserve System (US Fed)'s tapering of its stimulus will arguably find Romania much better prepared than during the 2008–2009 turbulences, owing to a major correction of its imbalances and the 'buffers' it has (NBR reserves and State Treasury funds). Table 15.2 and Figure 15.4 show the size of Romania's overall external debt, as compared to the newer EU member states.

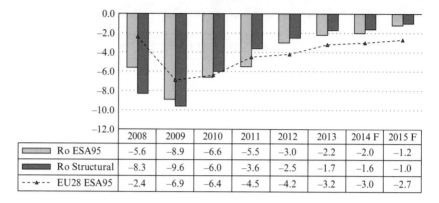

	2008	2009	2010	2011	2012	2013	2014 F	2015 F
Ro ESA95	−5.6	−8.9	−6.6	−5.5	−3.0	−2.2	−2.0	−1.2
Ro Structural	−8.3	−9.6	−6.0	−3.6	−2.5	−1.7	−1.6	−1.0
EU28 ESA95	−2.4	−6.9	−6.4	−4.5	−4.2	−3.2	−3.0	−2.7

Notes:
'RO ESA95' and 'EU28 ESA 95' refer to Romania's net lending (+)/borrowing (−) based on ESA 1995 methodology; 'Ro Structural' refers to Romania's structural budget balance.
F = forecast.

Sources: European Commission, autumn forecast 2014 in line with the European System of Accounts (ESA) 2010; Official estimates from the Budget Law Report of 2015.

Figure 15.1 Fiscal consolidation in Romania, 2008–2015

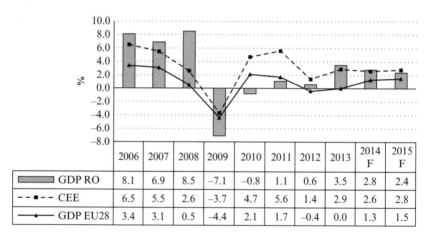

	2006	2007	2008	2009	2010	2011	2012	2013	2014 F	2015 F
GDP RO	8.1	6.9	8.5	−7.1	−0.8	1.1	0.6	3.5	2.8	2.4
CEE	6.5	5.5	2.6	−3.7	4.7	5.6	1.4	2.9	2.6	2.8
GDP EU28	3.4	3.1	0.5	−4.4	2.1	1.7	−0.4	0.0	1.3	1.5

Note: F = forecast.

Sources: The data for Central and Eastern Europe (CEE), Romania (RO) and the European Union (EU28) are derived from the annual macroeconomic (AMECO) database of the European Commission and own calculations (Bulgaria, Croatia, Hungary, Latvia, Lithuania, Former Yugoslav Republic of Macedonia, Montenegro, Poland, Romania, Serbia, Turkey). The data for 2014 and 2015 are based on the autumn forecast of the European Commission, in line with the European System of Accounts (ESA) 2010 methodology.

Figure 15.2 Real GDP growth rates (year on year in %), 2006–2015

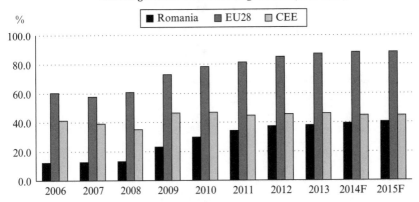

General government consolidated gross debt (% of GDP)

Note: EU28 = European Union, all 28 member states; CEE = Central and Eastern Europe.

Sources: European Commission (AMECO database) and own calculations (Bulgaria, Croatia, Hungary, Latvia, Lithuania, Former Yugoslav Republic of Macedonia, Montenegro, Poland, Romania, Serbia, Turkey). The data for 2014 and 2015 are based on the autumn forecast of the European Commission, in line with European System of Accounts (ESA) 2010 methodology (data for EU28 calculated on a non-consolidated basis).

Figure 15.3   Romania's public debt, 2006–2015

Table 15.2   Gross external debt* (% of GDP)

	2009	2010	2011	2012	2013	2014Q2
Romania	68.2	75.1	76.4	74.9	68.8	64.1
Bulgaria	104.8	100.7	90.5	92.1	91.0	89.9
Czech Republic	49.9	54.7	57.5	60.2	66.3	68.3
Hungary**	174.2	162.1	184.5	160.5	144.9	148.6
Poland	58.7	65.9	71.8	70.1	69.4	69.8
Slovakia	72.9	74.3	76.7	74.9	81.2	87.3

Notes:
 * Romania, Czech Republic, Hungary, Poland according to the methodology of the 6th edition of the *Balance of Payments Manual* of the International Monetary Fund (BPM6).
** including special purpose entities (SPEs).

Sources: National central banks and own calculations, in line with the European System of Accounts (ESA) 2010.

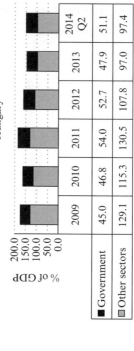

Poland

% of GDP	2009	2010	2011	2012	2013	2014 Q2
■ Government	18.2	23.0	25.7	28.6	27.9	28.7
▣ Other sectors	40.5	42.9	46.1	41.5	41.5	41.1

Hungary

% of GDP	2009	2010	2011	2012	2013	2014 Q2
■ Government	45.0	46.8	54.0	52.7	47.9	51.1
▣ Other sectors	129.1	115.3	130.5	107.8	97.0	97.4

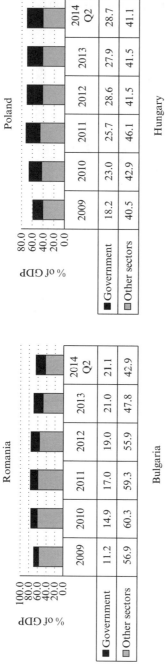

Romania

% of GDP	2009	2010	2011	2012	2013	2014 Q2
■ Government	11.2	14.9	17.0	19.0	21.0	21.1
▣ Other sectors	56.9	60.3	59.3	55.9	47.8	42.9

Bulgaria

% of GDP	2009	2010	2011	2012	2013	2014 Q2
■ Government	7.8	7.8	7.0	8.7	8.3	8.3
▣ Other sectors	97.0	92.9	83.6	83.4	82.6	81.5

Sources: National central banks and own calculations, in line with the European System of Accounts (ESA) 2010; Romania, Czech Republic, Hungary, Poland: according to the methodology of the 6th edition of the *Balance of Payments Manual* of the International Monetary Fund (BPM6).

Figure 15.4 External debt: public versus private sector, 2009–2014Q2

15.2   EARLIER-VINTAGE POLICY ISSUES AND DILEMMAS

Major pre-crisis and older concerns of Romanian policy-makers and of the NBR were related to 'structural strain' (how to deal with massive resource misallocation when prices are freed overnight), the pace of financial liberalization, the persistence of high inflation (expectations, moral hazard, exchange rate pass-through, and so on) and, not least, the move to inflation targeting.

15.2.1   Structural Strain

'Structural strain' (Daianu, 1994, 1997) can provide an analogy with over-burdened monetary policy during the financial and economic crisis that hit advanced economies in 2008. Following the collapse of the command system and a dramatic change in relative prices, many enterprises were found to be unprofitable and faced increasingly hard budget constraints. The system, due to its rigidities, more or less structural, was incapable of undergoing massive resource reallocation rapidly. Hence the need to subsidize firms and even sectors, involving the monetization of quasi-fiscal deficits. Moreover, firms themselves created their own pseudo-money via inter-enterprise arrears. This quasi-fiscal task of central banks during the initial stage of post-command transition resembles the quantitative easing practiced during the current financial crisis by major central banks in advanced economies; a similar fiscal dominance takes centre stage, blending two policy tools. Why the fiscal dominance now? Because, during the Great Moderation period, resources were misallocated on a large scale (Caruana, 2014). Unlike command systems, however, market mechanisms are not emasculated in free economies, and people and firms are free to make their own choices, thus allowing decisions to be driven by incentives and entrepreneurship. Moreover, inflation is very low in the economies afflicted by the financial crisis, whereas money printing after price liberalization in post-command economies created high inflation (since inflation expectations were pretty high after years of suppressed inflation, and because money balances were considerable[1]). This is due to an overwhelming liquidity trap and low or even declining inflation expectations in advanced economies. This difference explains why tolerating high inflation in the initial years of transition entailed the threat of entrenched high inflation expectations. This proved a handicap for the Romanian central bank in its efforts to subdue inflation later on, and forced a rethinking of its monetary policy regime about a decade ago.

15.2.2   Pace of Financial Liberalization

In an intense domestic debate on the pace of financial (capital account) liberalization going beyond the implications of the 'Tošovský dilemma',[2] supporters of fast financial liberalization, in tune with the Washington Consensus extolling the virtues of quick financial integration with the outer economy, faced proponents (Daianu and Vranceanu, 2002 [2003]) of a more cautious approach, considering structural features of emerging economies, the threats posed by hot money and the need to sequence financial liberalization. Notwithstanding the lessons of the Asian crisis of 1997–1998 and similar episodes of crisis in Latin American economies, international financial institutions continued to push for quick financial liberalization. While Romanian policy-makers did try to sequence the opening of the capital account, the EU rules of the game (the single market) forced a faster pace which, ultimately, enhanced a boom-and-bust cycle. The NBR's attempt to stem the skyrocketing pace of credits was of little avail due to euroization and parent bank funding, and possibly also due to little experience with macroprudential tools and the sheer size of capital inflows. One easily detects here Hélène Rey's insight that the 'impossible trinity' (trilemma) is, when a global financial cycle operates, basically a 'dilemma' (Rey, 2013), and that capital controls could play a useful role in mitigating the destabilizing features of massive capital flows. An ensuing inference is that major central banks, the Fed in particular, have a key responsibility in considering their monetary policies and ensuing externalities. Rey's 'dilemma' compounds the 'Tošovský dilemma', both indicating how hard it is to conduct an effective monetary policy in small open economies and when facing substantial capital flows.

The ample boom-and-bust cycle was not limited to Romania but also hit large parts of the EU (see Figure 15.5). While making sense, downhill flows did not move into tradable sectors in the main. Romania, the Baltic economies, Bulgaria, and euro zone economies such as Spain and Ireland, received enormous amounts of private capital, driving up external imbalances. One wonders whether a European financial cycle[3] was at play in the EU after the introduction of the euro and against the backdrop of the myopia of financial markets regarding the performance differences among various economies. Much of the inflow was private borrowing and, like in the Asian crisis of 1997–1998, financial markets were found in the end, to care about the overall external indebtedness of an economy, albeit driven by the private sector. One can draw an inference here about the importance of private borrowing in judging resilience to shocks and the triggering of balance-of-payments crises. Like other newer EU

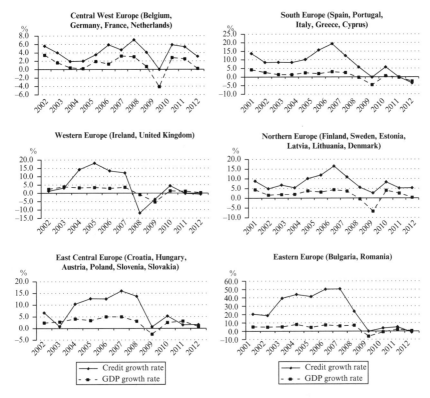

Source: Eurostat, European sector accounts (national central banks; other monetary financial institutions), own calculations.

Figure 15.5 Bank lending and GDP growth

member states, Romania faced a liquidity crisis as markets froze, with external financial support and the Vienna Initiative being instrumental in averting a worse scenario.

15.2.3 Which Type of Inflation Targeting?

For a long period of time, Romania was an outlier when it came to bringing inflation down to a reasonable (one-digit) level. A protracted transition, with many loss-making enterprises weighing heavily on budget deficits and entrenched high inflation expectations, made the mission of the NBR more difficult. The perspective of joining the EU prompted a more determined effort to combat high inflation, leading to the decision

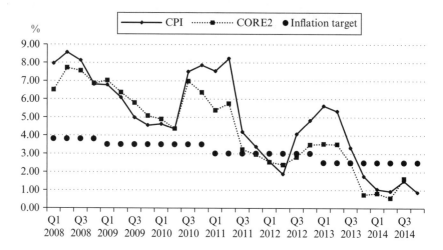

Note: CPI = consumer price inflation; CORE2 = CPI less administered prices, volatile prices, as well as tobacco and alcohol prices.

Sources: National Institute of Statistics (NIS), National Bank of Romania (NBR).

Figure 15.6   Disinflation in Romania (yoy, %)

to adopt flexible inflation targeting (IT) in 2005 (Popa et al., 2002; Daianu and Kallai, 2005).[4] The choice of 'light' IT (Isarescu, 2013) acknowledged the reality of a small open economy which is heavily euroized and for which wild gyrations of the exchange rate pose significant risks. This is why, de facto, managed floating was part and parcel of IT in practice. A sharp and persistent nominal appreciation (following massive capital inflows) can be highly detrimental to resource allocation (to the creation of comparative advantages[5]); likewise, brutal depreciations cause heavy losses via balancesheet and wealth effects. The NBR could not be complacent about erratic, wide exchange rate fluctuations, a stance that, arguably, has its merits.

Romania has witnessed disinflation in the period since 2008 (Figure 15.6), but with large deviations from target, due to various shocks. Disinflation around the world also helped in this regard, as did the large GDP gap after the crisis hit.[6] Inflation targeting relied also on administrative tools, such as substantial reserve requirements for both euro and Romanian lei funds. As mentioned, macroprudential tools (restraints on credit growth) operated during 2006–2008, but with little efficiency. The transmission mechanism has improved over the years, with smaller margins between the policy rate and lending rates, but it is still quite cumbersome. In addition, once the crisis erupted, supply-and-demand constraints took their toll, not unlike what can be seen in all economies where deleveraging and risk aversion have been ubiquitous.

Fiscal policy was procyclical after 2009 due to the forex constraint and the big structural budget deficit. Why output bounced back starting with 2011 is a legitimate question that will be tackled in the next section, as a recent-vintage dilemma. Monetary policy easing took place during 2014, but while being firm, it took into account unwelcome effects of possible excessive exchange rate depreciation. On top of this, when the transmission mechanism breaks down, lower policy rates are less effective owing to credit supply-and-demand constraints. There is an asymmetry at work here, for rises in policy rates can prolong and deepen a recession.[7] In a heavily euroized economy, monetary conditions (the policy stance) are to be assessed by examining both the dynamics of the policy rate (real policy rates) and the dynamics of the real effective exchange rate (Figure 15.7).

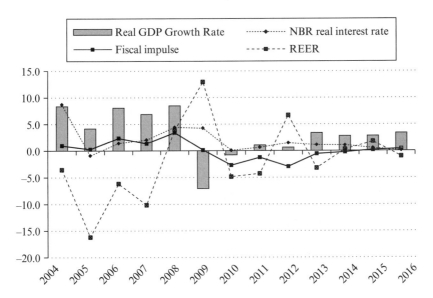

Sources: National Institute of Statistics (NIS), National Bank of Romania (NBR), European Central Bank (for real effective exchange rates = REER).

Figure 15.7 REER, GDP growth, policy rate, fiscal impulse

15.3　RECENT-VINTAGE DILEMMAS: A NEW AGE?

After what the Great Recession has entailed paradigm-wise, policy-wise and as an overall mood of the people, a gripping new 'age of uncertainty',[8] of disruptions, would be a proper term to capture these sentiments and changes.[9] I will now sum up what appears to make up the dramatically changed environment in which policy-makers (central bankers included) operate.

15.3.1　The Overall Environment: Cognition and Policies

The Great Recession has questioned cognitive and operational models. The search for suitable models has to take into account:

- An oversized financial sector (ESRB, 2014[10]), with destabilizing features (Stiglitz, 2010; Blanchard and Ostry, 2012) and a derailed institutional culture,[11] in spite of major efforts to reform financial sector regulation and supervision.
- How to model non-linearities (tail events) is a big challenge, as is the integration of finance in macroeconomic models (Brunnermeier et al., 2012; Borio, 2012 [2014][12]).[13]
- A paradigm shift: price stability is not sufficient for economic stability.
- Proliferation of conventional and non-conventional shocks (including cyber attacks), and a decline in robustness and resilience (rising fragility).
- Complexity is on the rise and there is frequent inability to understand; hence the need for more simple, more transparent and more robust financial sectors.
- An overburdening of central banks' functions'; central banks can no longer rely on simple rules (like Taylor's rule). This makes central banking much more complicated and obfuscates the delimitations between monetary policy and other policies, especially when financial stability takes centre stage.
- The development of capital markets brings about new systemic risks. Regulators and supervisors of these markets will arguably think increasingly like central bankers, to the extent that shadow banking creates new systemic risks (think just about the role central counterparties are asked to play, the volume of funds moved by hedge funds and money market funds worldwide, and sudden stops that can occur in these markets).
- The spectre of much lower growth in the industrialized world (a balancesheet recession, secular stagnation) due to demographics,

income inequality (e.g. Piketty and Saez, 2013), technical change and zero sum games in the world economy, and so on (Summers, 2014; Gordon, 2014; Crafts, 2014; Eichengreen, 2014; Koo, 2011; Jimeno et al., 2014).

- Social and political implications of economic slowdown and recession.
- Ineffective international policy coordination.

As far as Europe is concerned, several observations are relevant to this discussion:

- The spectre of debt deflation in the euro zone is real; debt deflation could rekindle the menace of a euro zone break-up.
- The link between sovereign debt and bank balancesheets has not been severed; and it may be quite unrealistic to think that a total delinking is feasible. After all, governments are the only entities with taxation power;
- Market fragmentation has continued, although the periphery (except Greece) pays much less than it used to for issuing its debt, due to the ECB's special operations.
- Internal demand in most of the euro zone is very weak and suffering from the negative loops between weak activity, fragile banks, weak firms, diminished incomes and the need for fiscal consolidation.
- The bottom-line question in the euro zone is: how to foster economic growth, avoid debt deflation? Unless this is achieved the seeds of a new crisis are planted, which would impair the state of the banking sector again (in spite of its efforts to increase own capital, and reduce leverage).
- The fragility of the growth model that relies on debt; this is particularly relevant for the newer EU member states from Central, Eastern and South-Eastern Europe (CESEE), which need to reinvent their growth model, enhance domestic savings and orient more resources toward tradables.
- The fallout from the Ukraine crisis on economic recovery in Europe, and the return of major geopolitical risks. This development is especially relevant in an environment which is already very severely influenced by risk aversion. The fall in price of oil and gas hardly offsets the economic impact of the additional uncertainty on CESEE economies.
- Capital flow reversals are a significant threat in view of the disconnect between booming asset markets worldwide and the very slow economic growth rates in most of Europe. The search for yield

would quickly be arrested were the Fed to taper its stimulus in a significant way.

15.3.2   Dilemmas of Recent Vintage: The Domestic Context

Observations are made next on a range of policy issues and dilemmas which confront the NBR.

The policy space issue

Economists are fond of extolling the virtues of fiscal space, and the European Commission and the International Monetary Fund (IMF) keep prodding governments to build up fiscal space through buffers and countercyclical measures. But the broader concept of *policy space* is no less important. For economies to adjust smoothly to shocks, they need to rely on highly flexible markets and be able to resort to an array of adjustment tools; Jan Tinbergen got his Nobel prize for highlighting just this tenet in 1969. In a single currency area, where the monetary policy and exchange rate policy are gone, the tasks for policy-makers can easily turn into a 'mission impossible' unless local markets are sufficiently flexible and productivity gains in the local economy match those of neighbouring economies.

When to join the European Banking Union and the euro area

The policy space issue and the pains the single currency area is going through make joining the euro area (which is a must according to the accession treaties) a more complicated journey. There is caution among the newer EU member states in this regard. After all, a key lesson of the euro zone crisis is that real convergence and a better functioning of the single currency area are badly needed in order to make accession successful. Solid fiscal underpinnings are an absolute must in the euro area, while fiscal rectitude is not sufficient in this regard. It should be said that the Ukraine crisis has brought geopolitical concerns into the pros of joining the euro area (in the case of Baltic economies in particular).

The banking union project might provide a solution to enhancing the cohesiveness of the euro zone. But there are important technicalities, of a fiscal nature in particular, and sequencing problems that need clarification. And there is hardly any talk about a collective deposit insurance scheme, which would make sense in a monetary union. National budgets will essentially be the main financial backstops in case of emergencies, notwithstanding lending-of-last-resort operations by the European Central Bank (ECB) and the European Stability Mechanism (ESM). Since member states' financial fortunes are very different, inferences are not hard to make.

The bailing-in procedures are likely to increase funding costs, in the short term at least. There is also the need for a strong and timely financial back-stop (the €55 billion common resolution fund is pretty small, and its time of coming into being, 2024, is pretty remote).[14] Other policy arrangements, going beyond the operations of a banking union, are required to make the euro zone, the EU, function properly. This said, one also needs to consider that banking sectors in the newer EU countries are heavily controlled by European groups and that participating in the working of the Single Supervisory Mechanism and the Single Resolution Fund presents benefits.

A threat of the zero lower bound?
Diminishing inflation has allowed monetary policy to be eased lately; the policy rate moved from 5.25 per cent in December 2013 to 2.75 per cent in December 2014, and reserve requirements were also brought down several times. In January 2015 the policy rate was cut further to 2.5 per cent and in February to 2.25 per cent. If inflation continues to be considerably below forecasts (not least due to the oil price fall) the NBR has the room to lower its policy rate further. It is telling that 2014 ended with an inflation rate of 0.8 per cent (considerably below 1.5 per cent, which is the lower bound of the band around the target of 2.5 per cent). A caution note for moving drastically further down would be linked with balancesheet effects and rising global risk aversion. One can infer that a threat of the zero lower bound in Romania is highly improbable in the near future.

Financial stability policy
Financial stability is a concern not quite of recent vintage. High euroiza-tion has always suffused the NBR's monetary policy with a concern for the balancesheet effect and for financial stability (apart from the concern to avoid bank failures, as happened in the late 1990s). The thinking at the NBR, which is shared more widely in the local policy-making community, is that financial stability policy should be a preserve of the central bank. This is due to the need to have thorough access to information and the ability to respond quickly to a crisis. The Cyprus crisis vindicated this approach, for Cypriot banks operate in Romania, too. The NBR had to act swiftly in coordination with the European authorities (ECB) and the central bank of Cyprus. How one can avoid conflicts of interest in formu-lating monetary policy and financial stability policy is not a trivial issue, but the experience available and the need to act coherently when things go wrong would arguably support the choice made until now.[15] Concern for financial stability implies measures to diminish the degree of euroization, even if accession in the euro area is an ultimate goal. And it is good that there is a tendency for the level of euro-denominated credits to come down

simultaneously with the relative rise in the share of lei-denominated credits lately. One can argue that a more active presence of local banks would be a favourable evolution, by considering the deleveraging undertaken by banks that operate EU-wide and which, sometimes, cater less to the needs of local markets.[16] Having said this, one should not underestimate the lessons from the collapse of Santo Espirito in Portugal and the failure of a couple of domestic banks in neighbouring Bulgaria. It may be good to have more domestic capital in local banking, but how banks are managed is the key issue in the end.

A puzzle with credit?

In CESEE countries, public debts and private debts are much lower than in most of the EU: is there a puzzle with credit?[17] In spite of deleveraging and the importance of general external funding requirements (GEFR) for the way financial markets judge sovereign creditworthiness, public and private sector debt is much higher in the mature EU economies than in the EU's newer member states in Central and Eastern Europe.[18] One explanation could be that the latter, and CESEE in general, enjoyed the 'benefits' of the Great Moderation (rising indebtedness) later. But there could be other explanations as well, such as: they also experienced boom-and-bust dynamics; there was substantial resource misallocation, with much investment in non-tradables (which shows up in the volume of non-performing loans); trade and finance and foreign direct investment (FDI), link CESEE organically with the rest of the EU (deleveraging is a facet of this financial integration); local market sentiment hinges on EU-wide dynamics; banks have tightened credit conditions and many firms are reluctant to borrow more because of their debts; and household debt must be judged in conjunction with people's incomes and their wealth (lending takes into account the assets of individuals and firms).[19]

Although local banks rely increasingly on deposits, domestic savings are still low. Therefore, parent banks' policies and overall credit conditions in the EU will continue to shape bank landing in CESEE in the years to come. There is a powerful size effect at work here, for these are small economies and their growth prospects depend on what happens in the hard core of the euro zone.

A creditless recovery?

Why did GDP bounce back after 2011, despite the dwindling stock of credit? Is there a 'credit-less recovery' in Romania?[20] Here it is important to distinguish between stock and flows (especially in case of massive write-offs): new credits condition economic recovery; big recessions are followed by recoveries that may not involve credit expansion, for there is already much liquidity in the system (when dormant liquidity wakes up, it may make new lending redundant); there is fragmentation in the credit markets, with small and medium-sized enterprises being in much pain and some of them being priced out of markets for the wrong reasons; there is a substantial underground economy that is not captured by statistics and which can lubricate a financial system that has partially broken down; commercial credit can be a substitute for bank lending, and arrears too can play a role in this regard. Finally, EU funds can add liquidity, to the tune of several percentage points of GDP. Moreover, export growth was key in driving economic recovery in recent years; productivity gains were also important. With regard to the distinction between credit stock and credit flow, it is possible that deleveraging (which shows up in the decrease of the stock[21]) should not preclude new bank lending, especially in an economy in which capital markets play a minor role.

Macroprudential considerations and macroeconomic policy
One has to consider that many of the macroprudential tools recommended by the European Systemic Risk Board (ESRB) or the Financial Stability Board (FSB), and so on, are poorly tested, and in some instances the experience gained is not highly relevant. Spain's poor record in spite of its dynamic provisioning and prudent fiscal policy is quite telling in this respect. Romania's own experience with trying to stem massive capital inflows indicates the limited room of manoeuvre in the context of the 'single market'. Likewise, the crisis that started in 2008 forces us to revisit the pluses and minuses of deep financial markets in relation to the size of the economy. In addition, one wonders whether the use of highly sophisticated financial products is warranted when markets can be so erratic and volatile. The experience of emerging markets in dealing with massive capital flows allows a series of inferences:

First, the macro picture:

- Macroeconomic fundamentals (external imbalances, gross external debt and short-term debt, budget deficits, and so on) matter much, but they do not provide insulation against massive tidal waves, such as: (1) the size of liquidity that poured into emerging markets since 2005: emerging markets attracted about $7 trillion since then through a mix of FDI, mergers and acquisitions, and investment in stocks and bonds, according to International Institute of Finance data; between 2010 and 2013, private capital flows jumped to 6 per cent of emerging markets'cumulated GDP; (2) much borrowing has taken place primarily via bond markets (capital markets); (3) the emergence of index-tracking exchange-traded funds, which has

increased the indiscriminate nature of emerging market flows, and
which leaves them vulnerable to across-the-board withdrawals.
- Sound macroeconomic fundamentals can make the difference
  between a recession and a balance of payments crisis (a 'sudden
  stop').
- Private indebtedness matters as much as public debt.
- External indebtedness, of gross external financing requirements
  (GEFR), is important in explaining the fragility of emerging markets
  in respect of external shocks.

Second, capital markets and fragility to external shocks:

- The size of domestic saving and the base of domestic investors help
  to make an economy less fragile (more robust).[22]
- Deep financial markets entail pluses and minuses (non-resident
  investors' share of local currency-denominated bond issues).
- Despite much improved economic policies in many emerging
  markets, investors tend to lump them together in times of sell-off.
- There are capital markets instruments which entail an indiscriminate
  impact on emerging economies (exchange-traded funds).
- Capital controls are hardly effective in the event of massive outflows.
- Political instability amplifies economic instability and risk aversion.

Third, policy responses:

- Rises in monetary policy rates do not, frequently, have a decisive
  impact (see Turkey, India in the autumn of 2013), while there can be
  a severe impact on economic activity.
- The cost of funding goes up when policy rates increase.
- European emerging markets are, arguably, better prepared now than
  during 2008–2009 (some of them had awful macroeconomic imbalances before the crisis hit), but high external indebtedness and substantial GEFR continue to make some of them vulnerable.

Capital markets move with financial cycles. What drives a European
financial cycle (if there is any) is of utmost importance for the emerging
markets of Europe, whose macroeconomic policies are heavily influenced
by what happens in the core economies. A European cycle depends on
crisis management policies at the EU level and its intrinsic drivers. The
latter also depend on the paradigms policy-makers embrace. It appears
that there is a clash of visions in this regard: 'the Basel view' takes a long-
term perspective and stresses factors and policies which have amplified

boom-and-bust dynamics and led to the misallocation of resources. Not delaying policy rate increases would be a means to combat future booms and busts, and new big crises. Another view highlights the threat of debt deflation, especially in Europe, of being stuck in a very bad equilibrium with intense hysteresis phenomena that may invite social and political troubles.[23] Income inequality and highly skewed wealth distribution, which would impair economic growth, is a factor that should be factored into both visions; it can bring them closer and reconcile policies that can bolster aggregate demand (for the sake of avoiding debt deflation) with measures that take into account resource misallocation.

When it comes to world capital markets, we seem to be at the beginning of a bumpy ride, at a time when the crisis is not yet over (in Europe, the impact of the financial crisis blends with the crisis of the euro zone). It is never futile to stress how important for global markets is the international policy regime, and what big players in the global economy do.

Economic recovery in the euro zone

This concern is of utmost importance since it conditions the very sustainability of economic growth in the newer EU member states via many channels, including finance. Were debt deflation to happen in wide stretches of the euro zone, this would quite likely bring the Romanian economy to very slow motion, or even a halt. Economic recovery in the euro zone depends not only on national economic policies, but also on euro area-level policies: on whether there is a significant bolstering of aggregate demand at the euro area level which should help avoid debt deflation (is the Juncker plan sufficient in this regard?), the operations of the ECB[24] and, not least, structural reforms in various countries.[25] More debt restructuring may be needed to help the private sector be reignited (Borio, 2012 [2014], 2014).

A middle-income trap?

This is a concern rooted in the need for a catching-up economy to have a mix of policies which favour education, innovation and constant upgrading of value added in the economy. It is not an easy task for policy-makers when the economy is small, deeply integrated in outer markets, and with local markets dominated by international groups. Why should a central bank have this concern? Because its policies are increasingly under pressure due to the need to protect financial stability in view of internal and external imbalances and their impact on the robustness and resilience of the economy. A huge challenge for policy-makers here is how to mobilize substantial efficiency reserves, which in the Romanian case are ubiquitous at micro and macro levels.

15.4   THE WIDER CONTEXT

15.4.1   A Trade-Off between Economic Growth and Financial Stability?

This is probably the most profound '*grosse Frage*' for academic econo-mists and policy-makers nowadays. One could say that this issue sets a Basel view against a view that is more concerned with the level of resources used in the economy, with the need to combat high unemploy-ment and avoid poor equilibria. One view takes a longer-term perspective. The other pays attention to what may push an economy toward a bad equilibrium and keep it stuck there because of hysteresis phenomena. A related question is the growth potential of mature economies. Gordon (2014) would say that it is lower than in the past, owing to a range of structural factors including demographics and education. Others would argue that this growth potential may be eroded by not adopting the right policies now, in the wake of the current crisis. In contrast, there is a line of reasoning, the Basel view included, which fears that attempts to foster short-term growth may sow the seeds of future crises by enhancing the search for yield and risky behaviour (Borio, 2014; Rajan, 2013). Is there a way out of this conundrum? Summers (2014) seems to be quite pes-simistic in this regard. One would also have to consider the relationship between economic growth and income distribution. It is quite an amazing change to hear top officials of major central banks voicing concerns in this regard: their worries that income distribution may hurt economic growth (Yellen, 2014; Mersch, 2014; Haldane, 2014); IMF and OECD experts voice similar concerns.[26] The debate encompassing these issues is of enormous importance to central banks, for their mission cannot be divorced from what policy-makers do in order to resuscitate their economies.

15.4.2   The Governance of the Euro Zone and its Fiscal Underpinnings

Fiscal rectitude is not sufficient for rescuing the euro zone. There is a need for elements of fiscal integration (the issue of common bonds, eventu-ally), tools for dealing with asymmetric shocks (such as insurance for unemployed people) and stronger means for fostering economic conver-gence. Fiscal capacity, as put forward by former EU President Herman van Rompuy, encapsulates such requirements.[27] It is justified to decry, as some do, the insufficient resources that the EU budget assigns to research and development-based activities, to innovation, as a means to help EU member states cope with the challenges posed by the emerging economic powers. But it is also wrong to underestimate the impact on the euro zone, on the EU in general, of growing economic cleavages among member states.

15.4.3 The Reform of Finance: Its Size, Content, and Shadow Banking

The Larosiere and Liikanen reports commissioned by the European Commission, the Turner, Vickers and Tyrie reports in the United Kingdom (UK), the Dodd–Franck legislation and Volcker's proposals in the United States (US), and what the FSB and the Bank for International Settlements (BIS) do, indicate a logic and action of overall reform.[28] Measures have been taken in order to bolster capital and liquidity requirements, reduce leverage, limit pay, enhance transparency and discourage excessive risk-taking, and so on. But, arguably, more has to be done. For example, dealing with the 'too big to fail' syndrome requires the application of antitrust legislation, as it happens in various industrial sectors; this would imply splitting big financial entities. A sort of Glass–Steagall legislation should be restored, as after the Great Depression. Ring-fencing retail from trading activities is, arguably, not sufficient for protecting taxpayers.[29] More own capital (Admati and Hellwig, 2013) and less reliance on debt (as against the Modiglian–Miller theorem, which says that where capital comes from does not matter), and rules that prohibit the use of depositors' money for the own trading of banks, would also contribute to making systems more robust.

The robustness and resilience of financial systems has been much diminished by interconnectedness and the spreading use of derivatives. Via widespread unsound securitization banks have, arguably, relinquished their mission of due diligence in lending, and have gone much beyond what is prudent business conduct. In order to reduce its fragility, to make it more robust, the financial (banking) system needs to be 'modularized' (Haldane and May, 2011). This can be achieved, in spite of stern opposition from the financial industry: by promoting more simple banking (finance), downsizing large groups, separating activities, prohibiting the use of certain financial products, regulation of the shadow banking sector (hedge funds and private equity funds included), forcing transactions on open venues and mandating reporting and transparency standards, and severely punishing frauds and market-rigging. More should be done when it comes to diminishing the casino-like activities and regulating shadow banking, enforcing ethical standards, and tackling the threats posed by rising electronic (algorithmic) trading and cyber-attacks.

One could argue that what hedge and private equity funds use in their modelling is their exclusive business; that banks and insurance companies are in a different league, which would make them objects of public scrutiny and regulation when it comes to risk modelling. But hedge funds and other asset management funds, and shadow banking in general, do create systemic risks through their operations that can be huge and can destabilize markets.

15.4.4   Trilemma or 'dilemma'

BIS experts highlight that the 'financial cycle' has much lower frequency than business cycles and is much more ample time-wise. In this context, the observation that the financial cycle depends critically on policy regimes (Borio, 2012) is of exceptional relevance. For, although cycles can hardly be precluded, the amplitude of boom-and-bust dynamics is influenced by policies, as is the size of the financial industry – which is oversized in more than a few advanced economies.

15.4.5   A New Bretton Woods is Needed

We need to rediscover the Bretton Woods logic and spirit for the sake of tackling three formidable crises which blend into each other: a financial crisis, the euro zone crisis, and the crisis of the international regime against the backdrop of shifting power in the world economy. The future international economic system will, quite likely, be carved out amongst three major currency blocs, with the US, the EU and China providing the lynchpins. A reshaped international regime would involve rules for the realignment of major currencies and measures in order to mitigate destabilizing capital flows, including financial transactions taxes; rules for preserving an open trade regime, but that would consider the needs of the poorest countries at a time when ecological degradation and food safety are a rising global concern. The functioning of the IFIs would have to keep in mind the shifting power redistribution in the world and lessons of economic modernization. The Group of Twenty (G-20) has not been effective enough in this respect. A new international regime would have to combat tax evasion and avoidance, not least because of the heavy burden bank rescues operations have put on public budgets, and on taxpayers. In this respect, legislation that limits tax havens to the utmost would make sense economically, socially and ethically. In domestic finance, restoring a sort of Glass–Steagall legislation would be more than welcome, together with measures that deal with the 'too big to fail' syndrome, limit over-risky activities (trading), and downsize finance and bring it back to reason, making it more simple. The EU and the US have the key role in promoting uniform norms in the regulation and supervision of finance. The FSB could help enforce this new framework. The main aim in this respect is not the avoidance of arbitrage attempts by firms, but the very function of finance in the service of economies. The US and the EU have the key role in reinventing the logic and spirit of Bretton Woods, in taming finance, for the sake of regaining economic stability and avoiding 'dark corners' (Blanchard, 2014), in order to defend democratic order.

15.5 FINAL REMARKS

Central bankers have a much more complicated and difficult job nowadays. Not only has the impact of the financial crisis combined with a persistent euro zone crisis, but cognitive and operational models have been questioned. It is a period of increasing uncertainty, when central banks navigate in uncharted territory, aptly captured by the diplomatic euphemism of 'unconventional policies'. Furthermore, a threat of 'secular stagnation' and the menace of debt deflation in the euro area foreshadow years of painstaking efforts to keep the boats afloat. Central banks in the newer EU member states have their tasks shaped by membership, or not, in the euro area, the size of domestic macroeconomic imbalances and of public and private debt, the degree of euroization, the intensity of deleveraging, and so on. Preserving financial stability is crucial and this mission hinges enormously on the health of the banking sector in Europe, and on the effectiveness of macroprudential tools. This goal will influence monetary policy, and inflation-targeting regimes. Joining the banking union is an option under consideration in view of the heavy presence of international banks on local financial markets. But the deep interest and concern of any lucid policy-makers is to see the functioning of a 'complete' banking union, which should help to fine-tune the policy and institutional arrangements of the euro area. An adequate design and better policies in the euro area would help to prevent debt deflation and combat the threats to the very existence of the EU.

Romania has gone through a very painful process of macroeconomic adjustment since 2009. Its 'new age' dilemmas are fundamentally linked with challenges facing all EU member states.

ACKNOWLEDGEMENTS

The views expressed in this chapter are the author's own and do not necessarily represent the position of the institutions he is affiliated with. The author thanks Adrian Alter (IMF and Konstanz University), Cosmina Amariei (Centre for European Policy Studies, CEPS-Brussels), Valentin

Lazea (NBR), and Laurian Lungu (Cardiff Business School) for their comments. The author also thanks Amalia Fugaru and Cristian Stanica for assistance in the technical processing of data.

NOTES

1. Kornai, with his masterpiece (1980), and Kolodko and MacMahon (1987) analyse repressed inflation in a command system.
2. For the Tošovský dilemma and the way IMF viewed its significance, see Lipschitz et al. (2002).
3. Were it to operate, a European financial cycle would mix with what BIS experts (Borio, 2012 [2014]) call the 'global financial cycle'.
4. 'The characteristics of the Romanian economy do not favor the "divine coincidence" if hard inflation targeting is implemented. The economy still needs substantial relative price adjustments, wages have to be more flexible, the economic structure shows too much power and the tax system is still pretty distorting. . . Since the NBR has announced its intention to introduce IT in 2005 a 'soft' form is, arguably, a better choice than a hard version' (Daianu and Kallai, 2005, in Liebscher et al., 2005, p.138).
5. Dynamic comparative advantages lay behind Asian economies' rejection of real appreciation of their currencies. There was another reason as well: the build-up of forex reserves as buffers against an unfavourable international environment. The crisis of 1997–1998 taught them a very painful lesson.
6. The GDP gap ante- and post-crisis is quite controversial. The Basel view would see the gap close substantially in view of the need to consider the financial cycle.
7. This is Svensson's (2014) argument when he discourages the use of the policy rate as a means to forestall a bubble when the economy is weak. Instead, he asks for the use of macroprudential tools. On the other hand, there is the view that emphasizes the use of the policy rate as a means to mitigate the amplitude of financial cycles (Borio, 2014; Caruana, 2014). Woodford (2012) seems to take a mixed position on this matter.
8. This concept was used by the Harvard economist John Kenneth Galbraith in a 1977 TV series, *The Age of Uncertainty*, in which he tried to portray the world in the way he saw it at that time.
9. Krugman (1997) talked about 'diminished expectations' as a proper description of entering the new century. Luttwak (1999) and Reich (2008) highlighted insecurity in modern society, in a global economy.
10. The group, which was chaired by Ugo Pagano and assisted by Sam Langfeld, included Viral Acharya, Arnoud Boot, Markus Brunnermeier, Claudia Buch, Martin Hellwig, Andre Sapir and Ieke van den Burg.
11. As Mark Carney (2014), the head of the Financial Stability Board and Vice-Chairman of the ESRB says, by echoing William Dudley and Minouche Safik, 'the succession of scandals mean it is simply untenable to argue that the problem is one of a few bad apples. The issue is with the barrels in which they are stored.'
12. As Borio (2012 [2014]) puts it, 'macroeconomics without the financial cycle is like Hamlet without the prince'. Monetary policy regimes and inflation targeting are going to be influenced by this new outlook regarding financial stability.
13. Buch and Holtemoeller (2014), while examining dynamic stochastic general equilibrium (DSGE) models, acknowledge their weaknesses in explaining crises in developed economies and allude to the modelling of balance-of-payments crises in emerging economies (Calvo, 1995; Krugman, 1998, quoted in Buch and Holtemoeller, 2014; Velasco, 1987). Borio and BIS experts favour a financial cycle-based, disequilibrium (Minsky-type) approach. For an explanation of crises in the euro zone see Stein (2014).

14. All this implies that national budgets would have to step in, in order to deal with banks' failure.
15. The Governor of the NBR is the head of its Monetary Policy Committee while the First Deputy Governor is the head of its Supervision Committee. Ultimately, it is the Board of the NBR which makes the key decisions with regard to monetary policy and financial stability policy.
16. The local bank Transylvania took over the operations of Volksbank in Romania at the end of 2014.
17. Borio (2012 [2014], p.29) argues that a main indicator for the financial cycle is credit. In the CESEE it is probably the speed of credit expansion (and less its stock) together with poor resource allocation that lies behind the boom-and-bust dynamic.
18. For example, in 2012, according to Eurostat, the public debt and the private debt (except financial institutions) were, as a share of GDP, in Germany 81 per cent and 107 per cent, respectively; in the Netherlands they were 71.3 per cent and 219 per cent, respectively; in the UK, 89 per cent and 178 per cent respectively; in Italy, 127 per cent and 126.4 per cent, respectively. Whereas the figures, in the same year, in Poland were 55.6 per cent and 74.8 per cent, respectively; in Slovakia, 52.7 per cent and 73 per cent, respectively; in the Czech Republic, 46.2 per cent and 72.4 per cent, respectively; in Romania, 38 per cent and 73 per cent, respectively.
19. According to Eurostat, in 2012, salaries in the EU-15 (the better-off countries) had an average share of the GDP of more than 50 per cent, as against 33 per cent in Romania. In the same year, this share was 51.6 per cent in Germany, 52 per cent in Finland, 54 per cent in Sweden, 53 per cent in France, 45 per cent in Hungary, 38.6 per cent in Bulgaria. In 2012, the share of profits in GDP was 38.4 per cent in the EU-15, while it was 54.5 per cent in Romania, 48.4 per cent in Bulgaria and *circa* 40 per cent in Hungary.
20. The stock of credit, as a share of GDP, went down in Romania during the crisis years. This tendency would validate a delinking between credit and economic activity after episodes of crisis and when access to external finance is pretty difficult – so-called 'creditless recoveries' (Calvo et al., 2006; Takats and Upper, 2013).
21. Foreign banks have reduced their exposure to the Romanian economy by more than €5 billion in recent years (NBR statistics).
22. According to NBR data, non-resident holdings of sovereign titles (domestic market issues) were 19.4 per cent of the total in September 2014.
23. See Posen and Ubide (2014).
24. A problem for the ECB to replicate the Fed's and the Bank of England's experience with QEs is that capital markets play a much smaller role in finance in Europe; this limits the room for repairing a broken transmission mechanism.
25. Mario Draghi's speech in Jackson Hole, in August 2014, in which he highlighted these three components, is quite indicative in this regard. Giavazzi and Tabellini (2014) consider that there is need for a much larger boost to aggregate demand than what the Juncker plan suggests. See also Butiglione et al. (2014) and Wolff (2014) in this respect.
26. Korinek and Kreamer (2014), from the BIS, observe that financial deregulation favours Wall Street (as against Main Street), and that it has important redistributive effects. Market imperfections would ask for regulatory interventions which would increase (upside and downside) risk-sharing between finance and the rest of society. For the linkage between economic growth and income distribution, see also Piketty (2014), Piketty and Saez (2013) and Ostry et al. (2014).
27. Studies made for the European Commission, more than three decades ago, highlighted the need for a euro zone budget, which should go over 5 per cent of the cumulated GDP of the member states (the MacDougall report). There is talk nowadays, too, about the need to create a euro zone budget; see, *inter alia*, the Glienicker Group (2013) report in Germany, and the Eiffel Group (2014) report in France.
28. One of the legislative pieces of the European Parliament dealing with the need to reform the regulation and supervision of financial markets is a report by Ieke van den Burg

and Daniel Daianu (2008) and the related resolution of the European Parliament of 9 October 2008.
29.   The proposal made by the US Senators John McCain and Elisabeth Warren does make sense and should be considered in Europe too. As a *Financial Times* editorial stresses, 'it would eradicate the testosterone-charged culture of investment banking from retail activities' ('Split the Banks', 13 July 2013). See also Laeven et al. (2014) and Gapper (2015).

REFERENCES

Admati, A. and M. Hellwig (2013), *The New Bankers'Clothes: What's Wrong with Banking and What to Do about It*, Princeton, NJ: Princeton University Press.
Blanchard, Olivier (2014), 'Where danger lurks', VoxEu, 3 October.
Blanchard, O. and J. Ostry (2012), 'The multilateral approach to capital controls', VoxEU.
Borio, Claudio (2012 [2014]),'The financial cycle and macroeconomics: what have we learned and what are the policy implications', BIS Working Papers No. 395, December 2012; and in E. Nowotny, D. Ritzberger-Gruenwald and P. Backe (eds) (2014), *Financial Cycles and the Real Economy: Lessons for CESEE Countries*, Cheltenham, UK and Northampton, MA, USA: Edward Elgar Publishing, pp. 10–36.
Borio, Claudio (2014),'The financial cycle, the debt trap and secular stagnation', presentation at the BIS General Meeting, Basel, 29 June.
Brunnermeier, Markus K., T. Eisenbach and Y. Sannikov (2012), 'Macroeconomics with financial frictions: a survey', NBER Working Paper no. 18102.
Buch, Claudia and Oliver Holtemoeller (2014), 'Do we need new modeling approaches in macroeconomics?', in E. Nowotny, D. Ritzberger-Gruenwald and P. Backe (eds), *Financial Cycles and the Real Economy: Lessons for CESEE Countries* Cheltenham, UK and Northampton, MA, USA: Edward Elgar Publishing, pp. 36–58.
Burg, I. van den and D. Daianu (2008), 'Resolution of 9 October 2008 with the Recommendations to the Commission on Lamfalussy follow up: future structure of supervision', 2008/2148(INI), Brussels: European Parliament.
Butiglione, L., P. Lane, L. Reichlin and V. Reinhart (2014), 'Deleveraging? What deleveraging?', Geneva Reports on the World Economy 16, London: CEPR Press.
Calvo, C.A. (1995),'Varieties of capital market crises', Inter-American Development Bank, Working Paper No.4008, Research Department, Washington, DC.
Calvo, G., A. Izquierdo and E. Talvi (2006), 'Phoenix miracles in emerging markets', NBER Working Paper No. 12101.
Carney, Mark (2014), 'The future of financial reform', speech at the 2014 Monetary Authority of Singapore Lecture, Singapore, 17 November.
Caruana, Jaime (2014), 'Stepping out of the shadow of the crisis: three transitions for the world economy', speech at the General Meeting, BIS, Basel, 29 June.
Crafts, N. (2014), 'Secular stagnation: US hypochondria and EU disease?', in R. Baldwin and C. Teulings (eds), *Secular Stagnation: Facts, Causes and Cures*, VoxEU eBook, pp. 91–101, http://www.voxeu.org/content/secular-stagnation-facts-causes-and-cures.

Daianu, Daniel (1994), 'Inter-enterprise arrears in a post-command economy', IMF Working Papers, 54.

Daianu, Daniel (1997), 'Resource misallocation and strain: explaining shocks in post-command economies', Working Paper No. 96, November, Davidson Institute, Ann Arbor, MI.

Daianu, D., G. Basevi, C. D'Adda and R. Kumar (eds), *The Euro Zone Crisis and the Future of Europe*, London: Palgrave Macmillan.

Daianu, D. and E. Kallai (2005), 'Disinflation and monetary policy arrangements in Romania', in K. Liebscher, J. Christl, P. Mooslechner and D. Ritzberger-Grünwald (eds), *European Economic Integration and South East Europe*, Cheltenham, UK, and Northampton, MA, USA: Edward Elgar Publishing, pp.119–44.

Daianu, D. and R. Vranceanu (2002 [2003]), 'Opening the capital account of developing countries: some policy issues', William Davidson Institute Working Paper No. 511, 2002; also published by Acta Oeconomica, No. 3, 2003.

Draghi, Mario (2014), 'Unemployment in Europe', speech at the annual Central Bank Symposium, Jackson Hole, August.

Eichengreen, B. (2014), 'Secular stagnation: a review of the issues', in R. Baldwin and C. Teulings (eds), *Secular Stagnation: Facts, Causes and Cures*, VoxEU eBook, pp.41–7, available at: http://www.voxeu.org/sites/default/files/Vox_secular_stagnation.pdf.

Eiffel Group (2014), 'For a Euro Community', report, Bruegel, 14 February, available at www.bruegel.org/about//person/view/389-the-eiffel-group.

ESRB (2014), 'Is Europe overbanked?', Reports of the Advisory Scientific Committee, No. 4, ESRB, June.

Glienicker Group (2013), 'Towards a Euro Union', Report, Bruegel, 18 October, available at http://www.bruegel.org/nc/blog/detail/article/1173-towards-a-euro-union/ (first published in German by *Die Zeit*, 17 October 2013).

Gordon, Robert (2014), 'The Turtle's progress: secular stagnation meets the headwinds', in R. Baldwin and C. Teulings (eds), *Secular Stagnation: Facts, Causes and Cures*, a Vox eBook, pp.47–60, available at http://www.voxeu.org/sites/default/files/Vox_secular_stagnation.pdfBaldwin and Teulings.

Haldane, Andrew (2014), 'Twin Peaks', speech at the Kenilworth Chamber of Trade Business Breakfast, Kenilworth, 17 October.

Haldane, A and R.M. May (2011), 'Systemic risks in banking systems', *Nature*, January, Vol. 469.

Gapper, John (2015), 'Regulators are right to cut the biggest banks down to size', *Financial Times*, 8 January, p.9.

Giavazzi, F. and G. Tabellini (2014), 'How to jumpstart the euro zone economy', VoxEU, 21 August.

Isarescu, Mugur (2013), 'Relations between euro and non-euro countries within the banking union', speech at the Unicredit 15th International Advisory Board, Rome, 10 July.

Jimeno, J., F. Smets and J. Yiangou (2014), 'Secular stagnation: a view from the Eurozone', in R. Baldwin and C. Teulings (eds), *Secular Stagnation: Facts, Causes and Cures*, VoxEU eBook, pp.153–61, available at http://www.voxeu.org/sites/default/files/Vox_secular_stagnation.pdf.

Kolodko, W.G. and W.W. MacMahon (1987), 'Stagflation and shortageflation: a comparative approach', *Kyklos*, 40 (2), 176–97.

Koo, Richard (2011), 'The world in balance-sheet effect recession: causes, cure and policies', *Real World Economics Review*, 58, 19–37, available at http://www.paecon.net/PAEReview/issue58/whole58.pdf.

Korinek, A. and J. Kreamer (2014), 'The redistributive effects of financial deregulation: Wall Street vs. Main Street', BIS Working Papers, No. 468, October.

Kornai, J. (1980), *The Economics of Shortage*, Amsterdam: North Holland.

Krugman, Paul (1997), *The Age of Diminished Expectations*, Cambridge, MA: MIT Press.

Krugman, Paul (1998), 'What happened to AsiaAsia – or – bubble, boom, crash, theoretical notes on Asia's crisis', mimeo.

Laeven, L., L. Ratnovski and H. Tong (2014), 'Bank size and systemic risk', IMF Discussion Note, May.

Lipschitz, L., T. Lane and A. Mourmouras (2002), 'The Tošovský dilemma: capital surges in transition economies', *Finance and Development*, 39(3), available at http://www.imf.org/external/pubs/ft/fandd/2002/09/lipschit.htm.

Luttwak, Edward (1999), *Turbo Capitalism: Winners and Losers in the Global Economy*, New York: Harper&Collins.

Mersch, Yves (2014), 'Monetary policy and income inequality', speech at the Corporate Credit Conference, Muzinich, Zurich, 17 October.

Ostry, J.D., A. Berg and C. Tsangarides (2014), 'Redistribution, inequality and growth', IMF Discussion Note, February.

Piketty, Thomas (2014), *Capital in the Twenty-first Century*, Cambridge, MA: Harvard University Press.

Piketty, T. and E. Saez (2013), 'Top incomes and the Great Recession: recent evolutions and policy implications', *IMF Economic Review*, 61(3), 456–78.

Popa, C. et al. (2002), 'Inflation targeting: a new monetary policy regime for Romania', NBR Occasional Paper No. 1.

Posen, A. and A. Ubide (eds) (2014), 'Rebuilding Europe's common future', PIIE Briefing No. 14–5, December.

Rajan, R. (2013), 'A step in the dark: unconventional monetary policy after the crisis', Andrew Crockett Memorial Lecture, Basel, BIS, 23 June.

Reich, R. (2008), *Supercapitalism: The Transformation of Business, Democracy and Everyday Life*, New York: Random House.

Rey, Hélène (2013), 'Dilemma not trilemma: the global financial cycle and monetary policy independence', *Global Dimensions of Unconventional Monetary Policy*, Proceedings of the Federal Reserve Bank of Kansas City Symposium, Jackson Hole, 22–24 August.

Stein, J.L. (2014), 'The diversity of debt crises in Europe', in D. Daianu, G. Basevi, C. D'Adda and R. Kumar (eds), *The Euro Zone Crisis and the Future of Europe*, London: Palgrave Macmillan, pp. 25–39.

Stiglitz, J. (2010), 'Contagion, liberalization, and the optimal structure of globalization', *Journal of Globalization and Development*, 1(2), article 2.

Summers, Larry (2014), 'Reflections on the "new secular stagnation hypothesis"', updated version in R. Baldwin and C. Teulings (eds), *Secular Stagnation: Facts, Causes and Cures*, a Vox eBook, available at http://www.voxeu.org/sites/default/files/Vox_secular_stagnation.pdf.

Svensson, Lars E.O. (2014), 'Inflation targeting and "leaning against the wind"', *International Journal of Central Banking*, June, pp. 103–14.

Takats, E. and C. Upper (2013), 'Credit and growth after financial crises', BIS Working Papers No. 416, July.

Velasco, Andres (1987), 'Financial and balance of payments crises: a simple model of the Southern Cone experience', *Journal of Development Economics*, 27(1–2), 263–83.

Wolff, Guntram (2014), 'Monetary policy cannot solve secular stagnation alone', Brussels, Bruegel, 19 August, available at http://www.bruegel.org/nc/blog/detail/ article/1415-monetary-policy-cannot-solve-secular-stagnation-alone/; in Coen Teulings and Richard Baldwin (eds), *Secular Stagnation: Facts, Causes and Cures*, VoxEU eBook, available at http://www.voxeu.org/sites/default/files/Vox_ secular_stagnation.pdf.

Woodford, Michael (2012), 'Inflation targeting and financial stability', *Sveriges Riksbank Economic Review*, 1, 1–29.

Yellen, Janet (2014), 'Perspectives on inequality and opportunity from the survey of consumer finances', speech at the Conference on Economic Opportunity and Inequality, Federal Reserve Bank of Boston, Boston, MA, 17 October.

16. The monetary policy framework of the central bank of Montenegro: is financial stability a feasible central bank goal?

Nikola Fabris

16.1 A BRIEF HISTORY OF THE CENTRAL BANK OF MONTENEGRO

The idea of establishing a Central Bank of Montenegro (CBCG) was born in the early twentieth century, but in the end it was the Ministry of Finance rather than a central bank that issued the first Montenegrin money, in 1906. After World War I, Montenegro lost its independence and became a part of the Kingdom of Serbs, Croats and Slovenes, and afterwards of Yugoslavia. Yugoslavia had a dual financial system, consisting of the central monetary institution – the National Bank of Yugoslavia (NBY), which was the core of the system – and six national banks of the member republics. Therefore, the Central Bank of Montenegro existed in this period as an integral part of the NBY framework, with some degree of independence. Its status and functions changed throughout history, but it was essentially never authorized to pursue an independent monetary policy because that authority was in the hands of the National Bank of Yugoslavia, headquartered in Belgrade.

After the disintegration of the Socialist Federal Republic of Yugoslavia (SFRY), two former member republics – Montenegro and Serbia – formed the Federal Republic of Yugoslavia (FRY) on 28 April 1992. In the new country, the monetary system was recentralized, with the National Bank of Montenegro losing its autonomy. A high level of monetary and financial centralization was established, providing policy-makers with great leverage for manipulation.

As a result of the war in the former Yugoslavia and sanctions imposed by the United Nations, monetary policy was used to finance the budget and social issues. A huge bureaucratic apparatus of the former FRY supported an increase in inflation, generated by printing money. Most of the apparatus remained in Belgrade, showing not the slightest intention of dealing with fiscal adjustments in the existing situation, although it was obvious that the war spreading in 1992 would not be short-lived. Consequently, the former FRY recorded one of the highest hyperinflations in the world, with Montenegro and the National Bank of Montenegro lacking the instruments to influence these policies, but suffering all the consequences of hyperinflation.

This situation nourished the wish of Montenegro of pursuing an independent course of monetary policy regardless of its participation in the FRY. Building on the practice of both private individuals and the business sector of transacting and saving in German Marks that had evolved over the years, the Montenegrin government opted for a dollarization model. Instead of the dinar, the world's worst currency at the time, as estimated by Hanke (2000) in November 1999, Montenegro introduced a parallel currency system, one in which the German Mark (DEM) was made legal tender and allowed to freely float alongside Montenegro's other legal tender, the dinar. The entire process was conducted swiftly and without any support or guidance of the International Monetary Fund (IMF). As of January 2001, the German Mark became the only legal tender, with the euro taking over as the official means of payment as of June 2002.

The Monetary Council[1] governed the National Bank of Montenegro from the moment the German Mark was adopted until the establishment of the Central Bank of Montenegro. This body enacted numerous regulations which enabled the German Mark to be fully accepted as the means for payments, accounting and hoarding. The Central Bank was established in March 2001 (Fabris et al., 2004).

Montenegro also met all theoretical requirements for a successful implementation of dollarization. It was a small, highly open country with experience of hyperinflation in the past, with almost no seigniorage income, with a great share of foreign trade with the European Union (EU), and substantial flexibility of the labour force (a great number of people were employed outside Montenegro).

Following the introduction of dollarization, the situation in the monetary, financial and banking sectors of Montenegro slowly but surely began to show signs of increasing levels of confidence in the new monetary regime. Modest at first, an increase in deposits soon became notable, and during 2003 loans, primarily the short-term ones, grew significantly. However, it should also be stressed that at this time long-term loans also recorded growth.

16.2   THE MONETARY POLICY FRAMEWORK OF THE CENTRAL BANK OF MONTENEGRO

The Central Bank of Montenegro operates within the established euroization regime, with corresponding monetary policy objectives and instruments. Its main monetary policy objective, which is also defined by the Constitution, is to preserve financial stability.

When it comes to price stability, the statutory mandate of the CBCG is to contribute to the accomplishment of price stability. The reason for this somewhat specific objective is reflected in the absence of monetary policy instruments, that is, in the low efficiency of the existing instruments. After all, inflation, the traditional objective of the central bank, cannot be influenced with the existing monetary policy instruments. However, in the conditions of a highly open and liberal economy, the euroization system looks like a kind of self-balancing mechanism. This means that if the inflation rate is viewed over a longer period, it is actually at the level of average inflation rates in the euro area. Broken down by individual years, deviations are obvious in both directions, but in the long term, the inflation rate returns to the euro area average. This means that there are time lags, which are not too long.

Given that the CBCG is not an issuing central bank, it does not set a reference interest rate. The performance of open market operations is possible in theory if capital and reserves available to the CBCG are used. However, bearing in mind their limitations, this instrument has not been used in practice so far. Also, there are several different credit lines for liquidity support to banks.

This leaves the reserve requirement as the only real monetary policy instrument. There was a lot of experimenting with this instrument in the past: trying to stimulate lending activity, lower interest rates, improve the maturity structure of deposits. However, when it comes to these objectives, the practice has shown, and studies have confirmed, a poor efficiency of this instrument (Kalezić, 2006). Therefore, this instrument is currently used to support the preservation of financial stability.

Maintaining financial stability in Montenegro can be described via three lines of defence. The first line is prevention, the second is increasing the system's resilience to shocks, and the third line is crisis management. All three dimensions are equally important (Figure 16.1).

The CBCG has developed mechanisms to monitor and preserve financial stability. The key challenges that the CBCG is facing in implementing the framework for preserving financial stability include limited instruments, the absence of reliable time series, and limited experience in implementing the framework. The key threat to financial stability is a relatively high level of non-performing loans.

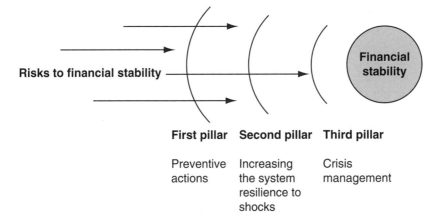

Source: Žugić and Fabris (2014).

Figure 16.1   *Three-dimensional approach to preserving financial stability*

Maintaining confidence in the banking sector is of vital importance to avoid massive bank runs and maintain financial stability. Fast payout to depositors and limiting negative economic effects of bank bankruptcy or liquidation on the remaining parts of the banking sector may boost public confidence. Quick bank resolution implies lowering costs and minimizing the loss of assets and franchise values. Allowing problem banks to continue operating causes market disruptions and increases moral hazard and the costs of problem bank resolution. In order to prevent or at least mitigate crisis in some banks, the CBCG may provide liquidity support to solvent banks to ensure their regular operation or, in exceptional circumstances, when it assesses that providing financial assistance is necessary to prevent negative repercussions on the banking sector's stability and soundness.

A Financial Stability Council (FSC) has also been established. The Council is chaired by the Governor of the CBCG, and the members include the Minister of Finance, the President of the Securities and Exchange Commission and the President of the Council of the Insurance Supervision Agency. The FSC serves to coordinate discussion about all potential risks to the financial stability and coordinates activities for preserving financial stability. The FSC passed the National Contingency Plan and the proposal of the Lex Specialis to be sent for adoption to Parliament in case of a crisis, which would increase the rights of institutions included in the financial crisis resolution. Moreover, the Lex Specialis allows the use of additional instruments other than those prescribed under the existing legislation.

16.3   IS FINANCIAL STABILITY A FEASIBLE CENTRAL BANK OBJECTIVE?

Price stability is the prevailing objective of modern central banks. As the global financial crisis has shown, by aiming to achieve a narrow price stability objective, central banks may come to neglect developments in credit growth and asset prices. They may then miss a build-up of credit and leverage in the system that, over a longer horizon, proves unsustainable (Nier, 2009). Had the United States Federal Reseve System (Fed) reacted to the emergence of asset bubbles in the property market in a timely manner, the global financial crisis would have probably been much less severe.

Historically, some central banks, such as the Fed, were established for the very purpose of preserving financial stability. Among the modern central banks, some pursue financial stability as their secondary objective, but the Central Bank of Montenegro is the only one with the primary mandate of preserving financial stability. This gives rise to the question of whether financial stability can and/or should become the goal of central banks. There is no consensus today about this issue since on one side we have economists who advocate that the central bank should be 'leaning against the wind', while on the other side we have those who emphasize, like Bernanke and Gertler (2001), that using interest rate policy in this way may not be powerful enough to dampen the upswing of asset prices and leverage, and that if it were used, it would create costs for the central bank's other objectives.

Financial stability does not have a generally accepted definition and, unlike inflation, it cannot be numerically expressed. As Crockett (2002) stated, monetary stability refers to price stability, while financial stability refers to the stability of key financial institutions and markets. Financial stability usually implies the absence of banking crises or large financial market fluctuations.

The Deutsche Bundesbank (2003) defined financial stability as a steady state in which the financial system efficiently performs its key economic functions and is able to do so even in the event of shocks, stress situations and periods of profound structural change. According to Gjedrem (2005), financial stability is achieved if households and enterprises may obtain optimal consumption and investment over time in the conditions of a well-functioning financial system that can intermediate between savers and borrowers and redistribute risk in a satisfactory manner, with an efficient allocation of real economic resources over time. Wieser (2005) defines financial stability as a financial system capable of absorbing severe shocks without triggering a financial crisis, that is, financial stress that has cross-sectoral spillovers with negative macroeconomic effects. Schinassy (2006) believes that a stable financial system allows market players to efficiently allocate economic resources, and to adequately determine the cost and manage financial risks and that a stable financial system is also able to perform these functions and when faced with external shocks and imbalances. The European Central Bank (2014) indicates that financial stability poses a:

> condition in which the financial system – comprising of financial intermediaries, markets and market infrastructures – is capable of withstanding shocks and the unravelling of financial imbalances, thereby mitigating the likelihood of disruptions in the financial intermediation process which are severe enough to significantly impair the allocation of savings to profitable investment opportunities.

On the other hand, there are authors who claim that financial stability cannot be defined, but only financial instability. Thus, Mishkin (1999) points out that financial instability occurs when shocks to the financial system interfere with information flows so that the financial system can no longer do its job of channelling funds to those with productive investment opportunities. Ferguson (2003) defines financial instability as a situation characterized by these three basic criteria:

- some important set of financial asset prices seems to have diverged sharply from fundamentals;
- market functioning and credit availability have been significantly distorted; and
- aggregate spending deviates significantly from the economy's ability to produce.

The global financial crisis has clearly shown that financial instability is a situation that is much more dangerous for central banks than inflation. An economy can operate in an inflation environment, albeit with difficulties, provided that inflation does not turn into hyperinflation. However, in case of a financial crisis, for example the banking system collapse, the entire economy becomes paralyzed. In the opinion of T. Padoa-Schioppa (2002), presented in a European Central Bank (ECB) study, 'the involvement of central banks in financial stability began when they undertook the issuance of money as paper currency (i.e. banknotes), which replaced previous metallic currencies'.

The first problem encountered when delegating the responsibility for financial stability to central banks is that not even the central banks with the broadest possible powers can cover all aspects of financial stability. Central banks are traditionally responsible for the banking system,[2] those with broader powers may also cover financial lease companies and insurance, but nowhere in the world does a central bank control the capital market, stock exchanges, investment funds, and the like.

Therefore, the issue of financial stability in most countries is not solely the responsibility of the central bank, but there is a division of responsibilities between central banks, finance ministries and supervisory agencies. Bearing in mind that the central bank may not be the only institution to be responsible for financial stability, this begs the question why financial stability is considered as an objective of central banks. The answer lies in the fact that there is a plethora of evidence to support the hypothesis that a future financial crisis is predicted by the expansion of money and banking loans (Goodhart, 2005). Also, the opinion is quite widespread that financial stability and price stability always go hand in hand (Cukierman, 1996; Schwartz, 1995; Issing et al., 2006). At the same time, monetary cycles can boost real cycles. The best example is the Asian crisis in the 1990s when the weaknesses in the financial sector triggered a drop in economic activity and strengthened the impact of shocks on the real economy. Also, most frequent causes of financial crises originate from banks which are often subject to the supervision and regulation of central banks.

Another problem relates to the fact that financial stability and price stability can be conflicting objectives. For example, inflationary pressures require a contractionary monetary policy which may adversely affect liquid assets in the banking system and, consequently, financial stability. However, the absence of stable prices is a major threat to financial stability. Deflation could lead to recession, which in turn could lead to financial instability. Deflation tends to trigger a vicious circle of an increasing real value of debt and a decreasing value of assets, which leads to defaults. Also, high inflation, and especially hyperinflation, is a serious threat to financial stability, because hyperinflation primarily damages the financial system. All previous hyperinflation episodes were followed by a collapse of the banking system and other financial institutions (Dimitrijević and Fabris, 2012). Therefore, financial stability and price stability are complementary objectives in the long term, but sometimes trade-offs have to be made in the short term. One should also take into account the complementarity of the lender-of-last-resort function to financial stability preservation.

The aforesaid indicates that while the central bank cannot be the institution that will be solely responsible for financial stability in developed market economies, the neglect of financial stability can lead to a number of risks to the central bank:

- a collapse of the banking system that would prevent the pursuit of monetary policy;

- loss of credibility for the central bank because the financial system is traditionally associated with the central bank;
- occurrence of inflation due to the injection of significant bailout funds in the banking system;
- cessation of the transmission mechanism functioning;
- capital flight, with negative implications for the exchange rate, inflation, monetary policy pursuit, and the like.

A study of the Bank for International Settlements (BIS) shows that even those central banks that do not have an explicit mandate consider the pursuit of systemic stability and the stability of payment and settlement systems as one of their key duties. Although central banks cannot cover all aspects of financial stability, there are currently no other institutions that have been set up to perform this task, nor are there institutions other than central banks whose instruments can affect financial stability – with financial instability generating immeasurable costs in terms of losses in production, employment and financial resources (needed for bank resolution), as well as a long-term loss of credibility.

The risk of financial cycles becoming stronger, and economic booms and busts more disruptive, could grow in the future. This could endanger financial stability, even though a sound supervisory framework reduces the risk. The way forward is to enhance cooperation among central banks and supervisory authorities in addressing financial instabilities, and to combine more system-wide and countercyclical supervisory policies with the willingness of central banks to address financial stability concerns (Padoa-Schioppa, 2002). What is clear from the ongoing crisis is that it is by no means always easy or costless for monetary authorities to 'clean up the mess'. Monetary policy may lose its effectiveness in doing so when the unwinding of financial imbalances adversely affects or puts in doubt the solvency of the banking system (Nier, 2009). Therefore, it is no surprise that the Fed and the Bank of England called for further research on the ways in which macroprudential policy could strengthen preventive actions to preserve financial stability.

16.4   CONCLUDING REMARKS

The analysis has pointed to the complexity of financial stability as the central bank objective, but also to the danger of its neglect. As Corbo (2010) emphasized: 'Central banks have traditionally focused on treating financial crises, but they also have an important role in helping to prevent them.' This means that financial stability must be in the focus of central bank policy and attention. Although there is no consensus on this issue in the literature at this point, the critics of this view do not give any alternative suggestion of the institution to be responsible for maintaining financial stability.

When we talk about fully developed financial markets, monetary policy alone cannot ensure financial stability. In such circumstances, financial stability should be treated as a public good that the central bank will share with other institutions in the system which are responsible for specific segments of the financial system. Central banks should take into account developments in asset prices, leverage and credit growth. This means that financial stability should become a complementary objective to price stability.

However, in smaller economies where there is only one player in the financial market (bank-centric economies), as is the case in some economies in transition and some developing countries, the situation is somewhat different. Here the central bank can pursue its policy of financial stability because all internal risks essentially come from the banking system that should be the responsibility of the central bank. Of course, in such circumstances it is sometimes necessary to seek a trade-off between price and financial stability, but primarily in the short term. Also, the central bank must be given adequate powers.

When it comes to euroized (dollarized) economies, financial stability should be the primary objective of the central bank. In a euroized economy, the central bank cannot affect price stability with the instruments that are at its disposal, so there will be no conflict between price stability and financial stability and no case for questioning the need to pursue an independent policy of price and financial stability. The prerequisites for this are broad powers and an adequate authority of the central bank in the financial market.

Given the obvious bank-centricity of the financial system of Montenegro, euroization and the absence of numerous monetary policy instruments, setting financial stability as the main objective of the Central Bank of Montenegro is fully justified.

NOTES

1. The Regulation on the Appointment of the Members of the Monetary Council (*Official Gazette of the Republic of Montenegro*, 1999, 2000).
2. However, it should be taken into account that some countries have independent agencies that are responsible for banking system supervision.

REFERENCES

Bernanke, B.S. and M. Gertler (2001), 'Should central banks respond to movements in asset prices?' *American Economic Review*, 91, 253–57.

Bundesbank (2003), 'Monthly report – December 2003. Report on the stability of the German financial system', Frankfurt: Bundesbank.

Corbo, V. (2010), 'Financial stability in a crisis: what is the role of the central bank?', BIS Paper, No 51, available at http://www.bis.org/publ/bppdf/bispap51f. pdf.

Crockett, A. (2002), 'Central banking in the new millenium', in M.S. Ahluwalia, Y.V. Reddy and S.S. Tarapore (eds) *Macroeconomics and Monetary Policy: Issues for a Reforming Economy*, New York: Oxford University Press, pp. 129–46.

Cukierman, A. (1996), 'The economics of central banking', Center for Economic Research, Discussion Paper No. 96–31.

Dimitrijević, B. and N. Fabris (2012), 'Ekonomska Politika', Faculty of Economics, Belgrade University.

European Central Bank (2014), 'Monetary policy glossary', available at https://www.ecb.europa.eu/home/glossary/html/act4f.en.html.

Fabris, N., D. Vukajlović-Grba, T. Radunović and J. Janković (2004), 'Economic policy in dollarized economies with special review of Montenegro', Working Paper No. 1, Central Bank of Montenegro.

Ferguson, R.W. (2003), 'Should financial stability be an explicit Central Bank objective?', in P.C. Ugolini, A. Schaechter and M.R. Stone (eds), *Challenges to Central Banking from Globalized Financial System*, Washington, DC: IMF, pp. 208–24.

Gjedrem, S. (2005), 'The macroprudential approach to financial stability', *Proceedings*, 33rd Economics Conference, Monetary Policy and Financial Stability, Oesterreichische Nationalbank, Vienna, pp. 10–22.

Goodhart, C.A.E. (2005), 'The links between fiscal and monetary policies on the one hand, and financial stability on the other', *Proceedings*, 33rd Economics Conference, Monetary Policy and Financial Stability, Oesterreichische Nationalbank, Vienna, pp. 22–38.

Hanke, S. (2000), 'The beauty of a parallel currency', available at www.cato.org/cgi-bin/scripts/printtech.cgi/dailys/01/14/00/html.

Issing, O., V. Gaspar, O. Tristani and D. Vestin (2006), *Imperfect Knowledge and Monetary Policy*, Cambridge: Cambridge University Press.

Kalezić, Z. (2006), 'Empirijsko istraživanje uticaja obavezne rezerve na osnovne finansijske varijable u Crnoj Gori', Working Paper No. 9, Central Bank of Montenegro.

Mishkin, F. (1999), 'Global financial instability: framework, events, issues', *Journal of Economic Perspectives*, 13(4), 3–20.

Nier, E.W. (2009), 'Financial stability frameworks and the role of central banks: lessons from the crisis', IMF Working Paper, No. 09/70, Washington, DC.

Official Gazette of the Republic of Montenegro (1999 and 2000), 'The Regulation on the Appointment of the Members of the Monetary Council', No. 41/99, 45/99 and 39/00.

Padoa-Schioppa, T. (2002), 'Central banks and financial stability: exploring a land in between', Second ECB Central Banking Conference, The Transformation of the European Financial System, European Central Bank.

Schinassy, G.J. (2006), *Safeguarding Financial Stability*, Washington, DC: International Monetary Fund.
Schwartz, A. (1995), 'Why financial stability depends on prices stability', *Economic Affairs*, 15(3), 21–35.
Wieser, T. (2005), 'Comments on Charles A.E. Goodhart – the links between fiscal and monetary policies on the one hand and financial stability on the other', 33rd Economics Conference, Monetary Policy and Financial Stability, Oesterreichische Nationalbank, Vienna, pp. 33–48.
Žugić, R. and N. Fabris (2014), 'Framework for preserving financial stability in Montenegro', *Journal of Central Banking Theory and Practice*, 3(1), 27–41.

17. Inflation targeting and use of the exchange rate as a monetary policy instrument: the CNB experience

Miroslav Singer

The Czech National Bank (CNB) has been targeting inflation continuously since 1998. The inflation targeting framework has undergone enormous changes since then. This chapter reviews the CNB's experience with inflation targeting. It goes on to summarize the action the CNB took to weaken the domestic currency in November 2013, and concludes by assessing the CNB's experience with using the exchange rate as a monetary policy instrument.

17.1 SEVENTEEN YEARS OF EXPERIENCE WITH INFLATION TARGETING

17.1.1 Form of the Target

The Czech National Bank introduced inflation targeting at the start of 1998 (Coats, 2000). Initially, it targeted 'net' inflation, that is, headline inflation net of administered prices. This, however, proved difficult for the public to understand, making it hard, or even impossible, for the CNB to shape inflation expectations. Consequently, in 2002 the CNB switched to targeting headline inflation, which is much easier for the public to grasp.

17.1.2 Escape Clauses

In November 1998, a few months after the introduction of inflation targeting, the CNB announced a number of *ex ante* exceptions from fulfilling the inflation target. The adoption of these 'escape clauses' implied a switch to flexible inflation targeting. Given an unexpected undershooting of its inflation targets for 1998 and 1999, the CNB initially announced the following explicit escape clauses:

- major deviations in world prices of raw materials, energy-producing materials and other commodities from their predictions;
- major deviations of the Czech koruna's exchange rate from its prediction which are not connected with domestic economic fundamentals and domestic monetary policy;
- major changes in the conditions for agricultural production having an impact on agricultural producer prices;
- natural disasters and other extraordinary events having cost and demand impacts on prices.

Following the switch from net inflation targeting to headline inflation targeting, the set of escape clauses was expanded to include:

- changes in administered prices whose effects on headline inflation would exceed 1–1.5 percentage points a year;
- step changes in indirect taxes.

In subsequent years, the escape clauses were applied unsystematically and on the borderline between the *ex post* and *ex ante* approaches. Economic reality and monetary policy communication was too multifaceted to allow the issue of escape clauses to be resolved in advance with a simple list. An explicit and pre-announced list of escape clauses proved to be rather unnecessary for routine communication.

17.1.3 Forecasting

The CNB's forecasting techniques have also evolved over time. During the first few years of inflation targeting, the quarterly inflation reports were significantly backward-looking: they chiefly described developments observed in the past quarter and contained only very brief inflation forecasts based solely on expert judgement. This focus provided readers with only a sketchy idea about the CNB's view of the future, which again made it difficult to shape inflation expectations. In later years, detailed and typically model-based forecasts were to become a key part of the inflation reports.

In July 2002, the bank introduced a Quarterly Projection Model (QPM), which put the whole forecasting process on a much firmer and rather well-structured footing. By the same token, the forecast switched from conditional to unconditional. This required well-designed communication to explain to the public that the CNB's interest rate and exchange rate forecasts were not commitments. In mid-2008, the CNB switched to a new structural model, a dynamic stochastic general equilibrium (DSGE) model internally referred to as the 'g3 model' (Andrle et al., 2009). This DSGE model is far more sophisticated than the previous QPM and ranks the CNB among the world's leading central banks in this regard. Understandably, the reliability of modelling techniques decreased during the acute phase of the 2008–2009 financial crisis. As a result, the forecasts were supplemented to a larger extent with expert judgement (Brůha et al., 2013). Despite all the criticism of this class of model, the DSGE model has proved itself and performs better as an analytical and forecasting tool in a zero lower bound situation.

17.1.4 Increasing Transparency

The CNB has been systematically increasing its monetary policy transparency over the years. These efforts have been based on the conviction that pursuing an open, comprehensible, accountable and therefore credible monetary policy is an essential part of fulfilling its statutory mandate. The many different actions it has taken to increase transparency have included:

- disclosure of voting ratios in votes on policy interest rates (since 2001);
- the introduction of regular meetings with analysts (since 2005);
- publication of the forecast-consistent interest rate path in the form of a fan chart (since 2008);
- publication of the forecast-consistent exchange rate path in the form of a fan chart (since 2009);
- publication of a graph of risks to the inflation projection (since 2011).

Numerous studies from other countries (see, e.g., Fracasso et al., 2003) have repeatedly and convincingly shown that the CNB is currently one of the most open central banks in the world.

17.1.5 Positives and Negatives of IT

The inflation targeting (IT) regime has functioned as a consistent decision-making framework, proving effective even at the height of the financial and economic crisis. It has provided for successful disinflation and anchoring of inflation expectations. It has also contributed to the macroeconomic stabilization of the Czech economy. Moreover, it has facilitated long-term real and nominal convergence of the Czech economy to developed economies. Finally, the flexible inflation targeting framework allowed the exchange rate to be added to the list of instruments used to ease the monetary conditions in November 2013 (see below).

Although the CNB's experience with inflation targeting has been mostly positive, there have been some negatives. The first problem has been frequent undershooting of targets. In the initial period of inflation targeting, the net inflation target was undershot by 3.8 percentage points in December 1998, 2.5 percentage points in December 1999, and 0.5 percentage points in December 2000. The headline inflation target was undershot by 3.1 percentage points in 2003Q1. Further undershooting episodes occurred after the financial crisis erupted and again in 2014. These episodes were mostly due to anti-inflationary shocks coupled with shortcomings in the forecasting system, although different factors had different degrees of importance in different phases of inflation targeting (Šmídková, 2008). The second problem has been relatively high volatility of the exchange rate. An appreciation bubble against the euro began to emerge in 2001, reaching 12.2 per cent year on year on a monthly basis in July 2002. The bubble was eventually eliminated by means of interest rate cuts and foreign exchange interventions. A special sterilization account was set up to eliminate the exchange rate impacts of the capital inflows resulting from sales of state-owned property. This was a key component of the strategy to stabilize the koruna during specific periods. The second appreciation bubble in 2008 was even bigger, as the appreciation reached 17 per cent in July. On the other hand, the koruna depreciated by 12.2 per cent year on year in February 2009 based on monthly data.

17.2 WEAKENING OF THE KORUNA IN NOVEMBER 2013

The CNB lowered its monetary policy interest rates to the zero lower bound in November 2012. This meant that it could not ease the monetary conditions any further via interest rates. The CNB announced that if it became necessary to ease monetary policy further, it would do so by weakening the exchange rate of the Czech koruna.

During 2013 the CNB made verbal interventions aimed at weakening the Czech currency. These interventions had some effect (tenths of a koruna), but their effectiveness gradually faded over time. Meanwhile, disinflationary and deflationary tendencies strengthened across the entire Czech economy.

In response to these developments, the CNB Bank Board decided on 7 November 2013 to weaken the koruna to around CZK 27 to the euro. This was roughly equivalent to cutting rates by one percentage point. The CNB expressed a (one-sided) exchange rate commitment to prevent excessive appreciation of the koruna below CZK 27 to the euro by intervening on the foreign exchange market, that is, by selling koruna and buying foreign currency. On the weaker side of the CZK 27 level, the CNB decided to allow the exchange rate to float according to supply and demand on the foreign exchange market. The exchange rate thus became a new tool in the inflation targeting regime (Franta et al., 2014).

The weakening of the koruna was aimed at:

● averting the real threat of deflation;
● attaining the inflation target earlier;
● helping the economy to recover faster;
● exiting the zero lower bound earlier (and returning to the use of the main monetary policy instrument – interest rates – sooner).

By historical standards, the November weakening of the koruna was not at all unusual (see Figure 17.1).

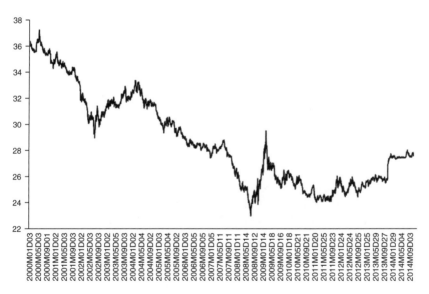

Source: Eurostat.

Figure 17.1 *Koruna–euro exchange rate, 3 January 2000–17 November 2014*

Table 17.1   Key macroeconomic indicators

	y-o-y change in %			
	Available on 7 Nov 2013		Available on 6 Nov 2014	
GDP (s.adj.)	II/13	−1.3	II/14	2.5
Household consumption (s.adj.)	II/13	0.0	II/14	1.9
Gross capital formation (s.adj.)	II/13	−14.0	II/14	6.3
CPI	9/13	1.0	9/14	0.7
Monetary policy-relevant inflation (without taxes)	9/13	0.2	9/14	0.6
Unemployment – age 15–64 years (s.adj., in %)	III/13	7.0	III/14	6.0
Average nominal wage in business sector	II/13	1.1	II/14	2.5
Number of vacancies	9/13	39,040	9/14	56,600
Gross operating surplus of non-financial enterprises	II/13	1.3	II/14	14.5
Composite confidence indicator	10/13	88.9	10/14	94.1
Retail sales incl. cars (s.adj.)	9/13	0.3	9/14	4.5
Industrial production (s.adj.)	9/13	1.8	9/14	5.6
Construction output (s.adj.)	9/13	−12.7	9/14	8.4

Source: Czech Statistical Office (CZSO).

17.3   ASSESSMENT OF THE WEAKENING OF THE KORUNA

The key macroeconomic indicators in the Czech Republic were develop-ing much more favourably in 2014 than they were before November 2013 (see Table 17.1). Except for lower inflation, the developments were in line with what was envisaged when the koruna was weakened. The low (but non-negative) inflation was fostered by more deflationary (than expected) producer price developments in the euro area and a deeper decline in domestic administered prices.

Most importantly, the Czech economy avoided deflation and emerged from recession in 2014. This growth was fostered by three factors: (1) the weakening of the koruna; (2) the end of budgetary restrictions; and (3) a recovery abroad (albeit weaker than had been expected). Monetary policy faced no adverse trade-offs during the crisis. The weakening of the koruna stimulated economic activity, which in turn helped to lift inflation towards the CNB's inflation target.

The CNB will not discontinue the use of the exchange rate as a mon-etary policy instrument before 2016. It does not expect the koruna to appreciate significantly after the exit. The main risks to future growth are linked with developments in the euro area. To conclude, the weakening of the koruna turned out to be beneficial and even more necessary than it had seemed in November 2013.

REFERENCES

Andrle, M., T. Hlédik, O. Kameník and J. Vlček (2009), 'Implementing the New Structural Model of the Czech National Bank', Working Paper Series 2/2009, Czech National Bank.

Brůha, J., T. Hlédik, T. Holub, J. Polanský and J. Tonner (2013), 'Incorporating Judgments and Dealing with Data Uncertainty in Forecasting at the Czech National Bank', Research and Policy Note No. 2/2013, Czech National Bank.

Coats, W. (ed.) (2000), 'Inflation Targeting in Transition Economies: The Case of the Czech Republic', Czech National Bank and International Monetary Fund.

Fracasso, A., H. Genberg and C. Wyplosz (2003), 'How do Central Banks Write?' An Evaluation of Inflation Reports by Inflation Targeting Central Banks', Geneva Reports on the World Economy Special Report 2, Centre for Economic Policy Research.

Franta, M., T. Holub, P. Král, I. Kubicová, K. Šmídková and B. Vašíček (2014), 'The Exchange Rate as an Instrument at Zero Interest Rates: The Case of the Czech Republic', Research and Policy Note No. 3/2014, Czech National Bank.

Šmídková, K. (ed.) (2008), 'Evaluation of the Fulfilment of the CNB's Inflation Targets 1998–2007', Czech National Bank.

Index